AAT
PAYROLL
DIPLOMA
ASSESSMENT KIT

Payroll Administration (Finance Act 2000)

NVQ level 2

Units 71 to 74

In this October 2000 edition

- Material up to date at 1 October 2000 taking into account changes in the Finance Act 2000

FOR DECEMBER 2000 AND JUNE 2001 CENTRAL AND DEVOLVED ASSESSMENTS

BPP Publishing
October 2000

First edition October 2000

ISBN 0 7517 6251 2

British Library Cataloguing-in-Publication Data
*A catalogue record for this book
is available from the British Library*

Published by

*BPP Publishing Limited
Aldine House, Aldine Place
London W12 8AW*

www.bpp.com

*Printed in England by DACOSTA PRINT
35/37 Queensland Road
London, N7 7AH
(020 7700 1000)*

We are grateful to the Lead Body for Accounting for permission to reproduce extracts from the Standards of Competence for Accounting.

INTRODUCTION

How to use this Assessment Kit – Assessment technique –

Level 2 Standards of Competence - Assessment strategy

BPP PUBLISHING

HOW TO USE THIS ASSESSMENT KIT

Aims of this Assessment Kit

> To provide the knowledge and practice to help you succeed in the central and devolved assessments for Payroll Administration NVQ Level 2.

To pass the assessments you need a thorough understanding in all areas covered by the standards of competence.

> To tie in with the other components of the BPP Effective Study Package to ensure you have the best possible chance of success.

Tutorial Text

This covers all you need to know for the central and devolved assessments for Level 2. Icons clearly mark key areas of the text. Numerous activities throughout the text help you practise what you have just learnt.

Assessment Kit

When you have understood and practised the material in the Tutorial Text, you will have the knowledge and experience to tackle this Assessment Kit for Level 2. It contains the AAT's Specimen Central Assessment for Unit 74 plus other relevant questions.

Recommended approach to this Assessment Kit

(a) To achieve competence in all units, you need to be able to do **everything** specified by the standards. Study the text very carefully and do not skip any of it.

(b) Learning is an **active** process. Do **all** the activities as you work through the text so you can be sure you really understand what you have read.

(c) After you have covered the material in the Tutorial Text, work through this **Assessment Kit**.

The Kit is made up of three different types of question:

  (i) **Practice activities** are designed to help you practise techniques in particular areas of the Standards at a lower level than you will experience in the assessments themselves. They are 'warm-ups' which you may find it particularly useful to do if it is some time since you studied the Interactive Text and the activities it contains. The questions contain guidance notes which lead you through how to tackle the answer. The answers are preceded by tutorial notes which highlight tricky points in the question.

  (ii) **Full devolved assessment standard question** gives you practice in the type of question that comes up in the devolved assessment. It has a full answer with tutorial notes.

  (iii) The AAT's **Specimen Central Assessment** for Unit 74 with full answers provided by BPP.

(d) The structure of the main body of this Assessment Kit follows that of its companion Tutorial Text, with banks of practice questions for each area of the Standards. You may opt to do all the practice questions from across the range of the Standards first, or you may prefer to do questions of both levels in a particular area of the Standards before moving on. In either case, it is probably best to leave the Specimen Central Assessment until the last stage of your revision, and then attempt it as a 'mock' under 'exam conditions'. This will help you develop some key techniques in selecting questions and allocating time correctly. For guidance on this, please see **Assessment Technique** on page (vii).

(e)   This approach is only a suggestion. You college may well adapt it to suit your needs.

Remember this is a **practical** course.

(a)   Try to relate the material to your experience in the workplace or any other work experience you may have had.

(b)   Try to make as many links as you can to your study of the other units at this level.

ASSESSMENT TECHNIQUE

Passing assessments at this level is half about having the knowledge, and half about doing yourself full justice on the day. You must have the right **technique**.

The day of the assessment

1   Set at least one **alarm** (or get an alarm call) for a morning assessment.

2   Have **something to eat** but beware of eating too much; you may feel sleepy if your system is digesting a large meal.

3   Allow plenty of **time to get to where you are sitting the assessment**; have your route worked out in advance and listen to news bulletins to check for potential travel problems.

4   **Don't forget** pens, pencils, rulers, erasers.

5   Put **new batteries** into your calculator and take a spare set (or a spare calculator).

6   **Avoid discussion** about the assessment with other candidates outside the venue.

Technique in the assessment

1   *Read the instructions (the 'rubric') on the front of the paper carefully*

Check that the format of the paper hasn't changed. It is surprising how often assessors' reports remark on the number of students who attempt too few questions. Make sure that you are planning to answer the **right number of questions**.

2   *Select questions carefully*

Read through the paper once - don't forget that you are given 15 minutes' reading time - then quickly jot down key points against each question in a second read through. Select those questions where you could latch on to 'what the question is about' - but remember to check carefully that you have got the right end of the stick before putting pen to paper. Use your 15 minutes' reading time wisely.

3   *Plan your attack carefully*

Consider the **order** in which you are going to tackle questions. It is a good idea to start with your best question to boost your morale and get some easy marks 'in the bag'.

4   *Check the time allocation for each section of the paper*

Time allocations are given for each section of the paper. When the time for a section is up, you must go on to the next section. Going even one minute over the time allowed brings you a lot closer to failure.

5   *Read the question carefully and plan your answer*

Read through the question again very carefully when you come to answer it. Plan your answer to ensure that you **keep to the point**. Two minutes of planning plus eight minutes of writing is virtually certain to earn you more marks than ten minutes of writing.

6   *Produce relevant answers*

Particularly with written answers, make sure you **answer the question set,** and not the question you would have preferred to have been set.

7   *Gain the easy marks*

Include the obvious if it answers the question, and don't try to produce the perfect answer.

Don't get bogged down in small parts of questions. If you find a part of a question difficult, get on with the rest of the question. If you are having problems with something, the chances are that everyone else is too.

8   *Produce an answer in the correct format*

The assessor will state **in the requirements** the format in which the question should be answered, for example in a report or memorandum.

9   *Follow the assessor's instructions*

You will annoy the assessor if you ignore him or her. The **assessor will state** whether he or she wishes you to 'discuss', 'comment', 'evaluate' or 'recommend'.

10 *Lay out your numerical computations and use workings correctly*

Make sure the layout fits the **type of question** and is in a style the assessor likes.

Show all your **workings** clearly and explain what they mean. Cross reference them to your answer. This will help the assessor to follow your method (this is of particular importance where there may be several possible answers).

11 *Present a tidy paper*

You are a professional, and it should show in the **presentation of your work**. Students are penalised for poor presentation and so you should make sure that you write legibly, label diagrams clearly and lay out your work neatly. Markers of scripts each have hundreds of papers to mark; a badly written scrawl is unlikely to receive the same attention as a neat and well laid out paper.

12 *Stay until the end of the assessment*

Use any spare time **checking and rechecking** your script.

13 *Don't worry if you feel you have performed badly in the assessment*

It is more than likely that the other candidates will have found the assessment difficult too. Don't forget that there is a competitive element in these assessments. As soon as you get up to leave the venue, **forget** that assessment and think about the next - or, if it is the last one, celebrate!

14 *Don't discuss a central assessment with other candidates*

This is particularly the case if you **still have other assessments to sit**. Even if you have finished, you should put it out of your mind until the day of the results. Forget about assessments and relax!

Level 2 STANDARDS OF COMPETENCE

The structure of the Standards for Level 2 NVQ

The unit commences with a statement of the **knowledge and understanding** which underpin competence in the unit's elements.

The unit is then divided into **elements of competence** describing activities which the individual should be able to perform.

Each element includes:

(a) A set of **performance criteria** which define what constitutes competent performance

(b) **A range statement** which defines the situations, contexts, methods etc in which competence should be displayed

(c) **Evidence requirements,** which state that competence must be demonstrated consistently, over an appropriate time scale with evidence of performance being provided from the appropriate sources

(d) **Sources of evidence,** being suggestions of ways in which you can find evidence to demonstrate that competence.

The elements of competence for Level 2 NVQ units are set out below. Knowledge and understanding required for the Unit as a whole are listed first, followed by the performance criteria and range statements for each element. Performance criteria are cross-referenced below to chapters in the Level 2 Tutorial Text.

NVQ Level 2

Unit 71 maintain employee records

Knowledge and Understanding

The Statutory Framework

A working knowledge of statute law affecting payrolls.

- Employment Rights Act 1996
- Data Protection Acts 1984 and 1998
- Asylum and Immigration Act 1996

The organisation

A detailed understanding of:

- Procedures for the security and confidentiality of information
- Organisational requirements for information and the relevant sources
- External agency requirements for information
- Procedures for verifying information
- Sources of information for the resolution of discrepancies
- How to record, store and retrieve data
- Types of information input from external sources
- Signatories and authorisations
- Timescales and schedules for updating, presenting and despatching data
- Information flows within the organisation

Element 71.1 Verify and record employee personal data

Performance criteria		Chapters in this Text
(i)	All personal data required by statute and by the organisation are recorded	1
(ii)	Confidentiality and security of data is maintained at all times	1
(iii)	Any discrepancies in, or unusual features of, the data are investigated and resolved	1
(iv)	Where resolution does not fall within the discretion of the candidate, the matter is referred to the appropriate person	1
(v)	All organisational and statutory requirements relating to the storage of personal data are complied with	1
(vi)	All organisational and statutory timescales are complied with	1
(vii)	Source documentation is filed in accordance with the requirements of the organisation and in a logical and orderly manner	1

Range statement

1	Statutory data: name; title; address; date of birth; sex; NI number and category; tax code; starting date; leaving date; pensions status
2	Non-statutory data: marital status; single/multiple employment; employee number
3	Recording systems: manual; computerised
4	Documentation: tax notification; NI notification; evidence of appointment; building society/bank mandate; birth certificate; starting, change of status and termination forms; evidence to support change of name

Evidence guidance

The assesor must ensure that the volume of evidence produced is suffcient to demonstrate that the required level of knowledge and understanding has been achieved. The complexity of the payroll(s) on which the assessee works will determine the volume required. It is important that each performance criterion of the element is substantiated by evidence produced.

Evidence would normally be in the form of printed computerised records or those observed on screeen, and should be gathered **on a minimum of two occasions** from a sample of 10 records chosen at random from the payroll for which the assessee is responsible.

Evidence should be gathered in respect of at least two sets of data relating to the personal details of existing employees. Where all records are correct, oral questioning should be used to establish how the assessee would have dealt with a variety of errors or omissions in the data. Particular emphasis should be placed on the processes for the maintenance and compliance with privacy requirements.

Element 71.2 Verify and record contract terms and payments

Performance criteria	Chapters in this Text
(i) All employees are correctly classified in accordance with the organisation's specified practice and allocated to the appropriate payroll and financial code	2
(ii) Working hours, pay rates and entitlements are correctly recorded for all employees	2
(iii) All contractual entitlements are checked for proper authorisation and for consistency with the organisation's pay policies	2
(iv) Where entitlements are not consistent with policy, the matter is referred to the appropriate person for resolution	2
(v) Contractual arrangements for payments are checked for proper authority and discrepancies referred to the appropriate person for resolution	2

Range statement

1 Pay periods: weekly; multi-weekly; monthly; quarterly; supplementary payroll; irregular pay periods

2 Pay types: hourly; weekly; annual; piecework; commission

3 Enhancements, allowances and deductions: output bonus; shift pay; unsocial hours; performance-related pay; motor vehicles; payments in kind; expense entitlements

4 Other entitlements: statutory benefits (Statutory Sick Pay, Statutory Maternity Pay); occupational sick pay; occupational maternity pay; annual leave/holiday pay

5 Recording systems: manual; computerised

6 Methods of payment: cash; cheque; BACS

7 Documentation: authorised signatory list; starting, change of status and termination forms

8 Other information: building society/bank details; payslip destination; payment destination; pay day and date; pension status; duration of contract; financial code

Evidence guidance

The assessor must ensure that the volume of evidence produced is sufficient to demonstrate that the required level of knowledge has been achieved. The complexity of the payroll(s) on which the assessee works will determine the volume required. It is important that each performance criterion of the element is substantiated by evidence produced.

Evidence would normally be in the form of printed computerised records or those observed on screen, and should be gathered **on a minimum of two occasions** from a sample of 10 records chosen at random from the payroll for which the assessee is responsible.

Evidence should be gathered in respect of at least two sets of data to the contractual details of existing employees. Emphasis should be placed on the accuracy of the data recorded and compliance of the data with the policies of the organisation. Written or computer-based evidence should be backed up with oral questioning concerning the principles involved in secure storage of data.

BPP PUBLISHING

Unit 72 Validate and input variations

The Statutory Framework

A working knowledge of:

- Statute law affecting payrolls: Employment Rights Act 1996; Data Protection Acts 1984 and 1998; Asylum and Immigration Act 1996; PAYE regulations; Social Security regulations governing contributions

- The provision of the regulations for Statutory Maternity Pay, Statutory Sick Pay, Guarantee Payments and Redundancy Pay, and their interactions with occupational schemes

The organisation

A detailed understanding of:

- The functional position of payroll in the workplace

- The organisation's administrative requirements
  - Policies, practices and procedures for filing
  - Signatories and authorisations
  - Timescales and schedules for updating, presenting and despatching data
  - Information flows within the organisation
  - Procedures for the security and confidentiality of information
  - Organisational requirements for information and the relevant sources
  - Procedures for verifying information
  - Sources of information for the resolution of discrepancies
  - How to record, store and retrieve data
  - Types of information input from external agencies

Element 72.1 Process records of starters and leavers

	Performance criteria	Chapters in this Text
(i)	Proper authorisation of every appointment and cessation of employment is obtained before payroll is amended	3
(ii)	Personal and contract details are correctly input to new employee record	3
(iii)	All statutory regulations are met	3
(iv)	Starters are allocated to correct payroll, payment method and financial code	3
(v)	All necessary deletions from, and adjustments to, core payroll information are correctly executed	3
(vi)	Documents required to facilitate cessation of employment are completed accurately and promptly	3
(vii)	All organisational and statutory timescales are complied with	3

Range statement

1   Statutory data: name; title; address; date of birth; sex; NI number and category; tax code/basis; starting date; leaving date

2   Non-statutory data: marital status; single/multiple employment

3   Other information: building society/bank details; payslip destination; payment destination; pension status; duration of contract; hours of work

4   Recording systems: manual; computerised

5   Documentation: tax notification; NI notification; evidence of appointment or cessation; building society/bank mandate; Statutory Sick Pay notification; authorised signatory list

6   Pay periods: weekly; multi-weekly; monthly; quarterly; supplementary payroll; irregular pay periods

7   Pay types: hourly; weekly; annual; piecework; commission

8   Enhancements, allowances and deductions: output bonus; shift pay; unsocial hours; performance related pay; motor vehicles; payments in kind; expense entitlements

9   Other entitlements: statutory benefits; occupational sick pay; occupational maternity pay; annual leave/holiday pay; redundancy terms; *ex gratia* payments

10 Methods of payment: cash; cheque; BACS

Evidence guidance

The assessor must ensure that the volume of evidence produced is suffcient to demonstrate that the required level of knowledge and understanding has been achieved. The complexity of the payroll(s) on which the assessee works will determine the volume required. It is important that each performance criterion of the element is substantiated by evidence produced.

Evidence should normally be in the form of computerised printed records or observed on screen, and must be accompanied by the source documentation on which the variation is based. The primary source of evidence is the sampling of payroll records; where appropriate, the same samples may be used throughout the unit.

Evidence should be derived from a batch of six starters and six leavers chosen at random on two separate occasions from the payroll for which the assessee is responsible. Records must be traced from the prime documentation through to the completed record, covering as many of the items in the range indicator as are demonstrated from the evidence. Particular emphasis should be placed on the proper authorisation of employees starting and leaving. Where evidence does not cover the full range naturally, oral questioning should be used to supplement it and to establish the assessee's understanding of the procedures involved.

Element 72.2 Implement instructions from external agencies

Performance criteria		Chapters in this Text
(i)	All deductions requests are properly verified	4
(ii)	Instructions accompanied by a due date are acted upon within the timescale specified	4
(iii)	All other instructions are applied promptly and in accordance with statutory and organisational requirements	4
(iv)	Where deductions are non-statutory, requests are checked against organisational policy	4
(v)	All non-statutory deductions are authorised by the employee(s) concerned	4
(vi)	No requests for deduction is implemented unless compatible with the parameters of the payroll-processing system	4
(vii)	All properly authorised deductions are correctly processed	4
(viii)	All discrepancies are identified and are either resolved directly or by reference to the appropriate organisation or person	4
(ix)	Security and confidentiality of sensitive information is maintained at all times	4

Range statement

1   Statutory agencies: Inland Revenue; Contributions Agency; Child Support Agency; courts

2   Non-statutory bodies: pension funds; trades unions and associations; financial institutions charities

3   Recording systems: manual; computerised

4   Documentation: court orders; Inland Revenue documentation; Child Support Agency instructions; individual matters

Evidence guidance

The assessor must ensure that the volume of evidence produced is sufficent to demonstrate that the required level of knowledge and understanding has been achieved. The complexity of the payroll(s) on which the assessee works will determine the volume required. It is important that each performance criterion of the element is substantiated by evidence produced.

Evidence should normally be in the form of computerised printed records or observed on screen, and must be accompanied by the source documentation on which the variation is based. The primary source of evidence is the sampling of payroll records; where appropriate, the same samples may be used throughout the unit.

Evidence should be derived from a batch of six starters, six leavers and six existing employees chosen at random on two separate occasions from the payroll for which the assessee is responsible. Where evidence does not cover the full range naturally, oral questioning should be used to supplement it and to establish the assessee's understanding of the procedures involved.

Element 72.3 Evaluate and record variations to payroll

Performance criteria	Chapters in this Text
(i) All data received is evaluated for accuracy and reasonableness	5
(ii) All data received is checked for proper authorisation	5
(iii) Permanent variations to core payroll information are correctly processed	5
(iv) Temporary variations are actioned in an accurate and timely manner	5
(v) Records supporting variations are retained in accordance with organisational policy and statutory requirements	5
(vi) All retained documents are filed in a logical and accessible manner	5

Range statement

1   Permanent variations: status (promotion, demotion, change of grade; nature of employment (temporary to/from permanent); contract hours; pay rate; payment method; payment frequency; voluntary deduction (pensions contributions, subscriptions, give-as-you-earn; save-as-you-earn); shift allowance; changes in personal circumstances (marital status, name, address, bank/building society details)

2   Temporary variations: Absence from work (sickness, holiday, industrial action, maternity leave, jury service); variations in hours worked (overtime, on-call time, shift variations); retrospective pay adjustments, variations in output (piecework, commission, bonus); special payments (expenses, subsistence, travel costs, reimbursements); extra duty payments

3   Recording systems: manual; computerised

4   Documentation: pay card/docket; time sheet; clock card; swipe card; authorised signatory list

Evidence guidance

The assessor must ensure that the volume of evidence produced is sufficent to demonstrate that the required level of knowledge and understanding has been achieved. The complexity of the payroll(s) on which the assessee works will determine the volume required. It is important that each performance criterion of the element is substantiated by evidence produced.

Evidence should normally be in the form of computerised printed records or observed on screen, and must be accompanied by the source documentation on which the variation is based. The primary source of evidence is the sampling of payroll records; where appropriate, the same samples may be used throughout the unit.

Evidence should be derived from a batch of six starters, six leavers and six existing employees chosen at random on two separate occassions from the payroll for which the assessee is responsible. Records must be traced from the prime documentation through to the completed record, covering as many of the items in the range indicator as are demonstrated from the evidence. Particular emphasis should be placed on the proper authorisation of employees starting and leaving. Where evidence does not cover the full range naturally, oral questioning should be used to supplement it and to establish the assessee's understanding of the procedures involved.

Unit 73 ascertain gross pay

Knowledge and Understanding

General information

An understanding of:

- The parameters of payroll calculations
  - ○ Positive and negative payrolls
  - ○ Pay frequency
  - ○ Pay intervals
- Payroll processing methods
  - ○ Computerised in-house
  - ○ Computerised bureau
  - ○ Manual

The Statutory Framework

A working knowledge of:

- Statutory law affecting payrolls
  - ○ Employment Rights Act 1996
  - ○ Asylum and Immigration Act 1996
  - ○ PAYE regulations
  - ○ Social Security regulations governing contributions
- The provisions of the regulations for:
  - ○ Statutory Maternity Pay
  - ○ Statutory Sick Pay
  - ○ Guarantee Payments
  - ○ Redundancy Pay

  and their interaction with occupational schemes

The organisation

An understanding of the principles underlying the calculation of:

- Basic pay and contractual obligations
- Allowances, enhancements and benefits
- Statutory and occupational sick pay
- Statutory and occupational maternity pay

A detailed understanding of:

- The functional position of payroll in the workplace
- Administrative requirements of the organisation
  - ○ Timescales and schedules for updating, processing and despatching data
  - ○ Information flows within the organisation
  - ○ Procedures for the security and confidentiality of information
- The common components of remuneration and benefits packages
- The application of statutory parameters to pay items

Element 73.1 Determine basic entitlements

Performance criteria	Chapters in this Text
(i) Details of employees' basic pay rates and contractual conditions are verified for accuracy and authorisation	6
(ii) Variations in working hours are checked for accuracy and authorisation	6
(iii) Employees covered by positive payrolls are clearly identified and relevant details are correctly inserted	6
(iv) Rates for overtime payments are checked against scales for each type of employee affected	6
(v) The treatment of permanent allowances and enhancements is correctly identified with respect to tax, National Insurance and pensions deductions	6
(vi) All permanent allowances and enhancements supplementary to basic pay are identified and input correctly to payroll	6

Range statement

1   Documentation: pay card/docket; time sheet; clock card; swipe card

2   Allowances: shift pay; unsocial hours; stand-by payments; contractual overtime; standard bonus; lump sums (vehicles, accommodation, tools, clothing)

3   Processing systems: manual; computerised

Evidence guidance

The assessor must ensure that the volume of evidence produced is sufficient to demonstrate that the required level of knowledge and understanding has been achieved. The complexity of the payroll(s) on which the assessee works will determine the volume required. It is important that each performance criterion of the element is substantiated by evidence produced.

Evidence should be derived primarily from a random sample of five employees from the payroll for which the assessee is responsible taken from three different payroll runs. The completed records must be in **manual** form as though in preparation for the processing of the payroll following manual procedures.

The five records should contain evidence relating to basic personal and contractual details relevant to that payroll run. Oral questioning should be used to supplement the written evidence where it does not give rise naturally to the full breadth of performance designated in the standard.

Element 73.2 Input additional pay and allowances

Performance criteria	Chapters in this Text
(i) All relevant temporary allowances are identified and correctly affected	7
(ii) Where relevant, payment of temporary allowances is checked for proper authorisation in accordance with organisational requirements	7
(iii) Monetary values of temporary payments are checked against payroll parameters applicable to the type of employee concerned	7
(iv) The treatment of temporary pay and allowances is correctly identified with respect to tax, National Insurance and pensions deductions	7
(v) Where variations arise as a result of sickness, maternity leave or holidays, the appropriate action is taken to apply the terms of statutory and organisational payment schemes	7

Range statement

1   Documentation: Pay card/docket; time sheet; clock card; swipe card; pay scales; contractual details; statutory benefit regulations; pensions fund regulations; authorised signatory list

2   Temporary: sick pay; maternity pay; holiday pay; variable overtime; shift pay; retrospective pay

3   Allowances: adjustments; production bonus; performance-related pay; special payments (expenses, subsistence, travel costs, reimbursements); *ex gratia* payments

4   Compensatory payments: redundancy; pay in lieu of notice

5   Processing systems: manual; computerised

Evidence guidance

The assessor must ensure that the volume of evidence produced is sufficient to demonstrate that the required level of knowledge and understanding has been achieved. The complexity of the payroll(s) on which the assessee works will determine the volume required. It is important that each performance criterion of the element is substantiated by evidence produced.

Evidence should be derived primarily from a random sample of five employees from the payroll for which the assessee is responsible taken from three different payroll runs. The completed records must be in **manual** form as though in preparation for the processing of the payroll following manual procedures.

The five records should contain evidence relating to basic personal and contractual details relevant to that payroll run. Oral questioning should be used to supplement the written evidence where it does not give rise naturally to the full breadth of performance designated in the standard.

Unit 74 Determine individual and aggregate payments

Knowledge and Understanding

General information

An understanding of:

- The parameters of payroll calculations
  - Positive and negative input
  - Pay frequency
  - Pay intervals
  - Methods of payment
- Payroll processing methods
  - Computerised in-house
  - Computerised bureau
  - Manual
- Role and influence of regulatory bodies
  - Inland Revenue
  - National Insurance Contributions Office
  - Courts
  - Local authorities
  - Child Support Agency

The Statutory Framework

A working knowledge of:

- Statutory law affecting payrolls
  - Employment Rights Act 1996
  - Data Protection Acts 1984 and 1998
  - Asylum and Immigration Act 1996
  - PAYE regulations
  - Social Security regulations governing contributions
- The provisions of the regulations for:
  - Statutory Maternity Pay
  - Statutory Sick Pay
  - Guarantee Payments
  - Redundancy Pay

    and their interaction with occupational schemes

The organisation

An understanding of the principles underlying the calculation of:

- Statutory, contractual and voluntary deductions
- Basic pay and contractual obligations
- Allowances, enhancements and benefits

An understanding of the general principles underlying the operational pension scheme.

A detailed understanding of:

- The functional position of payroll in the workplace
- Administrative requirements of the organisation
  - Timescales and schedules for updating, processing and despatching data

- ○ Information flows within the organisation
- ○ Procedures for the security and confidentiality of information
- ○ Procedures for initiating and monitoring payments
- ○ Principles of payroll accounting and the reconciliation of periodic balances
- ○ Methods of disbursement
- ○ Information and timescale requirements of systems for transmission of disbursement to employees

Element 74.1 Identify and input deductions

	Performance criteria	Chapters in this Text
(i)	All relevant temporary deductions are identified and correctly applied to employees affected	11
(ii)	Temporary deductions are checked for proper authorisation in accordance with organisational and legal requirements	11
(iii)	Permanent deductions are identified by reference to core payroll data	11
(iv)	Taxable pay is correctly identified for each employee	8, 9
(v)	Pay subject to National Insurance contributions is correctly identified for all eligible employees	10
(vi)	Pensionable pay is correctly identified for all eligible employees	11
(vii)	All deductions are compared with payroll parameters and any which fall outside are referred to the appropriate person for resolution	11
(viii)	All organisational and statutory timescales are complied with	11

Range statement

1 Statutory deductions: tax; National Insurance; attachment of earnings; Council Tax/Community Charge orders (Scotland - arrestments); child support orders

2 Non-statutory deductions: pension contributions (basic, supplementary and additional voluntary contributions); incomplete work period; recovery of overpayments; advances and contributions to payments in kind; voluntary deductions (union subscriptions, give-as-you-earn, save-as-you-earn); repayment of loans

3 Documents: tax tables; NI regulations; pensions funds regulations; authorisation for voluntary deductions; statutory orders; authorised signatory lists

4 Processing systems: manual; computerised

Evidence guidance

The assessor must ensure that the volume of evidence produced is sufficient to demonstrate that the required level of knowledge and understanding has been achieved. The complexity of the payroll(s) on which the assessee works will determine the volume required. It is important that each performance criterion of the element is substantiated by evidence produced.

Evidence for this element should be derived in similar fashion as for Unit 73 – from a random sample of five employees from the payroll for which the assessee is responsible taken from three different payroll runs. The completed records must be in **manual** form as though in preparation for the processing of the payroll following manual procedures.

The five records should contain evidence relating to basic personal and contractual details relevant to that payroll run. Oral questioning should be used to supplement the written evidence where it does not give rise naturally to the full breadth of performance designated in the standard.

Element 74.2 Calculate and verify net pay

Performance criteria	Chapters in this Text
(i) Net pay is calculated accurately and in accordance with requirement deadlines for all employees	12
(ii) Deductions of tax, National Insurance and pensions contributions are made in accordance with the applicable regulations with regard to: - tax/NI/pensions rate - taxable/NI/pensionable income	12
(iii) Net pay totals are checked to ensure that the full range of applicable allowances and deductions has been made	12
(iv) The payroll status of all employees is checked for validity	12
(v) Net pay figures are checked against the parameters for the payroll concerned and any discrepancies are dealt with or referred to the appropriate person for resolution	12

Range statement

1   Pay periods: weekly, multi-weekly; monthly; quarterly; supplementary payroll; irregular pay periods

2   Processing systems: manual; computerised

3   Allowances: shift pay; unsocial hours; stand-by payments; permanent overtime; standard bonus; lump sums (vehicles, accommodation, tools, clothing); sick pay; maternity pay; holiday pay; variable overtime; shift pay allowances; retrospective pay adjustments; production bonus; performance related pay; special payments (expenses, subsistence, travel costs, reimbursements), *ex gratia* payments

4   Compensatory payments: redundancy pay; pay in lieu of notice

5   Statutory deductions: tax; National Insurance; attachment of earnings; Council Tax/Community Charge orders (Scotland - arrestments); child support orders

6   Non-statutory: pensions contributions (basic, supplementary and additional voluntary deductions contributions); incomplete work period; recovery of overpayments; advances and contributions to payments in kind; voluntary deductions (union subscriptions, give-as-you-earn, save-as-you-earn); repayment of loans

7   Documents: tax tables; NI regulations; pension fund regulations; authorisation for voluntary deductions; statutory orders

Evidence guidance

The assessor must ensure that the volume of evidence produced is sufficient to demonstrate that the required level of knowledge and understanding has been achieved. The complexity of the payroll(s) on which the assessee works will determine the volume required. It is important that each performance criterion of the element is substantiated by evidence produced.

Evidence for this element should be derived in similar fashion as for Unit 73 – from a random sample of five employees from the payroll for which the assessee is responsible taken from three different payroll runs. The completed records must be in **manual** form as though in preparation for the processing of the payroll following manual procedures.

The five records should contain evidence relating to basic personal and contractual details relevant to that payroll run. Oral questioning should be used to supplement the written evidence where it does not give rise naturally to the full breadth of performance designated in the standard.

Element 74.3 Ascertain and reconcile aggregate payroll totals

	Performance criteria	Chapters in this Text
(i)	Actual payroll totals are reconciled against authorised totals	12
(ii)	Aggregate employer's National Insurance and pensions contributions are correctly calculated and reconciled against control totals	12
(iii)	Amounts relating to National Insurance Class 1A contributions are included in NI totals in accordance with the calculation and payment methodology chosen by the organisation	12
(iv)	Aggregate Statutory Sick Pay and Statutory Maternity Pay are checked against control totals	12
(v)	Sums recoverable from NICO in respect of statutory payments are correctly calculated and netted off against payments due	12
(vi)	Where applicable, aggregate small employer's refund of Statutory Maternity Pay is calculated promptly and accurately	12
(vii)	Roundings to facilitate cash payments are accurately aggregated and reconciled to control totals	12
(viii)	Aggregate amounts payable to external bodies in respect of statutory and voluntary deductions are correctly calculated and reconciled against control totals	12
(ix)	Total charges to organisational budgets are reconciled against payroll totals and are correctly coded for allocation	12
(x)	Where discrepancies arise, these are resolved wherever possible, and where they cannot be they are referred for action to the appropriate supervisor(s)	12
(xi)	All organisational and statutory timescales are complied with	12

Range statement

1. Pay periods: weekly; multi-weekly; monthly; quarterly; supplementary payroll; irregular pay periods

2. Processing systems: manual; computerised

3. Statutory payments: employer's National Insurance contributions classes 1 and 1A

4. Non-statutory payments: employer's pension contributions (basic and supplementary)

5. Statutory deductions: tax; National Insurance; attachment of earnings; Council Tax/Community Charge orders (Scotland - arrestments); child support orders

Evidence guidance

The assessor must ensure that the volume of evidence produced is sufficient to demonstrate that the required level of knowledge and understanding has been achieved. The complexity of the payroll(s) on which the assessee works will determine the volume required. It is important that each performance criterion of the element is substantiated by evidence produced.

Evidence for this element should be derived from the samples used for Elements 74.1 and 74.2. Two consecutive sets of these samples should be used to carry out manually a cumulative exercise covering the various items specified in the range indicators. Oral questioning should be used to supplement the written evidence where it does not give rise naturally to the full breadth of performance designated in the standard, with particular emphasis being placed on the differences arising as a result of different pay frequencies.

Element 74.4 Generate and distribute payslips

Performance criteria	Chapters in this Text
(i) All payslips are: - legible/comprehensible - mathematically correct - completed in accordance with statutory requirements - completed in accordance with organisational requirements	12
(ii) The number of the payslips generated is reconciled promptly with the number of employees on the payroll	12
(iii) The number of no pays and actual pay is reconciled promptly with the number of employees on the payroll	12
(iv) Payslips are distributed to employees in accordance with statutory requirements and organisational procedures	12
(v) Where emergency or exceptional payments are required, these are produced in accordance with organisational requirements, to the deadlines agreed and are fully and validly documented	12
(vi) All supporting documentation is retained in accordance with statutory and organisational requirements and is filed in a logical and accessible manner	12
(vii) Payment procedures are initiated in accordance with organisational procedures	12
(viii) All organisational and statutory timescales are complied with	12

Range statement

1   Pay periods: weekly, muli-weekly; monthly; quarterly; supplementary payroll; irregular pay periods

2   Processing systems: manual; computerised

3   Statutory requirements: gross pay; variable deductions; fixed deductions; net pay; allocation between pay methods

4   Other information: name; employee number/reference; distribution address; cumulative totals of pay; tax; NI and pensions contributions; NI number; tax code/basis; tax reference; other deductions

Evidence guidance

The assessor must ensure that the volume of evidence produced is sufficient to demonstrate that the required level of knowledge and understanding has been achieved. The complexity of the payroll(s) on which the assessee works will determine the volume required. It is important that each performance criterion of the element is substantiated by evidence produced.

Evidence for this element should be derived from the samples used for Elements 74.1 and 74.2. Two consecutive sets of these samples should be used to carry out manually a cumulative exercise covering the various items specified in the range indicators. Oral questioning should be used to supplement the written evidence where it does not give rise naturally to the full breadth of performance designated in the standard, with particular emphasis being placed on the differences arising as a result of different pay frequencies.

ASSESSMENT STRATEGY

The units at Level 2 are assessed by **devolved assessment only**, except for Unit 74 which is assessed by both **central and devolved assessment.**

An assessment is a means of collecting evidence that you have the **essential knowledge and understanding** that underpins competence. It is also a means of collecting evidence across the **range of contexts** for the standards and evidence of your ability to transfer skills, knowledge and understanding to different situations. Thus, although assessments will contain practical tasks linked to the performance criteria, they will also focus on the underpinning knowledge and understanding. You should in addition expect each assessment to contain tasks taken from across a broad range of the Standards.

Central assessment

The Assessment will last two hours plus 15 minutes reading time and will be divided into 2 sections:

- Operational Tasks
- Short Answer Questions

The Operational tasks contain exercises that require candidates to focus on issues surrounding payroll preparation. Candidates will be expected to know about various aspects of preparing payrolls including manual calculations plus knowledge of the rules concerning Statutory Sick Pay, Statutory Maternity Pay, deductions from pay including Court orders and Child Support Agency DEOs. They are given scenarios that require them to use their experience as well as the facts in order to completeb the relevant parts of the returns.

The Short Answer Questions are designed to explore the candidates' understanding of a miscellany of different issues relating to general payroll. Some questions require only yes/no answers and most a straightforward one or two sentence response will be required.

Operational Tasks

Example tasks

- Preparation of manual payslip
- Responding to memos received from colleagues

The tasks relate to a company callled Ruby & Stone situated in the theoretical town of Barcet. Candidates are not expected to have a detailed knowledge of the company as only relevant details will be provided and the tasks could be applicable to any other organisation.

Short Answer Questions

Example Tasks

- Consider issues surrounding general payroll matters in respect of tax, NI, SSP, SMP, court orders

EXTRACTS OF TAX TABLES

The following extracts of Tax Tables are provided in the Appendices at the end of this Assessment Kit. You will need to refer to these extracts as you work through this Kit. Due to the volume of the Tables, it would be impractical to reproduce them all in this Kit.

BPP PUBLISHING

Practice activities

1 Employee personal data

Practice activity 1.1 _____

What is the minimum period that PAYE documentation must be kept after the end of the tax year?

Practice activity 1.2 _____

Paula Mell works Mondays to Wednesdays for White Elephant Ltd, and Thursdays and Fridays for Budgie Wharf Ltd. She wants to be a freelance worker and asks you about her status.

(a) What are the relative pros and cons of self-employed status as opposed to employed status?
(b) What is the strict legal distinction between employment and self-employment?
(c) How would you assess Paula's case?

Practice activity 1.3 _____

What data must be kept on each employee by law?

Practice activity 1.4 _____

An employee tells you that he has changed his name and wants all his records altered. What evidence do you need to see?

Practice activity 1.5 _____

Your supervisor asks you to sort out a filing system for employees. There are only fifteen employees. In what order would you choose to file them?

Practice activity 1.6 _____

An employee come up to you and says 'I'm sick of PAYE. Can't I go self-employed or freelance?'

What do you say to him? What do you do?

2 Ascertaining rates of pay

Practice activity 2.1

How would you ensure that you are paying an employee the agreed rate?

Practice activity 2.2

What would you expect to see in a contract of employment?

Practice activity 2.3

What are the implied terms in a contract of employment?

Practice activity 2.4

Joe Johnson has just moved from sales to the accounts department. Your organisation uses the following codes:

Sales	S01
Purchases	P01
Financial	F01
Administration	A01

Which department code should be used for Joe's new department?

Practice activity 2.5

Joe Johnson queries his first pay received after moving to the accounts department. When in sales, his pay was increased by commission. He wants to know why he is no longer receiving this. You are paying an increased basic salary but no commission in accordance with instructions received from personnel. Explain the situation to Joe.

Practice activity 2.6

You have been on holiday. On your return you notice that Joe's salary has been paid into a different bank account. However, there is no change of account noted in the employee records. What do you do?

Practice activity 2.7

What are the four main requirements for payroll processing?

3 Starters and leavers

Practice activity 3.1 _____

This activity requires the correct completion of a P45 for a leaver.

You are the payroll officer of Shepherds Brushes Ltd, 3 Long Road, Dutton, Worcs DT2 3BP. You receive notification that Alan Wilson, an employee, will be leaving the company on 26 September 2000 (Week 25).

You check his P11 and find the following information.

        Starting date 1.8.91
        National Insurance no   AB225518C
        Date of birth   8/7/73
        Tax code   547H
        Week 25
                Total pay to date   £3,550.00
                Total free pay to date £2,634.50
                Total taxable pay to date £915.50
                Total tax due   £113.60

His address is 5 River Street, Dutton, Worcs DT13 9XX.

You have already calculated the final wage payable on 25 September and this is included above. Your company's Tax Office reference is 123/B1234.

Task

Prepare a P45 (blank Part 1 provided) for Alan Wilson.

		Details of employee leaving work Copy for Tax Office	P45 Part 1

Inland
Revenue

		District number	Reference number
1	PAYE Reference	123	B123H

2	Employee's National Insurance number	AB 22 55 18 C

(Mr Mrs Miss Ms)

3	Surname (in capitals)	WILSON	MR

	First name(s) (in capitals)	ALAN

4	Leaving date (in figures)	Day 26	Month 09	Year 2000	5 Continue Student Loan Deductions (Y)	

6	Tax Code at leaving date. *If week 1 or Month 1 basis applies, write 'X' in the box marked Week 1 or Month 1*	Code S47H	Week 1 or Month 1

7	Last entries on *Deductions Working Sheet* (P11) **Complete only if Tax Code is cumulative.** *Make no entry here if Week 1 or Month 1 basis applies. Go to item 7.*	Week or month number	Week 25.	Month
		Total pay to date	£ 3550	00 p
		Total tax to date	£ 113	60 p

8	This employment pay and tax. ■ *No entry needed if Tax Code is cumulative and amounts are same as item 6 entry.*	Total pay in this employment	£	p
		Total tax in this employment	£	p

9	Works number/ Payroll number		10	Department or branch if any	

11	Employee's private address and Postcode	5 RIVER ST. DUTTON WORCS PT13 9XX

12 I certify that the details entered above in items 1 to 9 are correct

	Employer's name, address and Postcode	SHEPHERDS BRUSHES LTD 3 LONG ROAD DUTTON WORCS DT2 3BP

Date

To the employer *Please complete with care* ★

For Tax Office use

- Complete this form following the 'Employee leaving' instructions in the *Employer's quick Guide to PAYE and NICs* (cards CWG1). ★ **Make sure the details are clear on all four parts of this form**. Make sure your name and address is shown on Parts 1 and 1A.
- Detach Part 1 and send it to your Tax Office immediately.
- Hand Parts 1A, 2 and 3 (unseparated) to your employee when he or she leaves
- If the employee has died, write 'D' in this box and send all three parts of this form (unseparated) to your Tax Office immediately.

P45

BMSD9/99

Practice activity 3.2

You are the payroll officer of Gumm·Boots Ltd of 7 Worple Street, Haderton, Lancs HA1 2FT (PAYE ref 011/C2334). You receive notification on 24 July that an employee, David Ricketts, having been paid his weekly wage on 21 July 2000, walked out of his job after an argument with his supervisor and has not returned to work. He has therefore been dismissed.

From the P11 for David Ricketts you obtain the following information.

At 21 July (Week 16):

National Insurance no	DC986721B
Date of birth	30/3/70
Tax code	350T
Total pay to date	£2,420.50
Total free pay to date	£1,079.84
Total taxable pay to date	£1,340.66
Total tax due	£238.67

The last known address you have for Mr Ricketts is 17 River Mansions, Haderton, Lancs HA12 1YP.

You also notice on the P11 that Mr Ricketts only joined your company in May 2000, and you find Part 2 of the P45 from his previous employment, which shows the following information.

Inland Revenue

Details of employee leaving work
Copy for new employer

P45
Part 2

		District number	Reference number
1	Previous PAYE Reference	621	BM 1223

2	Employee's National Insurance number	DC 98 67 21 B

(Mr Mrs Miss Ms)

3	Surname	RICKETTS	Mr
	First name(s)	DAVID	

		Day	Month	Year
4	Leaving date	28	05	20 00

5 Continue Student Loan Deductions (Y)

Code — Week 1 or Month 1

6 Tax Code at leaving date. 'x' *in the box means Week 1 or Month 1 basis applies*
300T

7 Last entries on *Deductions Working Sheet (P11).* *If there is an 'X' at item 5, there will be no entries here*

	Week	Month
Week or Month number	8	
Total pay to date	£ 1,145	00 p
Total tax to date	£ 121	97 p

To the employee

This form is important to you, so take good care of it. Copies are not available. Keep Parts 2 and 3 of the form together and do not alter them.

Going to a new job

Give this form (Parts 2 and 3) to your new employer, or you will have tax deducted using the emergency code and may pay too much tax. If you do not want your new employer to know the details on this form, send it to your Tax Office immediately with a letter saying so and giving the name and address of your new employer. The Tax Office can make special arrangements, but you may pay too much tax for a while as a result.

Becoming self-employed

Let your local Tax Office know and ask for *Starting your own business* (leaflet CWL1).

Going abroad

If you are going abroad or returning to a country outside the UK ask for *Income Tax form for those Leaving the United Kingdom* (form P85) from any Tax Office or Tax Enquiry Centre.

Claiming jobseeker's allowance

Take this form to the benefit office. They will pay you any tax refund you may be entitled to when your claim ends, or at 5 April if this is earlier.

Not working and not claiming jobseekers allowance

If you have paid tax and wish to claim a refund ask for *Claim for income tax repayment* (form P50) from any Tax Office or Tax Enquiry Centre

To the new employer

Check this form, complete items 7 to 16 in part 3 and prepare a *Deductions Working Sheet* (form P11). Follow the instructions in the *Employer's Quick Guide to PAYE and NICs* (cards CWG1).

Detach part 3 of this form and send it to your Tax Office immediately. Keep part 2.

P45

Task

If you think that you should prepare a P45 for Mr Ricketts, prepare Part 1 of this form using the blank sheet provided, and explain what you would do with it. If you do not think you should prepare a P45 explain why.

Inland **Revenue**		**Details of employee leaving work** Copy for Tax Office	**P45 Part 1**

		District number	Reference number
1	PAYE Reference	O11	C2334

2	Employee's National Insurance number	DC 98 67 21 B

(Mr Mrs Miss Ms)

3	Surname (in capitals)	RICKETTS	MR.

	First name(s) (in capitals)	DAVID

4	Leaving date (in figures)	Day 21	Month 07	Year 20 00	5	Continue Student Loan Deductions (Y)	

Week 1 or Month 1

6	Tax Code at leaving date. *If week 1 or Month 1 basis applies, write 'X' in the box marked Week 1 or Month 1*	Code 350T

7	Last entries on *Deductions Working Sheet* (P11) **Complete only if Tax Code is cumulative.** Make no entry here if Week 1 or Month 1 basis applies. Go to item 7.	Week or month number	Week 16	Month
		Total pay to date	£ 2420 50 p	
		Total tax to date	£ 238 67 p	

8	This employment pay and tax. ■ *No entry needed if Tax Code is cumulative and amounts are same as item 6 entry.*	Total pay in this employment	£ 1275 50 p
		Total tax in this employment	£ 116 70 p

9	Works number/ Payroll number		10	Department or branch if any	

11	Employee's private address and Postcode	

12 I certify that the details entered above in items 1 to 9 are correct

Employer's name, address and Postcode

Date

For Tax Office use

To the employer   *Please complete with care* ★

- Complete this form following the 'Employee leaving' instructions in the *Employer's quick Guide to PAYE and NICs* (cards CWG1). ★ **Make sure the details are clear on all four parts of this form.** Make sure your name and address is shown on Parts 1 and 1A.
- Detach Part 1 and send it to your Tax Office immediately.
- Hand Parts 1A, 2 and 3 (unseparated) to your employee when he or she leaves
- If the employee has died, write 'D' in this box and send all three parts of this form (unseparated) to your Tax Office immediately.

P45   BMSD9/99

Practice activity 3.3

You are the payroll officer of Larks Ltd. On 11 November 2000 one of your company's salesmen, Gerald Wallet, died.

Details from his P11 are as follows.

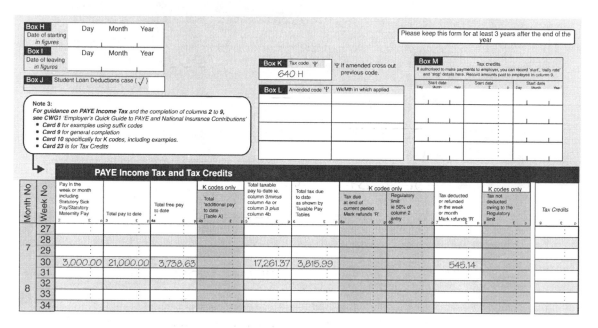

A P45 was completed and sent to the Tax Office on 13 November 2000. Mr Wallet's NI number is FG 23 32 45A and his payroll number is 622.

Mr Wallet's earnings from 1 to 11 November were not confirmed at that stage, as the Sales Director was at a conference. On her return, it was agreed that £1,600 was the gross pay due for the period. You have been authorised by your supervisor to make a payment on 30 November of the unpaid earnings to his widow, Mrs Mary Wallet (address 17 Cedar Avenue, Top Village, Herts HE2 4TP).

Your company's address is Larks House, 5 High Street, Borton, Herts, HE 17 1JK, and the PAYE reference for the company is 333/C2468.

Tasks

(a) Complete the P45 for Mr Wallet (below) on 13 November 2000.

(b) Following the payment to Mrs Wallet, do you prepare a further P45? Give reasons for your answer.

Inland Revenue	***Details of employee leaving work*** *Copy for Tax Office*	**P45 Part 1**

District number 333

Reference number C2468

1 PAYE Reference

2 Employee's National Insurance number: FG 23 32 45 A *(Mr Mrs Miss Ms)*

3 Surname (in capitals): WALLET.   MR.

First name(s) (in capitals): GERALD

4 Leaving date (in figures): Day 11 Month 11 Year 2000

5 Continue Student Loan Deductions (Y)

6 Tax Code at leaving date. *If week 1 or Month 1 basis applies, write 'X' in the box marked Week 1 or Month 1*

Code: 640 H   Week 1 or Month 1

7 Last entries on *Deductions Working Sheet (P11)* **Complete only if Tax Code is cumulative.** *Make no entry here if Week 1 or Month 1 basis applies. Go to item 7.*

Week or month number: Week 30   Month 7

Total pay to date: £ 21000 , 00 p

Total tax to date: £ 3815 , 99 p

8 This employment pay and tax. ■ *No entry needed if Tax Code is cumulative and amounts are same as item 6 entry.*

Total pay in this employment: £ , p

Total tax in this employment: £ , p

9 Works number/ Payroll number: 622.

10 Department or branch if any

11 Employee's private address and Postcode:

17 CEDAR AVE
TOP VILLAGE
HERTS
HE2 4TP

12 I certify that the details entered above in items 1 to 9 are correct

Employer's name, address and Postcode:

LARKS HOUSE
5 HIGH ST.
BORTON
HERTS HE17 1JK

Date

To the employer   *Please complete with care* ★

For Tax Office use

- Complete this form following the 'Employee leaving' instructions in the *Employer's quick Guide to PAYE and NICs* (cards CWG1). ★ **Make sure the details are clear on all four parts of this form**. Make sure your name and address is shown on Parts 1 and 1A.
- Detach Part 1 and send it to your Tax Office immediately.
- Hand Parts 1A, 2 and 3 (unseparated) to your employee when he or she leaves
- If the employee has died, write 'D' in this box and send all three parts of this form (unseparated) to your Tax Office immediately.

D

P45

BMSD9/99

- NO FUTURE P.45
- PUT DETAILS IN A LETTER TO TAX OFFICE + WIDOW
- APPLY INCOME TAX BUT NO NATIONAL INSURANCE TO EXTRA PAY.

Practice activity 3.4 _____

You are the payroll officer of Fry and Dice Ltd. Your company's tax reference number is 146/B1323. Its address is Home Works, Rudderton Estate, Gloucester, G99 1YY.

You ask to see two employees who have joined your company on 1 May 2000, and you obtain their P45s. Part 3 of each P45 is shown on the next pages.

Ms Williams supplies you with her personal details, as follows:

Address: 113 A Town St, Little Smeltings, Gloucs, G35 2HU
Date of birth: 12.12.1973

Mr Smith's address is 4 Constable Drive, Gloucester G22 4PQ. His date of birth is 29 May 1980.

Ms Williams, a quality control checker, has works number 351 and Mr Smith, a personnel assistant, has works number 724. Both are weekly paid.

Upon checking the tax tables you find that Ms Williams' tax due to week 4 is £62.30 and Mr Smith's £81.22.

Tasks

(a) Complete Part 3 of each P45, for despatch to your Tax Office.
(b) Complete the following extract from the tax side of a P11 for Mr Smith.

	Tax code	Amended WK/mnth											
W e e k	Pay in the week 2	Total pay to date 3	Total free pay to date 4a	K codes Total additional pay to date 4b	Total taxable pay to date 5	Total tax due to date 6	K codes Tax due at end of current period 6a	K codes Regul. limit 6b	Tax deducted or refunded in the week 7	K codes Tax not deducted owing to the regul. limit 8	Tax credits 9
1											
2											
3											
4		820.00	386.88		433.12	81.22					

Inland Revenue

New employee details
For completion by new employer

P45
Part 3

		District number	Reference number
1	Previous PAYE Reference	152	C 3124

2 Employee's National Insurance number — AB 23 45 67 C

           (Mr Mrs Miss Ms)

3 Surname — WILLIAMS   Ms

  First name(s) — KAREN ALICE

4 Date left previous employment — Day 30 Month 04 Year 20 00

5 Continue Student Loan Deductions (Y)

6 Tax Code at leaving date. 'x' in the box means Week 7 or Month 1 basis applies — Code 379 L   Week 1 or Month 1

7 Last entries on Deductions Working Sheet (P11). If there is an 'X' at item 6, there will be no entries here

  Week or Month number — Week 4   Month

  Total pay to date — £ 640 00 p

  Total tax to date — £ 62 30 p

To the new employer

Complete items 8 to 17 below and send this page of the form only to your Tax Office immediately.

8 New PAYE Reference — 1H6   B1323

9 Date employment started (in figures) — Day 01 Month 05 Year 20 00

10 Tick here if you want these details to be shown on tax code notifications — ✓

  Works/Payroll number — 351

  Department or branch if any

11 Enter P if employee will not be paid by you between date employment began and next 5 April

12 Enter code in use if different to code at item 6

13 If the tax figure you are entering on P11 differs from item 7 above (see CWG (1999) card 4) please enter your figure here — £

14 Employee's private address — 113 A TONN ST. LITTLE SMELTINGS   GLOUCESTER   Postcode GL3S 2HU

15 Employee's date of birth (if known) — 12 12 1973

16 Employee's job title or description — QUALITY CONTROL CHE

17 **Declaration.** I have prepared a *Deductions Working Sheet* (P11) in accordance with the details above.

  Employer — FRY + DICE LTD.

  Address — HOME WORKS, RUDDERTON ESTATE   GLOUCESTER   Postcode G99 1YY   Date

P45

O	Inland **Revenue**	*New employee details* **For completion by new employer**	**P45** **Part 3**

District number	Reference number
181	B 2697

1 Previous PAYE Reference

2 Employee's National Insurance number | LD 14 94 38 N

3 Surname | SMITH | (Mr Mrs Miss Ms) Mr

First name(s) | BENJAMIN PETER

4 Date left previous employment

Day	Month	Year	
30	04	20	00

5 Continue Student Loan Deductions (Y)

6 Tax Code at leaving date. 'x' in the box means Week 7 or Month 1 basis applies

Code: 502 H   Week 1 or Month 1

7 Last entries on *Deductions Working Sheet (P11)*. If there is an 'X' at item 6, there will be no entries here

	Week	Month
Week or Month number	4	
Total pay to date	£ 820	00 p
Total tax to date	£ 84	97 p

To the new employer

Complete items 8 to 17 below and send this page of the form only to your Tax Office immediately.

8 New PAYE Reference | 146 B1323

9 Date employment started (in figures)

Day	Month	Year
01	05	2000

10 Tick here if you want these details to be shown on tax code notifications ✓   Works/Payroll number Department or branch if any | 724

11 Enter P if employee will not be paid by you between date employment began and next 5 April

12 Enter code in use if different to code at item 6

13 If the tax figure you are entering on P11 differs from item 7 above (see CWG (1999) card 4) please enter your figure here | £ 81.22

14 Employee's private address | 4 CONSTABLE DRIVE | GLOUCESTER   Postcode G22 4PQ

15 Employee's date of birth (if known) | 29 05 1980

16 Employee's job title or description | PERSONAL ASSISTANT

17 **Declaration.** I have prepared a *Deductions Working Sheet* (P11) in accordance with the details above.

Employer | FRY + DICE LTD

Address | HOME WORKS RUDDERTON | GLOUCESTER   Postcode GA9 14Y   Date

P45

Practice activity 3.5 _____

You are the payroll officer of Health Audit Agency, a government agency. On 15 September 2000, you are visited by a new employee, a university graduate, who has just joined your organisation as a research officer. She has brought her National Insurance number, which is YC657891D. As she does not have a Form P45, she signed the attached Form P46.

You have already received the following information about her from her new departmental head in the research department, department 19.

Surname	**Carlyle**
First names	**Roberta Jane**
Address	**15 Crescent Lane**
	Willowby
	Bucks WL5 2TT
Date of birth	**19 August 1978**
Employment commenced	**8 September 2000**
Starting salary	**£13,500 pa**

Your company's PAYE reference is 186/D5432 and its address is Mussel House, Lymm Road, London EC5V 6QP.

Task

Complete the attached Form P46.

PAYE Employer's notice to Inland Revenue Office

Send in on the first pay day for employees who
- *do not have a form P45, or*
- *were previously paid below the PAYE threshold.*

Section 1 - to be completed by the EMPLOYEE

Read each statement carefully. Tick **each one** that applies to you. If none of them apply, do not sign the statement.

Statement A
This is my first regular job since leaving full-time education. I have not claimed Jobseeker's Allowance, or income support paid because of unemployment since then. ✓

Statement B
This is my only or main job. ✓

Statement C
I receive a pension as well as the income from this job. ☐

I confirm that I have ticked the statements that apply to me.

Signed R Carlyle

Date 15 / 9 / 00

Section 2 - to be completed by the EMPLOYER

Your employer's Quick Guide to PAYE and NICs (CWG1, Card 5) tells you how to complete this form.

Employee's details

National Insurance number Y C 6 5 7 8 9 1 D

Surname including title Mr/Mrs/Miss/Ms/Other
CARLYLE

First name(s)
ROBERTA JANE

Address 15 CRESANT LANE
WILLOWBY
BUCKS
Postcode WL5 2TT

Date of birth 19 / 08 / 1978

Male/Female *(enter M/F)* F

Works/payroll number, if any

Department/Branch, if any

Job title REASEARCH OFFICER

Date employment started 08 / 09 / 2000

P46

Coding information

Existing employee now above PAYE threshold
(enter X in box if this applies) ☐

New employee who has signed statement *(enter letter here)* A̶B̲

New employee who has not signed a statement ☐

Code operated for this employee 438 L

Enter X in box if code operated on week1/month 1 basis ☐

Employer's details

Employer's PAYE reference 186 / D5432

Name HEALTH AUDIT AGENCY

Address MUSSEL HOUSE
LYMNE ROAD
LONDON
Postcode EC5U 6QP

Date this form was completed 15 / 07 / 2000

Practice activity 3.6

Olly Whalley, a monthly paid employee assessed under Table D, left at the end of June, but was paid a regular bonus on July 15th, two weeks after he had left. What is the NIC treatment?

- YES NORMAL MONTHLY NATIONAL INSURANCE + TAX.

- USE RATES AS AT JUNE.

BPP
PUBLISHING

4 Instructions from external agencies

Practice activity 4.1

How can you verify that a deduction for pension contributions is correct?

Practice activity 4.2

You receive an attachment of earnings order from the Child Support Agency. This orders you to deduct £130 per month from Joe Johnson's pay, subject to a minimum protected rate of £350 per month. Joe Johnson's net pay for the following three months is as follows.

Month 1	£800	— 130
Month 2	£400	— 50
Month 3	£600	— 210

Task

Calculate the amount to be deducted each month under the CSA order.

Practice activity 4.3

The Child Support Agency has heard that Joe Johnson has had a pay rise. Joe comes to tell you that he doesn't want the CSA to be given details of his pay rise. Just after his visit, you receive a letter from the CSA demanding details of his pay rise. What do you do? *Give details*

Practice activity 4.4

You receive a letter from the local trade union, advising subscriptions have increased to £2 per month from £1.50 per month. Most employees have signed a form authorising payroll to deduct 'the current rate' for their trade union subscription. However, Marlene Ramsay's authority is specifically for £1.50 per month. What do you do?

*Take 150
but contact her
She must sign*

5 Recording payroll variations

Practice activity 5.1

It is your firm's policy that all employees who are sick need to supply a doctor's certificate after 5 working days' absence. Joe Johnson has been off sick for two weeks and has sent in self certification certificates for both weeks. The firm's rules state that sick pay can only be paid if the correct certificates are sent in. Can you pay Joe sick pay for either week? If you can not, what action should you take?

Practice activity 5.2

Joe Johnson tells you that he has been promoted and that his new salary rate is £20,000 pa. However, you receive a memorandum from personnel confirming the promotion, but stating that the new salary rate is £19,500 pa.

Tasks

(a) Which rate do you pay?
(b) Do you contact Joe Johnson about the pay rise?

Practice activity 5.3

Marlene Ramsay has claimed non-contractual overtime of 5 hours at double time this week. The overtime was worked on Sunday and her contract of employment confirms that Sunday overtime is paid at double time. Do you pay her the overtime?

Practice activity 5.4

Personnel inform you that the factory workers basic working week has been reduced to 35 hours from 40 hours and that hourly pay has increased to £4.00 per hour from £3.75.

Tasks

(a) Calculate basic pay before the change.
(b) Calculate basic pay after the change.

6 Basic pay

Practice activity 6.1

Alphonse is an hourly paid employee. His basic rate is £5 per hour for daytime shifts, £7.50 per hour for night shifts, £7.50 per hour for overtime (ie hours worked in excess of 40 hours a week) except weekends when the rate is always £10 per hour.

How much would he earn in the following cases, assuming an 8-hour day.

(a) For a 40 hour week of daytime shifts with no overtime?

(b) For a 40 hour week if one day is worked on Saturday?

(c) For a 40 hour week of nightshifts and an additional four hours overtime on Wednesday and Thursday?

Practice activity 6.2

Boris is a pieceworker, and is paid £5 for each of the first 60 widgets produced per week. However, he gets a guaranteed minimum wage of £144, and if he works more than 40 hours a week he gets £4 per hour as overtime. If he produces over 60 widgets per week he gets £6 per widget for the 61st and each subsequent widget. How much would he earn in each of the following weeks?

(a) In the week ending 13/3/X1 Boris made 50 widgets and did 4 hours of overtime.
(b) In the week ending 20/3/X1 he produced 10 widgets.
(c) In the week ending 27/3/X1 he produced 29 widgets.
(d) In the week ending 3/4/X1, Boris produced 70 widgets, and worked 6 hours overtime.

Practice activity 6.3

Cassandra works for a company which pays bonuses and commission. Her basic pay is £900 per month, but at the end of the month she receives commission of 5% of the sales she made in the previous month (so that at the end of May she will be paid the commission for April for example). If her sales exceed £10,000 in any quarter (ie three month period from 1 January to 31 March, 1 April to 30 June, 1 July to 30 September, 1 October to 31 December) she gets a one-off bonus of £1,000. These are paid in the month after the quarter.

Here are her sales figures for the first six months of 20X2.

Month	£
Jan	5,000
Feb	4,000
March	3,000
April	2,000
May	3,000
June	4,000

Her sales in December 20X1 were £5,000. Sales in the quarter to December 20X1 did not exceed £10,000.

What will be included in her gross pay at the end of each month from January to June inclusive?

BPP PUBLISHING

7 Additional pay and allowances

Practice activity 7.1 _____

Dilys is a salaried worker, who also receives overtime of £10 per hour for hours worked over 156 a month, and a productivity bonus of 5% of her basic monthly salary if the quality of her work exceeds expectations.

Her salary was £12,000 per year, payable in equal monthly instalments. This has been increased to £15,000 by agreement on 1 May, backdated to 1 January.

In May she worked 175 hours, and produced work of better quality than standard. For January to April the quality of her work exactly matched expectations.

What was her total gross pay for May?

Practice activity 7.2 _____

The following information relates to Mary Down, an employee.

	£
Employee's National Insurance contribution	10
Overtime	20
Back pay	15
Basic pay	150
Bonus	30
Award for staff suggestion	20
Income tax	25

Tasks

(a) What is Mary's gross pay?
(b) What is Mary's net pay?

Which would you expect to see on her pay cheque?

Practice activity 7.3 _____

You administer the payroll for Gosplan plc. The company runs two payrolls.

(a) A production payroll, for production workers.
(b) An administration payroll for all others.

The production payroll contains 20 employees.

You are provided with the following information, which applies to 20X1.

(a) A memorandum from the Board detailing wage rates, hours and overtime rates for 20X1.
(b) Timesheet summaries for Week 13 in 20X1.
(c) A list of employee names and job titles.

 22

(d)   A proforma payroll.

Task

Complete the proforma payroll for the week (see page 25) differentiating between basic pay and overtime.

GOSPLAN PLC INTERNAL MEMORANDUM

To: Personnel Department
         Finance Department   cc:Payroll Department
From: Board of directors   Date: 16/12/20X0

Settlement of wages claim for 20X1

The Board, after negotiations with the General and Provision Production Union, and with the Skilled Artisan Syndicalist Association, announce that the pay for production staff will be fixed at the following rates. Overall there has been a 10.6% rise since 20X0.

Grade title	*Hourly rate effective 1 January 20X1*
Foreman	£7.50
Underforeman	£6.50
Boilershutter	£5.75
Chargehand	£5.00
Templateer	£5.10
Hopper steerer	£5.20
Optical fibre twister	£7.00

Overtime remains at time and a half. It will be paid after 40 hours, as opposed to 41 hours. *All* Saturday working is paid at double time, irrespective as to how many hours have been worked previously.

By order of the Board

Anthony Paratchik

Anthony Paratchik
Company secretary

Timesheet summary

20X1 Week 13	Timesheet summary (hours)							
Employee	*Staff no*	*Mon*	*Tues*	*Wed*	*Th*	*Fri*	*Sat*	*Total*
Ashdown P	071	-	8	8	8	8	8	40
Baker K	659	8	8	8	8	7	-	39
Blair T	660	-	8	8	8	8	8	40
Callaghan J	661	12	12	12	4	-	-	40
Clarke K	624	7	7	7	7	7	-	35
Delors J	010	9	9	11	10	9	-	48
Heath E	970	8	8	9	9	-	-	34
Heseltine M	664	10	10	7	7	7	-	41
Hurd D	663	9	9	9	9	9	-	45
King T	662	-	-	10	10	10	10	40
Kinnock N	992	8	8	8	8	9	4	45
Lamont N	666	-	8	8	8	8	-	32
Lilley P	665	8	8	8	8	8	-	40
Major J	990	-	9	9	9	8	8	43
Patten C	696	9	8	8	8	-	-	33
Rifkind M	621	-	8	8	8	8	8	40
Scargill A	917	8	9	8	9	8	-	42
Thatcher M	999	8	8	8	8	8	8	48
Waldegrave W	721	8	8	8	8	8	-	40
Wilson H	964	-	-	8	8	12	12	40

Employee	*Staff number*	*Job title*
Ashdown P	071	Underforeman
Baker K	659	Templateer
Blair T	660	Boilershutter
Callaghan J	661	Optical Fibre Twister
Clarke K	624	Hopper steerer
Delors J	010	Foreman
Heath E	970	Chargehand
Heseltine M	664	Hopper Steerer
Hurd D	663	Boilershutter
King T	662	Templateer
Kinnock N	992	Underforeman
Lamont N	666	Hopper Steerer
Lilley P	665	Hopper Steerer
Major J	990	Chargehand
Patten C	696	Templateer
Rifkind M	621	Templateer
Scargill A	917	Boilershutter
Thatcher M	999	Chargehand
Waldegrave W	721	Templateer
Wilson H	964	Optical Fibre Twister

Payroll Proforma (please fill in)

PAYROLL – 20X1 WEEK 13 Employee	Staff number	Basic £ p	Saturday & overtime £ p	Total £ p
Ashdown P	071			
Baker K	659			
Blair T	660			
Callaghan J	661			
Clarke K	624			
Delors J	010			
Heath E	970			
Heseltine M	664			
Hurd D	663			
King T	662			
Kinnock N	992			
Lamont N	666			
Lilley P	665			
Major J	990			
Patten C	696			
Rifkind M	621			
Scargill A	917			
Thatcher M	999			
Waldegrave W	721			
Wilson H	964			
TOTAL				

Practice activity 7.4 _____

It is now 20X2. You, and all the production workforce, are still employed by Gosplan plc, even though Gosplan plc has been taken over by another company.

The new management are changing the pay and staff grading structure, and, after negotiating with the Trades Unions, have come up with an agreement.

It is Week 20 and you are required to work out the wages.

You have been given the following documents.

(a) A timesheet summary for Week 20, with details of good production.
(b) The new grades with payment details, and overtime details
(c) Details of the productivity and quality bonus scheme
(d) A note from the production director
(e) A list of the employees and their job titles in the old system (see Practice activity 7.3)
(f) A proforma payroll.

Practice activities

Task

Complete the payroll for Week 20 20X2.

20X2	Week 20			Timesheet summary (Hours)				
Employee	Staff no	Mon	Tues	Wed	Th	Fri	Sat	Total
Ashdown P	071	8	8	7	7	7	-	37
Baker K	659	9	7	7	7	9	-	39
Blair T	660	8	8	8	8	8	-	40
Callaghan J	661	10	10	-	10	10	-	40
Clarke K	624	-	8	10	8	-	10	36
Delors J	010	8	8	8	8	8	8	48
Heath E	970	-	-	9	9	9	9	36
Heseltine M	664	7	7	7	7	7	7	42
Hurd D	663	-	9	9	9	9	9	45
King T	662	9	9	8	8	8	-	42
Kinnock N	992	4	10	8	9	8	8	47
Lamont N	666	8	8	8	7	7	-	38
Lilley P	665	-	9	7	7	7	10	40
Major J	990	-	8	8	8	8	8	40
Patten C	696	7	6	6	9	9	-	37
Rifkind M	621	-	7	7	7	7	7	35
Scargill A	917	-	10	8	9	8	8	43
Thatcher M	999	9	7	7	9	9	-	41
Waldegrave W	721	6	7	7	7	7	7	41
Wilson H	964	9	9	9	9	-	-	36
TOTAL								803

Total number of units produced	1,273
Units rejected by quality control	153
Good units of production	1,120

GOSPLAN PLC INTERNAL MEMORANDUM

To: Payroll Department
From: Yashuhiro Tokugawa, Personnel Director
Date: 15/12/20X1

Before formal announcement of the deal, you might like to know the following grading structure is to be introduced from 1 January 20X2.

Old grade	New grade	Basic pay per week £	Overtime per hour £ p
Foreman	A	285	9.30
Underforeman	B	230	7.75
Boilershutter	B	230	7.75
Chargehand	C	180	6.30
Templateer	C	180	6.30
Hopper steerer	C	180	6.30
Optical fibre twister	A	285	9.30

Overtime

This will be paid at the rate per hour above for the first ten hours worked over 35 hours. Overtime hours over and above 10 hours should be paid at the above rate × 1.25.

There is no special rate for weekend working.

All employees are expected to work a standard 35 hours a week.

GOSPLAN PLC INTERNAL MEMORANDUM

To: Payroll Department
From: Yashuhiro Tokugawa, Personnel Director
Date: 16/12/20X1

Staff incentives

(1)   PRODUCTIVITY AND QUALITY BONUS

Production workers will be eligible for a group bonus each week. The scheme will commence on 1 January 20X2.

For every good unit produced over 1,000 units a £5 bonus will be paid. Units rejected by Quality Control are excluded from the calculation. The bonus is allocated equally between production employees.

(2)   STAFF SUGGESTION SCHEME

A reward of up to £5,000 will be offered for any idea to improve productivity or quality which is implemented. Amounts under £100 will be paid through the payroll. The rest will be paid by separate cheque.

BPP PUBLISHING

GOSPLAN PLC INTERNAL MEMORANDUM

To: Personnel Department
cc: Payroll Department
From: Toshiro Mifune, Production Director
Date: 2/5/20X2

The following employees are to be rewarded as follows for suggestions leading to increases in productivity or quality. Please pay in Week 20.

J Delors is to receive £30.

A Scargill is to receive £50.

PAYROLL PROFORMA (please fill in)

PAYROLL – 20X2 WEEK 20 *Employee*	*Staff number*	*Basic* £ p	*Over-time* £ p	*Bonus* £ p	*Other* £ p	*Total* £ p
Ashdown P	071					
Baker K	659					
Blair T	660					
Callaghan J	661					
Clarke K	624					
Delors J	010					
Heath E	970					
Heseltine M	664					
Hurd D	663					
King T	662					
Kinnock N	992					
Lamont N	666					
Lilley P	665					
Major J	990					
Patten C	696					
Rifkind M	621					
Scargill A	917					
Thatcher M	999					
Waldegrave W	721					
Wilson H	964					
TOTAL						

Practice activity 7.5 _____

How could the documentation with which you were provided for Additional exercises 7.3 and 7.4 have been better designed so as to make your calculations easier?

8 Income tax: simple cases

Practice activity 8.1

In Month 4 of the year, George Ghost earns £1,500 in gross pay. He earned £1,000 in each of Months 1, 2 and 3. His free pay to date is £603 (in Month 3 it was £452.25).

(a) What is his taxable pay to date?

(b) If, by the end of Month 3, George had paid £514.74 in tax, and tax due by the end of Month 4 was £796.53, how much would he pay in Month 4?

Practice activity 8.2

What is the significance of a person's tax code, and how is it notified to the payroll department?

Practice activity 8.3

What is the emergency code?

Practice activity 8.4

If an employee is taxable on Table B, what do you do about the Starting Rate relief?

Practice activity 8.5

The purpose of this activity is to test your ability to calculate correctly the PAYE income tax deductions for an employee who is paid weekly and taxed on a cumulative basis, and to fill in a P11 for him.

Ralph Thomas is a weekly paid worker with your company. Details about him are as follows.

BPP
PUBLISHING

National Insurance number	YY223344Y
Date of birth	3.9.71
Works number	626
Tax code	472T

On 8 April 2000, his total pay was £240.60.

On 15 April 2000, his total pay was £290.30, which includes an overtime payment of £49.70.

On 22 April 2000, his total pay was £260.00.

Tables A give the following free pay for code 472.

Week	Free pay
	£
1	90.95
2	181.90
3	272.85

Taxable pay tables are given in Appendix I at the end of this text.

Tasks

(a) Using the appropriate Tax Tables, calculate the total tax due in each of these three weeks.

(b) Fill in the following extract from the deductions working sheet for his PAYE income tax, as it should be as at 22 April 2000.

	Tax code	Amended											
		WK/mnth											
W e e k	Pay in the week 2	Total pay to date 3	Total free pay to date 4a	K codes Total additional pay to date 4b	Total taxable pay to date 5	Total tax due to date 6	K codes Tax due at end of current period 6a	K codes Regul. limit 6b	Tax deducted or reduced in the week 7	K codes Tax not deducted owing to the regul. limit 8	Tax credits 9
1											
2											
3											

Practice activity 8.6 _____

This activity is similar to Additional activity 8.5 except that it deals with a monthly-paid employee.

Barbara Walton is an employee of your company. Her monthly pay is £3,000 and her tax code is 505H. Staff are paid on the 22nd of each month.

Tables A give the following free pay.

		Month	
Code		1	2
		£	£
5		4.92	9.84
500		417.42	834.84
Boxed 500		416.67	833.34

Tasks

(a) Calculate the tax payable or refundable on the 22nd of (i) April 2000 and (ii) May 2000.

(b) Fill in the following extract from a P11 for this employee up to the end of May 2000.

	Tax code	Amended WK/mnth									
Month	Pay in the month 2	Total pay to date 3	Total free pay to date 4a	K codes Total additional pay to date 4b	Total taxable pay to date 5	Total tax due to date 6	K codes Tax due at end of current period 6a	K codes Regul. limit 6b	Tax deducted or reduced in the month 7	K codes Tax not deducted owing to the regul. limit 8	Tax credits 9
1											
2											

Practice activity 8.7

You are the payroll officer of Burnham Peters Ltd. During the course of a week in your job, you receive several queries from employees.

(a) Ellen Priestley is a pensioner, who now works for the company part time. She tells you that because she is now old enough for a state pension, and is only a part time worker, you shouldn't deduct any tax from her pay.

(b) Tina Rafferty is a temporary switchboard operator, who has been sent to your company by the Bright Sounds Employment Agency Ltd, an employment agency for temporary secretarial staff. She has been with your company for over three months, and has come to tell you that she would now like to be paid directly by you instead of by the agency. This is because the agency has been very slow recently to pay her weekly wages.

(c) Bob Harkins is a warehouse worker, who telephones you to say that his Tax Office has given him a code BR. He wants to know what it means.

(d) Simone Michel is a manager of your company who has just been posted to the overseas branch in Germany, where she expects to be (almost full time) for the next two to three years. She asks you whether her monthly salary will be subject to PAYE.

(e) Arthur Tildesley is a part-time worker in your company warehouse. He telephones you to say that he wants to become self-employed and that you shouldn't deduct any income tax from his pay.

(f) Alan Gorham tells you that he is on emergency code, and asks you what it means.

How would you deal with each of these queries?

9 Income tax: more complex cases

Practice activity 9.1 _____

Maria Pfeffer's salary as at 1 January 2000 was £15,000 per annum. On 1 January 2001 she received a pay rise of 5%. Her tax code at 6 April 2000 was 433L. On 22 July 2000 her employer received a P6(T) from the Tax Office notifying a change in Maria's tax code to 130L, to be used as soon as possible.

Tables A give the following figures.

Month	Code 130 Free pay £	Code 433 Free pay £
1	109.09	361.59
2	218.18	723.18
3	327.27	1,084.77
4	436.36	1,446.36
5	545.45	1,807.95
6	654.54	2,169.54
7	763.63	2,531.13
8	872.72	2,892.72
9	981.81	3,254.31
10	1,090.90	3,615.90
11	1,199.99	3,977.49
12	1,309.08	4,339.08

Task

Complete the extract from Maria's P11 for 2000/01 shown below, making (and stating) any further assumptions you think are necessary.

M o n t h	Pay in the month 2	Total pay to date 3	Total free pay to date 4a	K codes Total additional pay to date 4b	Total taxable pay to date 5	Total tax due to date 6	K codes Tax due at end of current period 6a	K codes Regul. limit 6b	Tax deducted or reduced in the month 7	K codes Tax not deducted owing to the regul. limit 8	Tax credits 9
1											
2											
3											
4											
5											
6											
7											
8											
9											
10											
11											
12											

Practice activity 9.2

Philip Phantom earns £1,500 in Month 1 and £2,000 in Month 2. Free pay for his tax code (498L) in Month 1 is £415.75 and in Month 2 is £831.50.

(a) What is his taxable pay to date in Month 1, and Month 2:

    (i)   on a Week 1/Month 1 basis?

    (ii)   on the normal cumulative basis?

(b) How much tax will he pay in Month 1 and 2:

    (i)   on a Week 1/Month 1 basis?

    (ii)   on a cumulative basis?

Practice activity 9.3

This additional activity is designed to test your awareness of taxation on a Week 1/Month 1 basis.

John David Rose is an employee of your company. He is paid a monthly salary of £3,000 before deductions on the 25th of each month. You receive the following P6(T) from your Tax Office.

Inland
Revenue

Issued by
H.M. Inspector of Taxes

LONDON 8

PAYE - Notice to employer of employee's tax
code (or amended code) and previous
pay and tax

SUNNY SERVICES LTD
5 BOX STREET
LONDON SW8 4BD

Date
20/4/00

Employer's PAYE reference
123/B1234

Employee's name

J D ROSE

National Insurance number
*(To be entered on the Deductions
Working Sheet and to be quoted
in any communication)*

YT 1324 57 C

Works/Payroll no., Branch etc.

Code:
The code of this employee is amended to

608 T Week 1/ Month 1

for the year to 5 April   2001

*Please use this code from the next pay day after you receive
this form and follow the instructions in Part A overleaf.*

Previous Pay and Tax
*Where there is an entry here
please follow the instructions in
both Parts A and B overleaf.*

Previous pay

Previous tax

P6 (T)

Tables A give the following figures.

Month	Code 108 £	Code 120 £	Code 500 £	Boxed 500 £
1	90.75	100.75	417.42	416.67
2	181.50	201.50	834.84	833.34
3	272.25	302.25	1,252.26	1,250.01

Tasks

(a) Complete the following extract from a P11 for this employee for his April and May salary payments, to show his PAYE income tax deductions.

(b) Complete the extract from the P11 for his June salary, after you have received notice from the Tax Office in June of a change in his tax code to 620H (cumulative basis).

	Tax code	Amended WK/mnth											
M o n t h	Pay in the month 2	Total pay to date 3	Total free pay to date 4a	K codes Total additional pay to date 4b	Total taxable pay to date 5	Total tax due to date 6	K codes Tax due at end of current period 6a	K codes Regul. limit 6b	Tax deducted or reduced in the month 7	K codes Tax not deducted owing to the regul. limit 8	Tax credits 9
1											
2											
3											

Practice activity 9.4

One of the unusual features of a tax year is a Week 53 payment, which will occasionally occur. This additional activity tests your ability to compute the PAYE income tax payable, and to fill in a P11 in this situation.

An employee is paid £300.00 every week, and in this particular year (2000/01), there are wage payments on (a) 29 March 2001 - Week 52 and (b) 5 April 2001 - Week 53.

His tax code, 329T, gives him free pay as follows.

Week	Free pay £
1	63.45
47	2,982.15
48	3,045.60
49	3,109.05
50	3,172.50
51	3,235.95
52	3,299.40

Task

Complete the following extract from a P11 for Weeks 47 to 53. Total pay to and including week 47 is £300 × 47 = £14,100 and total tax to and including week 46 is £2,280.87.

Week	Pay in the week 2	Total pay to date 3	Total free pay to date 4a	K codes Total additional pay to date 4b	Total taxable pay to date 5	Total tax due to date 6	K codes Tax due at end of current period 6a	K codes Regul. limit 6b	Tax deducted or reduced in the week 7	K codes Tax not deducted owing to the regul. limit 8	Tax credits 9
47											
48											
49											
50											
51											
52											
53											

Practice activity 9.5

This additional activity deals with another unusual feature of a payroll system, which is what to do when there is a strike or a lay-off of staff in your organisation.

Grade A staff at your company went on strike at the end of Week 1 of the 2000/01 tax year. Grade A each get £250 a week gross when not on strike. As a result of the strike, your company's management have had to lay off all Grade B staff immediately. Grade B staff are paid 25% of their normal basic wage of £200 per week during their lay-off (£50 per week per Grade B employee).

Blank extracts from the P11s of two of your employees are shown below.

(a) Paul Rodgers is a Grade A employee, who is on strike from Week 2.
(b) Richard Stout is a Grade B employee, who is paid £50 in Week 2.

35

(a) **Paul Rodgers**

W e e k	Tax code	Amended WK/mnth											
					K codes				*K codes*			*Tax deducted*	*K codes*	
	Pay in the week 2	Total pay to date 3	Total free pay to date 4a	Total additional pay to date 4b	Total taxable pay to date 5	Total tax due to date 6	Tax due at end of current period 6a	K codes Regul. limit 6b	or reduced in the week 7	Tax not deducted owing to the regul. limit 8	Tax credit. 9
1											
2											
3											

(b) **Richard Stout**

W e e k	Tax code	Amended WK/mnth											
					K codes				*K codes*			*Tax deducted*	*K codes*	
	Pay in the week 2	Total pay to date 3	Total free pay to date 4a	Total additional pay to date 4b	Total taxable pay to date 5	Total tax due to date 6	Tax due at end of current period 6a	K codes Regul. limit 6b	or reduced in the week 7	Tax not deducted owing to the regul. limit 8	Tax credit. 9
1											
2											

Each employee has a tax code of 300T, giving free pay of £57.87 for Week 1 and £115.74 for week 2.

Tasks

(a) Complete the P11s for Weeks 1 and 2 for each of these employees.

(b) What would you do about any tax refunds due to Paul Rodgers and Richard Stout?

Practice activity 9.6

(a) Why are some people given K codes?

(b) Carol Lewis, a senior manager in your company has just phoned to query the amount of PAYE income tax deducted from her salary last month. You promise to look into it and on checking you find that her code was changed from 94T to K321 last month. You call back but her assistant explains that she is out of the office for the rest of the day.

Task

Write Miss Lewis a memo explaining what has happened. Judging from your conversation she has no understanding of the PAYE system and you will need to explain about tax codes generally.

(c) Miss Lewis's office is only a few second's walk away. Should you leave the memo on her desk?

(d) Since Miss Lewis is away for the day, could this matter not be dealt with tomorrow?

Practice activity 9.7

Ahmed Mushtaq earns a salary of £36,000 per annum. His tax code is K149. Tables A give the following figures for code 149.

Month	Amount £
1	124.92
2	249.84
3	374.76

Complete the following extract from his P11 for Months 1 to 3.

	Tax code	Amended WK/mnth										
W e e k	Pay in the week 2	Total pay to date 3	Total free pay to date 4a	K codes — Total additional pay to date 4b	Total taxable pay to date 5	Total tax due to date 6	K codes — Tax due at end of current period 6a	K codes — Regul. limit 6b	Tax deducted or reduced in the week 7	K codes — Tax not deducted owing to the regul. limit 8	Tax credits 9
1											
2											
3											

Practice activity 9.8

Martin Carr's tax code is K491. Tables A give £409.92 for Month 1 and £819.84 for Month 2. He is still a director of MC Ltd although he has almost retired. He receives fees of £1,500 per annum for attending monthly meetings, drives a company car and receives other benefits.

Task

(a) Complete Martin Carr's P11 for Months 1 and 2.

	Tax code	Amended WK/mnth										
W e e k	Pay in the week 2	Total pay to date 3	Total free pay to date 4a	K codes — Total additional pay to date 4b	Total taxable pay to date 5	Total tax due to date 6	K codes — Tax due at end of current period 6a	K codes — Regul. limit 6b	Tax deducted or reduced in the week 7	K codes — Tax not deducted owing to the regul. limit 8	Tax credits 9
1											
2											

BPP PUBLISHING

Practice activities

(b) Complete Martin Carr's P11 for Months 1 and 2 assuming that the K code operates on Month 1 basis.

	Tax code	Amended WK/mnth										
W e e k	Pay in the week 2	Total pay to date 3	Total free pay to date 4a	**K codes** Total additional pay to date 4b	Total taxable pay to date 5	Total tax due to date 6	**K codes** Tax due at end of current period 6a	**K codes** Regul. limit 6b	Tax deducted or reduced in the week 7	**K codes** Tax not deducted owing to the regul. limit 8	Tax credits 9
1											
2											

10 National Insurance

Practice activity 10.1

Which of the NI tables would you use for:

(a) an employee under 16?
(b) a not contracted out man over 65 who has given you a certificate of age exemption?
(c) a married woman, aged 25, who had contracted out in a salary-related scheme?
(d) a man of 40 who had taken out a personal pension plan with his bank?

Practice activity 10.2

You earn £550 a week. How much is assessable to NICs payable by:

(a) you?
(b) your employer?

Practice activity 10.3

Earnings for NICs is the same amount as pay in the week or month for PAYE purposes.

True [   ]   **False** [   ]

Practice activity 10.4

When do employees normally pay NICs?

Practice activity 10.5

You are a payroll clerk for Water Babies plc, a company which manufactures educational toys for children.

One of the employees is Harold Childe. He has just recently joined the company as Office Factotum. Harold joined on 27 July 20X1, the day after he left school for good. Harold has been paid £80 a week for his services.

He is 16 years old on 25 August 20X1.

Task

What is the significance of Harold's sixteenth birthday as far as NICs and income tax are concerned?

BPP PUBLISHING

Practice activity 10.6 _____

Harold writes you a note asking why his pay is less than £80 after his 16th birthday and how you worked it out.

Write a simple reply to him, stating how you arrived at the figure, and the reasons for the deduction.

Practice activity 10.7 _____

Harold Childe asks you another question. 'I don't see why I have to pay NICs. Some of my friends say that they have contracted out, and pay less. Can't I do the same?'

Draft a memorandum in reply.

Practice activity 10.8 _____

Churne Orvill Ltd is a company which has two main activities.

(a) The manufacture of fireworks for sale.

(b) The arrangement of firework displays for local authorities and other bodies on days of celebration.

Staff employed in the manufacturing department are paid weekly. Staff who arrange the displays receive both a salary, and a bonus based on each successful display, and are paid on a monthly basis.

The company does not run a contracted out pension scheme.

The following information relates to four members of staff in Months 1, 2 and 3 of the year 2000/01.

Tasks

Complete the following extracts from the NIC side of the P11s provided for Months 1 to 3/Weeks 1 to 13.

(a) Diane Geness, aged 34, is a monthly paid employee, who has been responsible for many of the company's most innovative experiments.

   Her basic salary is £1,577.33 per month, but in Month 2 her pay rises to £2,200 a month basic (and stays at that level).

(b) Horace Inkley is a weekly paid employee, earning £180 per week, without variation. Horace reaches retirement age at the beginning of Week 7, and provides you with a certificate of age exemption. Although he is past retirement age, he continues to work for Churne Orvill Ltd.

(c) Maggie Knox earns £305 a month. She works three days a week, but has no other employment.

(d) Silas Izewell has been with the company since it was founded. He will be 70 on 4 May 2000. He is retained as his skill and artistry in designing displays is famed throughout the industry.

   His monthly salary is £2,000.

   In Month 1 he also earned a bonus of £300 which, as is the case with all his bonus payments, he gives to charity. In Month 3 he received another bonus of £350, although the bonus related to a display he gave on 1 June.

He has also given you a certificate of age exemption.

National Insurance tables are in Appendix II.

Practice activities

Diane Geness

National Insurance contributions *Note:*   **LEL** = Lower Earnings Limit,   **UEL** = Upper Earnings Limit

Month / Week	For employer's use only	Earnings details — Earnings at the LEL (where earnings reach or exceed the LEL) 1a £ p	Earnings above the LEL, up to and including the employee's Earnings Threshold 1b £ p	Earnings above the employee's threshold, up to and including the employer's Earnings Threshold 1c £ p	Earnings above the employer's Earnings Threshold, up to and including the UEL 1d £ p	Contribution details — Total of employee's and employer's contributions payable 1e £ p	Employee's contribution payable 1f £ p	Rebate details — NIC rebate due on amount 1b 1g £ p	NIC rebate due on the sum of the amounts in 1b and 1c 1h £ p	Statutory Sick Pay in the week or month included in column 2 1I £ p	Statutory Maternity Pay in the week or month included in column 2 1J £ p	Student loan 1k £ p
1 / 1												
2												
3												
4												
5 / 2												
6												
7												
8												
9 / 3												
10												
11												
12												
13												

Enter NIC Contribution Table letter here

End of Year Summary

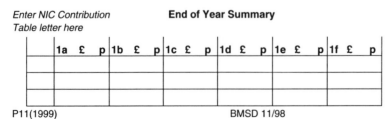

	1a £ p	1b £ p	1c £ p	1d £ p	1e £ p	1f £ p

P11(1999)   BMSD 11/98

Horace Inkley

National Insurance contributions *Note:*   LEL = Lower Earnings Limit,   UEL = Upper Earnings Limit

MONTH	WEEK	For employer's use only	Earnings details					Contribution details			Rebate details		Statutory Sick Pay in the week or month included in column 2	Statutory Maternity Pay in the week or month included in column 2	Student loan
			Earnings at the LEL (where earnings reach or exceed the LEL) 1a £ p	Earnings above the LEL, up to and including the employee's Earnings Threshold 1b £ p	Earnings above the employee's threshold, up to and including the employer's Earnings Threshold 1c £ p	Earnings above the employer's Earnings Threshold, up to and including the UEL 1d £ p	Total of employee's and employer's contributions payable 1e £ p	Employee's contribution payable 1f £ p	NIC rebate due on amount in 1b 1g £	NIC rebate due on the sum of the amounts in 1b and 1c 1h £ p		1l £ p	1l £ p	1k £ p
	W E E K N O														
	1														
	2														
	3														
1	4														
	5														
	6														
	7														
2	8														
	9														
	10														
	11														
	12														
3	13														

Enter NIC Contribution Table letter here   **End of Year Summary**

	1a £ p	1b £ p	1c £ p	1d £ p	1e £ p	1f £ p

43

Practice activities

Maggie Knox

National Insurance contributions *Note:*   LEL = Lower Earnings Limit,   UEL = Upper Earnings Limit

MONTH NO	WEEK NO	For employer's use only	Earnings details				Contribution details			Rebate details		Statutory Sick Pay	Statutory Maternity Pay	Student loan
			Earnings at the LEL (where earnings reach or exceed the LEL)	Earnings above the LEL, up to and including the employee's Earnings Threshold	Earnings above the employee's threshold, up to and including the employer's Earnings Threshold	Earnings above the employer's Earnings Threshold, up to and including the UEL	Total of employee's and employer's contributions payable	Employee's contribution payable	NIC rebate due on amount in 1b	NIC rebate due on the amount in 1b and 1c	in the week or month included in column 2	in the week or month included in column 2	
			1a £ p	1b £ p	1c £ p	1d £ p	1e £ p	1f £ p	1g £ p	1h £ p	1l £ p	1l £ p	1k £ p
	1												
	2												
	3												
1	4												
	5												
	6												
	7												
2	8												
	9												
	10												
	11												
	12												
3	13												

Enter NIC Contribution Table letter here   **End of Year Summary**

	1a £ p	1b £ p	1c £ p	1d £ p	1e £ p	1f £ p

P11(1999)   BMSD 11/98

44

Silas Izewell

National Insurance contributions *Note:*   LEL = Lower Earnings Limit,   UEL = Upper Earnings Limit

The following form is a P11 National Insurance contributions deductions working sheet with the following column structure:

Earnings details

- 1a £ p — Earnings at the LEL (where earnings reach or exceed the LEL)
- 1b £ p — Earnings above the LEL, up to and including the employee's Earnings Threshold
- 1c £ p — Earnings above the employee's threshold, up to and including the employer's Earnings Threshold
- 1d £ p — Earnings above the employer's Threshold, up to and including the UEL

Contribution details

- 1e £ p — Total of employee's and employer's contributions payable
- 1f £ p — Employee's contributions payable

Rebate details

- 1g £ p — NIC rebate due on amount in 1b
- 1h £ p — NIC rebate due on the sum of the amounts in 1b and 1c

- 1l £ p — Statutory Sick Pay in the week or month included in column 2
- 1l £ p — Statutory Maternity Pay in the week or month included in column 2
- 1k £ p — Student loan

Rows: Week (For employer's use only) No 1–13; Month No 1, 2, 3

Enter NIC Contribution Table letter here

End of Year Summary

	1a £ p	1b £ p	1c £ p	1d £ p	1e £ p	1f £ p

P11(1999)   BMSD 11/98

Practice activity 10.9 _____

The payroll department of Revolution-Art Ltd uses the exact percentage method of calculating NI contributions.

(a) Use the tables given in Appendix II to calculate how much in NICs would be paid for and by the following employees in a month or week. All are below pension age.

    (i)   P Morris earns £2,000 a month and is not contracted out.

    (ii)   B Jones earns £150 a week and is not contracted out.

    (iii)   F Sanders earns £80 a week and is not contracted out.

    (iv)   J Jellicoe earns £552.45 a week and is not contracted out.

    (v)   F Majid, who pays NICs under Table B at a reduced rate, earns £90 a week.

(b) Complete the following table, showing the entries to be made on each of the employees' P11s.

Name	Column 1a	Column 1b	Column 1c	Column 1d	Column 1e	Column 1f
P Morris						
B Jones						
F Sanders						
J Jellicoe						
F Majid						

Practice activity 10.10 _____

In Month 1, Penny Shaw earns £2,400 gross. Her employer, Executive Perks Ltd, runs a salary related occupational pension scheme which has the contracted out number S4 AB12CD3.

Penny contributes to the occupational pension scheme, which means that she is contracted out of SERPS, and the employer's and employee's contributions for Table D apply. As a result, the contribution rates are reduced for earnings between the earnings limits by 1.6% for employees and 3% for employers.

Penny makes pension contributions of £100 per month.

Task

Complete the following extract from Penny Shaw's P11. Use the exact percentage method to calculate NICs.

National Insurance contributions *Note:*   *LEL = Lower Earnings Limit,*   *UEL = Upper Earnings Limit*

		Earnings details				Contribution details		Rebate details		Statutory Sick Pay in the week or month included in column 2	Statutory Maternity Pay in the week or month included in column 2	Student loan
For employer's use only		Earnings at the LEL (where earnings reach or exceed the LEL)	Earnings above the LEL, up to and including the employee's Earnings Threshold	Earnings above the employee's threshold, up to and including the employer's Earnings Threshold	Earnings above the employer's Earnings Threshold up to and including the UEL	Total of employee's and employer's contributions payable	Employee's contribution payable	NIC rebate due on amount in 1b	NIC rebate due on the sum of the amounts in 1b and 1c			
		1a £ p	1b £ p	1c £ p	1d £ p	1e £ p	1f £ p	1g £	1h £ p	1i £ p	1j £ p	1k £ p
WEEK NO	1											
	2											
	3											
	4											
MONTH NO	1											

Practice activity 10.11 _____

(a) Tom Birmingham is an employee of Triton Ltd. He earns a salary of £40,000 per annum. £36,634.51 is paid in Week 1 and £65.99 per week in Weeks 2 to 52. He is not contracted out.

How much is due for the tax year 2000/01 in employee's and employer's NICs, using the exact percentage method?

(b) At the start of the following tax year Tom is promoted to the job of Director of Human Resources, but is not given a pay rise. His pay in Week 1 is £36,634.51 and in Weeks 2 - 52 he continues to receive £65.99 per week.

   (i)   Assuming that 2000/01 rates and limits still apply, how much is due in NICs for Weeks 1 and 2 of Tom's first year as a director? Use the exact percentage method.

   (ii)   How much is due for the year as a whole, using the exact percentage method?

11 Other deductions

Tutorial note: This section also contains some activities relating to Chapters 6 – 10, as revision.

Practice activity 11.1

Gilberta Sullivan has looked at her payslip. She doesn't understand why some deductions like income tax are deductions from gross pay and some aren't. Write a memo explaining the difference.

Practice activity 11.2

You work for Groddy Ltd, a company which sells recycled male cosmetics cheaply in the town of Bophinton. The town has a number of institutions of higher education. Your boss is thus never short of staff who can be paid a small sum for working a few hours a week.

At the beginning of the week you have three new employees to deal with. It is just after the end of the summer term.

(a) Charles Kingsley is nearly 16 years old, and has just left Dotheboys Hall, a local school. Mrs Groddy has written you a note saying that he is to be employed at £75 per week.

(b) Freddie Scullion is 19 and has just finished his first year at Porterhouse College, a college of one of the local universities. He has run up an overdraft, and wants to go on holiday in August. He has done no paid work during term time, nor in the Christmas or Easter vacations.

Mrs Groddy has agreed to employ Freddie Scullion at a salary of £70 a week for eight weeks.

(c) Oliver Spend, a 17 year old student at the Ned Ludd Technical College, works one evening a week from 6pm to 9.30pm for Mrs Groddy during term time, at £10 an evening.

What should you do in each case, with regard to tax and NICs?

Practice activity 11.3

Gill Tee Ltd of Workhouse Buildings, Almshouse Lane, Workington runs a payroll giving scheme for its employees. Each employee gives between £14 and £20 a month out of gross income to charities. Gill Tee Ltd does not charge for administration of the scheme. It is March 2001.

Gill Tee Ltd has a contract with the Charities Aid Foundation. The number of the contract is 9752. The following employees contribute to GAYE.

(a) Elizabeth Windsor (payroll number 02, NI number QE 201649 C) contributes £15 a month.
(b) Melani Ayre (payroll number 07, NI number AJ 999999 D) contributes £15 a month.
(c) R S I Croesus (payroll number 03, NI number KE 777777 B) gives £20 a month.
(d) John P Pope (payroll number 33, NI number ON 222222 A) gives £20 a month.

Tasks

(a) Fill in the GAYE listing form.

BPP PUBLISHING

(b) These donations are made gross.

Assuming that Elizabeth Windsor has taxable income of £10,000 per month:

(i)   how much is she saving in tax by participating in the payroll giving scheme?

(ii) how much is she saving in NICs?

INSTRUCTIONS FOR SUBMITTING DONATIONS

1. Quote your CONTRACT NUMBER and PAYROLL NAME on all documentation.

2. Check that the Employee identification number on each Charity Choice Form is correct.

3. Check that the Employee identification number which you quote on your monthly deduction list is also the same on the Charity Choice form.

4. Send us the completed TOP SECTION of the Charity Choice form AND keep a copy or the yellow carbonated copy on your file for future reference.

5. Please arrange for your monthly lists to be in this format or PHOTOCOPY FREELY and write or type the information required.

6. Please arrange for your monthly lists to show the MONTH OF DEDUCTION where possible.

7. Please submit donations by cheque. Other means of payment should be agreed with Give As You Earn prior to any change.

8. Please arrange for all Give As You Earn documentation to come to us in one monthly packet.

9. Use this as an example of the format needed for computer printouts.

10. It will help us if we could have both these numbers. If this poses a problem, please submit one or the other (see * overleaf).

GIVE AS YOU EARN EMPLOYEE DONATIONS   PAYLISTING/DEDUCTION STATEMENT

CONTRACT NUMBER: _ _ _ _ _ _ _ _ _ _   EMPLOYER NAME:_ _ _ _ _ _ _ _ _ _ _ _ _ _ _ _ _ _ _
MONTH OF DEDUCTION:_ _ _ _ _ _ _ _   EMPLOYER ADDRESS:_ _ _ _ _ _ _ _ _ _ _ _ _ _ _ _ _ _
PAYROLL NAME/ID/CODE:_ _ _ _ _ _ _ _ _ _ _ _ _   _ _ _ _ _ _ _ _ _ _ _ _ _ _ _ _ _ _

*NI NUMBER AND *PAYROLL NUMBER	DONATION	NAME	STARTER/ LEAVER
			—
			—
			—
			—
PAGE TOTAL			
OPTIONAL 5% ADMIN			
REMITTANCE ENCLOSED		MUST AGREE WITH ENCLOSED CHEQUE	

Additional activity 11.4

Sandy Shore is a weekly paid employee, whose basic weekly wage is £95, although she frequently does overtime. She is going on holiday.

At the end of Week 1, she asks for her pay for that week, which comprises basic of £95 plus £42 overtime, together with her basic pay of £95 for both Weeks 2 and 3. Sandy pays NICs based on Table A.

Her tax code is 419T, giving free pay as follows.

Week	Free pay
	£
1	80.75
2	161.50
3	242.25

Use National Insurance Table A (weekly pay) in the Appendix II.

Tasks

(a)   Fill in the weeks 1, 2 and 3 on the P11 provided.
(b)   What would she receive in her pay cheque at the end of Week 1?

National Insurance contributions *Note:*   *LEL = Lower Earnings Limit,*   *UEL = Upper Earnings Limit*

Month No	Week No	For employer's use only	Earnings details				Contribution details		Rebate details		Statutory Sick Pay in the week or month included in column 2	Statutory Maternity Pay in the week or month included in column 2	Student loan
			Earnings at the LEL (where earnings reach or exceed the LEL)	Earnings above the LEL, up to and including the employee's Earnings Threshold	Earnings above the employee's threshold, up to and including the employer's Earnings Threshold	Earnings above the employer's Earnings Threshold, up to and including the UEL	Total of employee's and employer's contributions payable	Employee's contribution payable	NIC rebate due on amount in 1b	NIC rebate due on the sum of the amounts in 1b and 1c			
			1a £ p	1b £ p	1c £ p	1d £ p	1e £ p	1f £ p	1g £ p	1h £ p	1I £ p	1J £ p	1k £ p
	1												
	2												
1	3												
	4												
	5												
	6												
	7												
2	8												
	9												
	10												
	11												
	12												
3	13												

Enter NIC Contribution Table letter here **End of Year Summary**

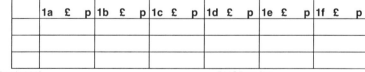

	1a £ p	1b £ p	1c £ p	1d £ p	1e £ p	1f £ p

P11(1999)   BMSD 11/98

| W e e k | Pay in the week 2 | Total pay to date 3 | Total free pay to date 4a | K codes | | Total taxable pay to date 5 | Total tax due to date 6 | K codes | K codes | Tax deducted or refunded in the week 7 | K codes | Tax credits 9 |
				Total additional pay to date 4b				Tax due at end of current period 6a	Regul. limit 6b		Tax not deducted owing to the regul. limit 8	
1												
2												
3												

Practice activity 11.5

Your procedures manual states:

'All employees who have been in permanent paid employment with the company for 6 months or more are eligible to join the company pension scheme.'

You have been asked to go through the personnel records of non-members of the scheme to assess whether to send out letters inviting them to join.

The date is 1 July 2000. You extract the following personnel details.

Name	Date joined company	Comments
R Dworkin	31/3/77	Personal pension plan from April 1991
A Foot	1/1/00	Temporary, first 3 months, then permanent since 1/4/00
Ian Grave	23/12/98	Director
R Hare	15/10/98	Aged 59
V Toombes	13/10/98	Working mother
B Quiet	4/2/00	Payroll clerk

Task

Which of them are eligible to join the pension scheme?

Practice activity 11.6

The employees of Panther Ltd are invited to join the company pension scheme. The pension fund trustees maintain two types of record:

(a) a service record
(b) a contribution record

for each member or prior member of the scheme. The pension scheme is only open to employees with over 6 months service. It only accepts joiners on 1 January of each year. Employee contributions are 6% of pensionable earnings per month and the company itself contributes 10%.

Tasks

(a) What details are necessary to keep a record of pensionable service?

(b) An employee, A Hopeful, decides to join the Panther Ltd pension scheme. Using the information below complete the proforma service record.

(c) How much would the employee's contributions to the scheme be in 2000?

53

(d)   How much would the employer's contributions to the scheme be in 2001?

(e)   How much would have been contributed to the scheme by A Hopeful, by Panther Ltd, and in total by 31 December 2001?

Pensionable earnings are basic salary at 1 January for most employees. For employees who earn a substantial amount of income as commission, this is added up for the year and added to the next year's basic to give an approximation (so that 2000's pensionable earnings will be basic pay at 1/1/00 plus the commission earned in 1999). Bonuses do not count as pensionable earnings.

A Hopeful joined Panther Ltd on 15 June 1999, at a salary of £20,000 pa. On 15 September 1999 his annual salary was increased to £22,000 pa. He joined the pension scheme on 1 January 2000.

On 3 January 2000 he changed jobs within the company, and his actual pay for the year was £12,000 basic plus £13,000 commission. On 1 January 2001 his basic salary increased to £14,500. His commission in 2001 was £15,000.

His NI number is WC963123X, and he was born on 3 June 1965. He intends to retire on his 65th birthday. His pension account number is H0943.

NAME:		NI NO:		A/C:	
SEX: M/F					
DATE JOINED COMPANY:			DATE JOINED SCHEME:		
ESTIMATED DATE OF RETIREMENT:			DATE LEFT SCHEME:		
YEARS (cross off)		1,2,3,4,5,6,7,8,9,10,11,12,13,14,15,16,17,18,19,20,21,22,23,24,25,26,27,28,29,30,31,32,33,34,35,36,37,38,39,40			

YEAR	PENSIONABLE EARNINGS (from 1/1)	YEAR	PENSIONABLE EARNINGS (from 1/1)	YEAR	PENSIONABLE EARNINGS (from 1/1)	YEAR	PENSIONABLE EARNINGS (from 1/1)
1		11		21		31	
2		12		22		32	
3		13		23		33	
4		14		24		34	
5		15		25		35	
6		16		26		36	
7		17		27		37	
8		18		28		38	
9		19		29		39	
10		20		30		40	
Pensionable earnings are earnings at 1 January of each year							

Practice activity 11.7

The occupational pensions scheme run for Harris Ltd takes 5% of the employee's pensionable earnings each month, and the company itself contributes 10% of the employee's pensionable earnings. 'Pensionable earnings' are the same as total pay in the month for PAYE purposes.

Jill Kernot earned a basic salary of £15,000 pa when she joined the scheme in January 2000. This rose to £17,000 pa from September 2000 and to £21,000 pa from September 2001. The standard working week is a 35 hour week. Occasionally she worked overtime and this was paid at time and a half.

Month	*Overtime hours*
March 2000	10
September 2000	5
October 2000	12
October 2001	14

(a) Complete the contribution record for Jill Kernot for years 1 and 2 of her membership of the scheme.

(b) If Jill were to leave the scheme at the end of Year 1 what would she receive with regard to her pension contribution?

(c) If she left after two years what would happen?

(d) Jill has said she wants to make some extra provision for the future. Draft a brief memo explaining what she can do.

NAME:									ACCOUNT:					
YEAR	B/F	JAN	FEB	MAR	APR	MAY	JUNE	JULY	AUG	SEP	OCT	NOV	DEC	C/F
EMP'EE														
1 EMP'ER														
EMP'EE														
2 EMP'ER														
EMP'EE														

Practice activity 11.8

Holmes plc contributes to an occupational pension scheme run on behalf of its employees who contribute up to retirement age. Not every employee is a member of the scheme, however, as some have opted out to invest in a personal pension plan instead.

Holmes plc pays its employees every month, using one payroll system. At the end of the report, a summary is printed of all the entries.

This totals up to the following for November 20X1.

	£
Gross pay	300,000
Income tax	50,000
NICs – employees	20,000
NICs – employer	30,000
Pension contributions – employees	18,000
Pension contributions – employer	30,000

£47,950 was eventually credited to the fund of contributions.

During November 20X1 the following occurred.

(a) One employee, Dr H Watson, reached 65 years old the day before pay day. His pension contributions were £100 a month. These had been deducted in error.

(b) The pension fund deducted 10 pence from every employee's contribution from the payroll as part of its statutory registration levy. There are 500 employees at Holmes Ltd.

(c) One employee made separately from the payroll an additional voluntary contribution of £78. It will form part of the payroll system next month. The employee pays tax at basic rate. The employee also makes FSAVCs of £50 per month to Piranha Funds Management Ltd. Holmes plc agreed to pay the tax relief of £22 on the AVC to the pension fund.

Task

Reconcile the pension deductions per the payroll with the amount actually credited to the pension fund at the end of November 20X1.

12 Net pay, aggregate payroll totals and payslips

Practice activity 12.1 _____

Some employees in your organisation are paid in cash, every Friday afternoon.

Your procedures manual states the following.

'Uncollected wage packets should be kept in the safe. Employees who do not, for whatever reason, collect their wage packets at the defined time should collect them before starting work on the next working day.

If the employee does not collect the wage packet then, he or she should be contacted over the public address system. The employee should then be contacted at home.

If the employee sends a representative to collect the wage, then the employee must provide a signed letter saying who the representative is, and the representative's address. The employee's signature on the letter should be checked against a specimen signature held by personnel department. The representative should bring evidence of identity so that the name and address can both be checked.'

(a) It is Friday 8 August, and you have been distributing wage packets to employees who still have the right to be paid in cash, and who insist on receiving wages this way.

   One employee, Lolita Humbert, has not turned up to collect her wage by the appointed time.

   What do you do?

(b) It is now Monday morning. You have come in early expecting to see Lolita Humbert. She is not there, so now what do you do?

(c) She does not appear to have turned up to work. Now what do you do?

(d) Suddenly, there is a knock on the door and a man walks in claiming to be Lolita's boyfriend. He tells you Lolita has been a bit out of sorts over the weekend and is ill. Could you give him the money? What should be your reply?

(e) He produces a letter from Lolita as follows.

13 James Mason St
Cambridge CB2
Mon 11 August

To: Payroll Dept

I authorise Vladimir Nabokov of 51 Russian Drive, Cambridge CB2, to collect my pay packet, which I should have picked up last Friday afternoon.

Yours faithfully

Lolita Humbert

He also produces the following driving licence.

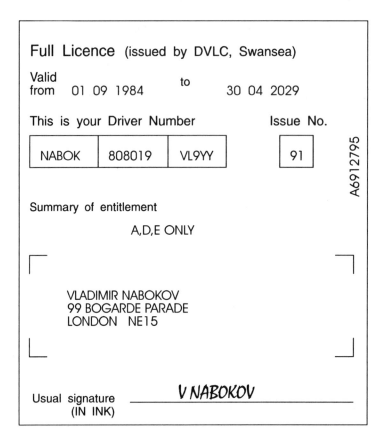

Full Licence (issued by DVLC, Swansea)

Valid
from   01 09 1984   to   30 04 2029

This is your Driver Number   Issue No.

| NABOK | 808019 | VL9YY |

91

A6912795

Summary of entitlement

A,D,E ONLY

VLADIMIR NABOKOV
99 BOGARDE PARADE
LONDON NE15

Usual signature _____ *V NABOKOV* _____
(IN INK)

What do you do?

Practice activity 12.2

You work in the payroll department of Astral Foods Ltd. The company is involved in gastronomic research, the results of which it publishes in its monthly magazine The Diner's Diet. Pay day is the last business day each month and each employee is paid by cheque.

Task

It is September 30. Prepare September 2000 (Tax Month 6) payslips for the following employees.

Sally Ami: Staff number 012, NI number TH123456E.

Victor Eel: Staff number 015, NI number SP123456I.

Abigail Tower: Staff number 031. NI number WA123456N. Abigail is given a round sum expense allowance of £1,000 a month in cash. Any over- or under-reimbursements are sorted out at the end of every six month period (normally in the March and September pay calculations) so that on April 1 and October 1 the balance on her account is zero.

All expense claims are dealt with in the month following that when they were incurred.

The following is also relevant.

(a) Each employee contributes £20 a month to a GAYE scheme

(b) An extract from the list of company loan accounts is also attached. These are repaid in equal instalments each month over the life of the loan. (The loans are given to the employees by way of cheques, not through the payroll.)

Blank payslips are provided on the following pages. Note that:

(a) 'deductions before tax' in the top half of the payslip refers to GAYE and employee's pension contributions;

(b) 'other deductions' include tax etc. (Note down employer's NICs at the bottom.)

ASTRAL FOODS LTD   EMPLOYEE LOAN ACCOUNT

ACCOUNT -	E1005 S AMI LOAN A/C	DR	CR	BAL
DATE	NARRATIVE	£	£	£
1/1/00	Season ticket 3-monthly	225		225
31/1/00			75	150
28/2/00			75	75
31/3/00			75	-
1/4/00	Season ticket 3-monthly	225		225
30/4/00			75	150
31/5/00			75	75
30/6/00			75	-
1/7/00	Season ticket 3-monthly	225		225
31/7/00			75	150
31/8/00			75	75

ASTRAL FOODS LTD

EXPENSE CLAIM

ATTACH VAT INVOICES FOR ALL EXPENSES

Employee name: Abigail Tower
Month: August 2000

	Item (Incl VAT) £
Client lunch	253.99
Caviare (for sampling research)	25.99
Champagne (for research purposes)	16.99
Hotel Gourmet, Paris (per Amex Bill)	234.81
Car Hire in Paris	178.90
Air tickets (Club Class)	700.00
	1,410.68

ABIGAIL TOWER'S EXPENSE ACCOUNT

Date	Narrative	£ DR	£ CR	£ DR/(CR)
1/4/00	Balance			-
15/4/00	March claim		963.90	(963.90)
30/4/00	April allowance	1,000		36.10
8/5/00	April claim		572.30	(536.20)
31/5/00	May allowance	1,000		463.80
8/6/00	May claim		371.94	91.86
30/6/00	June allowance	1,000		1,091.86
8/7/00	June claim		949.53	142.33
31/7/00	July allowance	1,000		1,142.33
8/8/00	July claim		1,250.01	(107.68)
31/8/00	August allowance	1,000		892.32
15/9/00	August claim		1,410.68	(518.36)

The following information has been extracted from your records. There have been a number of changes over the last few months to employees' salaries and tax codes.

	Ami £ p	Eel £ p	Tower £ p
Basic pay in tax year to 31/8	4,900.00	2,900.00	9,900.00
GAYE in tax year to 31/8	(100.00)	(100.00)	(100.00)
Basic pay 30/9	1,000.00	600.00	2,000.00
Bonus 1/9 - 30/9	100.00	60.00	150.00
GAYE 1/9 - 30/9	(20.00)	(20.00)	(20.00)
Income tax			
- 1/9 - 30/9	141.22	57.49	303.88
- to 31/8	763.08	255.01	1,788.42
NICs			
- in 1/9 - 30/9	77.20	33.20	182.00
- to 31/8	347.00	147.00	847.00
Employer's NIC 1/9 - 30/9	89.79	36.11	217.65
Tax code	270T	320T	400T

Employee:	Staff No:		Employer:	ASTRAL FOODS LTD	
NI No:	Tax Code:	Pay By:	Date:	Tax Period:	
DESCRIPTION				AMOUNT	THIS YEAR
PAY					
DEDUCTIONS BEFORE TAX					
TOTAL PAY >>>					
OTHER DEDUCTIONS					
NET PAY >>>					
OTHER ITEMS					
ADD EXPENSES REIMBURSED					
PER CHEQUE >>>					
Employer's NICs £					

Employee:	Staff No:		Employer:	ASTRAL FOODS LTD	
NI No:	Tax Code:	Pay By:	Date:	Tax Period:	
DESCRIPTION				AMOUNT	THIS YEAR
PAY					
DEDUCTIONS BEFORE TAX					
TOTAL PAY >>>					
OTHER DEDUCTIONS					
NET PAY >>>					
OTHER ITEMS					
ADD EXPENSES REIMBURSED					
PER CHEQUE >>>					
Employer's NICs £					

BPP
PUBLISHING

DESCRIPTION				AMOUNT	THIS YEAR
Employee:	Staff No:		Employer: ASTRAL FOODS LTD		
NI No:	Tax Code:	Pay By:	Date:	Tax Period:	
PAY					
DEDUCTIONS BEFORE TAX					
	TOTAL	PAY	>>>		
OTHER DEDUCTIONS					
	NET	PAY	>>>		
OTHER ITEMS					
ADD EXPENSES REIMBURSED					
		PER CHEQUE	>>>		
Employer's NICs £					

Practice activity 12.3

Greater London Supplies Ltd has fifteen employees.

The net pay owing to each employee is listed on the payroll extract below.

	Net pay £	Payment method
Mr Barnet	175.91	Cash
Mrs Bromley	213.43	Cash
Mr Camden	141.32	Cheque 10855
Mr Ealing	132.10	Cash
Mrs Enfield	241.53	Cheque 10856
Mr Hackney	113.95	Cheque 10857
Mrs Hammersmith	204.11	Cheque 10858
Mr Haringey	123.45	Cheque 10859
Mrs Islington	67.89	Cheque 10860
Mr Kensington	232.91	Cash
Mrs Lambeth	184.32	Cheque 10861
Mr Redditch	166.66	Cheque 10862
Mr Southwark	297.43	Cheque 10863
Mrs Wandsworth	148.04	Cash
Mr Westminster	159.91	Cash
Total	2,602.96	

Tasks

(a) Complete the form below to order the right amount of notes and coins from the bank, analysed by employee. Use the largest denomination notes and coins possible. Fill in how many of each denomination you will need.

(b) Reconcile your cash and cheque payments to the total on the payroll.

Denom- ination	Mr Barnet (no)	Mrs Bromley (no)	Mr Ealing (no)	Mr Kensington (no)	Mrs Wandsworth (no)	Mr Westminster (no)	Total (no)	Total (£)
£50								
£20								
£10								
£5								
£2								
£1								
50p								
20p								
10p								
5p								
2p								
1p								
Total (£)								

Practice activity 12.4

Your employer has decided to cease payment by cash or cheque, and use Direct Credit instead.

An employee who has heard about the plan through the 'grapevine' phones you up protesting that he does not understand what Direct Credit is. He says he does not have a bank account.

Draft a memorandum explaining to the employee what Direct Credit is, and its advantages. Your employer is prepared to give a one-off payment of £50 to every employee for accepting payment this way, and is prepared to help employees open bank or building society accounts if they so choose.

Practice Devolved Assessment

Practice Devolved Assessment
Radio Gaga Ltd

Notes on completing the Assessment

This Assessment is designed to test your ability to deal with the payroll affairs of one individual who has a rather complicated life.

You are provided with data (pages 67 to 68) which you must use to complete the tasks on page 68. Tax tables, plus relevant free pay and NI tables, will be found in the Appendices.

You are allowed 3 hours to complete your work. A high level of accuracy is required. Check your work carefully. Correcting fluid may be used but should be used in moderation. Errors should be crossed out neatly and clearly. You should write in black ink, not pencil.

You are advised to read the whole of this Assessment before commencing as all of the information may be of value and is not necessarily supplied in the sequence in which you might wish to deal with it.

A full answer is provided on page 161 of this Kit.

Data

You are employed as a payroll clerk by Radio Gaga Ltd of 132 Marconi St, Valveton, W Midlands, PM1 AM2, a small independent radio station in the West Midlands. Radio Gaga Ltd gains most of its revenue from producing advertisements for local businesses and selling air-time. It broadcasts music, targeted to different audiences during the day, and local news. Radio Gaga has the following structure.

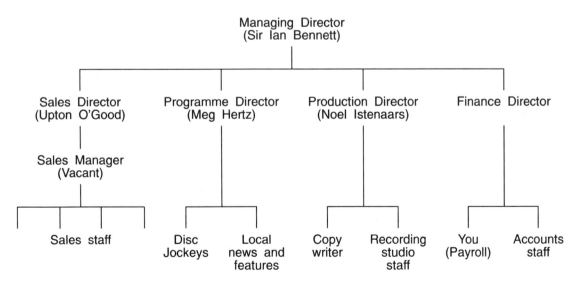

A new sales manager has been appointed. His name is Orpheus Switch. He has joined from a competing radio station, Crystal Radio. He had to leave owing to an acrimonious divorce action with his wife, the Finance Director.

Orpheus is paid a basic salary, but the bulk of his pay is provided by commission.

Orpheus leaves the company later on in the tax year to go to a new company.

There are a number of other items relating to his tax affairs that you must deal with.

You have been provided with the following documents.

(a) Orpheus Switch's employment contract.
(b) Sales figures, on which to base his commission during his employment.
(c) A P45 for you to fill in when he leaves.
(d) Forms P6(T) to adjust his tax code.
(e) Details of his monthly expenses, which have to be authorised by Sir Ian Bennett.
(f) A P14.
(g) Details of Orpheus Switch's company car and a loan to him.
(h) A memo about Orpheus Switch's resignation.
(i) A blank P11.
(j) Payslips.
(k) The P45 from the previous employment, to be completed on joining.
(l) A letter and a memo requiring a response.
(m) Amount of free pay for various codes taken from Tables A.

Other information is as follows.

(a) Orpheus's works number at Radio Gaga Ltd is 345.

(b) Radio Gaga Ltd's tax district and reference is DDY/2422.

(c) Orpheus was born on 21 January 1955. His address is 13 Lyre Street, Hadeston, W Midlands, PL2 UT0.

(d) Expenses are reimbursed one month in arrears (ie September expenses are reimbursed in the October pay packet). All Orpheus's expenses are legitimate business expenses supported by invoices.

(e) Orpheus took no holiday in January or February 2001.

Tasks

(a) State the date on which the contract of employment between Radio Gaga Ltd and Orpheus Switch became legally binding.

(b) From the period Orpheus starts to the period he leaves complete his P11, having reviewed his P45, received when he joined, for accuracy, and having completed Part 3.

(c) Complete payslips for each payday until Month 11.

(d) Complete Orpheus's P45 on leaving.

(e) Prepare a P14.

(f) Respond as you think appropriate to the letter from Mrs Switch.

(g) Respond as fully as possible to the memo dated 11 April 2001.

Amounts of 'Free pay' taken from Tables A are shown overleaf.

Month	Code 100	Code 340	Code 440
1	84.09	284.09	367.42
2	168.18	568.18	734.84
3	252.27	852.27	1,102.26
4	336.36	1,136.36	1,469.68
5	420.45	1,420.45	1,837.10
6	504.54	1,704.54	2,204.52
7	588.63	1,988.63	2,571.94
8	672.72	2,272.72	2,939.36
9	756.81	2,556.81	3,306.78
10	840.90	2,840.90	3,674.20
11	924.99	3,124.99	4,041.62
12	1,009.08	3,409.08	4,409.04

PRIVATE AND CONFIDENTIAL

Dear Orpheus Switch,

This letter sets out the terms and conditions of your employment with Radio Gaga Ltd ('the Company').

1   *Commencement*

Your employment will commence with effect from 1 September 2000. Your continuous period of employment, for the purposes of the Employment Protection (Consolidation) Act 1978 as amended, will commence on that date.

2   *Job description and duties*

You are employed as sales manager or in such other position of like status as the company shall determine from time to time with such duties as are normally associated with your position and/or such other duties as the company shall determine from time to time.

3   *Remuneration*

Your basic salary is at the rate of £18,000 per annum payable monthly in arrears on or around the last day of each month. You will receive commission of 10% of all fees you earn personally, payable at the end of the month to which the commission relates. The basic salary will be increased to £21,000 subject to satisfactory completion of a probation period of six months.

The company shall be entitled to deduct from your salary all sums due from time to time owing from you to it.

4   *Hours of work*

Normal office hours are from 9.30am to 5.30pm Monday to Friday with one hour for lunch, unless pressure of business requires otherwise, in which case you shall be required to work such additional time as the company considers necessary. You are also required to travel to clients' premises on business if appropriate.

5   *Holidays*

The holiday year runs from 1 January to 31 December.

You are entitled to 20 working days holiday in every holiday year in addition to statutory and bank holidays. The timing of your holidays must be agreed in advance with the managing director. Holiday entitlement accrues at the rate of $1^2/_3$ days per completed calendar month.

Holidays must be taken in the holiday year in which they are earned, unless otherwise agreed in advance with the company.

On termination of your employment, you will be entitled to be paid pro rata for any unused holiday entitlement in the holiday year at a rate of 1/261 of your annual salary per day not taken, and the company shall have the right to deduct from your salary payment for any holiday taken in excess of your accrued entitlement at the rate of 1/261 of your annual salary for each excess day.

6   *Notice*

Subject to clause 7, your employment may be terminated by the company or you providing not less than the following period of prior written notice.

Length of service	*Notice*
Less than 4 years	1 month
Between 4 and 12 years	1 week for every complete year of service, or one month, whichever is greater
More than 12 years	12 weeks

The company reserves the right to offer payment in lieu of notice in either case. Where employment is ended during a calendar month, the pay shall be calculated as 1/261 of the annual salary per working day.

7   *Summary termination*

The company may terminate your employment with immediate effect if you:

(a)   are incapacitated by any cause whatsoever from efficiently performing your duties hereunder for an aggregate of 60 days in any 12 month period; or

(b)   are guilty of any serious misconduct.

8   *Sickness*

If you are sick or injured and will be absent from work, you must notify the sales director of your intended absence by 10.00am or as soon as reasonably practicable thereafter on the first day of such absence. If such absence continues for up to four days, then you must again notify the sales director on that (or the next working) day.

If you are absent from work for more than seven consecutive days, you must, on the eighth day, send to the company a doctor's certificate and shall send further certificates on a weekly basis unless otherwise agreed with the company in respect of any continued absence.

If you are absent through sickness or injury you will be entitled to sick pay at a rate equivalent to your basic salary for an aggregate of 60 days' absence in any 12 month period. This sick pay shall include any statutory sick pay or sickness benefits which you may be entitled to receive.

The company shall be entitled at any time to require you to attend (or, as appropriate, be visited by) a medical practitioner designated by it for the purpose of a medical examination. The company will pay all costs associated with such examination. You hereby authorise such medical practitioner to disclose to and discuss with the company the results of such examination provided that such disclosure is confined to matters which could affect your employment.

9   *Pension*

The company does not currently operate a pension scheme in respect of your employment.

10   *Place of work and secondment*

Your normal place of work will be at the company's offices in Valveton, although it is anticipated that you will travel elsewhere. The company reserves the right to change your place of work at its discretion and/or to require you to work for any associated or subsidiary company (on terms no less favourable than those set out in this letter).

11   *Disciplinary and grievance procedure*

Any query or grievance you may have relating to your employment should be raised in the first instance with the sales director. If the matter is not settled at that level, then it may be referred to the managing director.

If a disciplinary matter arises involving you, the company will generally apply its disciplinary procedure then in force. Such disciplinary procedure does not form part of your contract of employment.

12   *Expenses*

The company shall reimburse to you all reasonable expenses properly incurred by you in the proper performance of your duties subject to production of receipts where required by the company.

13   *Motor car*

The company shall provide you with a car for use for work and also for your private use. The company shall pay for any maintenance, insurance and other bills, excepting fines for traffic offences. The company shall also pay for fuel.

Yours sincerely,

Sir Ian Bennett

Sir Ian Bennett
For and on behalf of the company

I agree and accept the above.

Signed: *Orpheus Switch*

Dated: 23 July 2000

Expenses forms:

			NET	VAT	TOTAL
Radio Gaga		MOTOR CAR EXPENSES			
EXPENSES CLAIM					
PETROL, TELEPHONE BILLS & ROUND SUM ALLOWANCES		Parking	£	£	£
		Repairs/Service	£	£	£
NAME Switch, O MONTH Sept '00		Car Tax	£	£	£
		Insurance	£	£	£
		Taxis	£	£	£
	Amount (inc VAT) £	VAT (office use)	Petrol	£	£	£
HOTEL	50				
		PROFESSIONAL SUBSCRIPTIONS			
		Professional subscriptions	£	£	£
BUSINESS ENTERTAINING					
		OTHER (to be authorised)			
ROUND SUM ALLOWANCES					
		TOTAL CLAIMED			£
GRAND TOTAL	£ 50	£	CAR MILEAGE	200	

Claimant's signature *O Switch*

Signature of authority *Ian Bennett*

Claimant's signature *O Switch*

Signature of authority *Ian Bennett*

			NET	VAT	TOTAL
Radio Gaga		MOTOR CAR EXPENSES			
EXPENSES CLAIM					
PETROL, TELEPHONE BILLS & ROUND SUM ALLOWANCES		Parking	£	£	£
		Repairs/Service	£	£	£
NAME Switch, O MONTH Oct '00		Car Tax	£	£	£
		Insurance	£	£	£
		Taxis	£	£	£
	Amount (inc VAT) £	VAT (office use)	Petrol	£	£	£
HOTEL	300				
		PROFESSIONAL SUBSCRIPTIONS			
		Professional subscriptions	£	£	£
BUSINESS ENTERTAINING					
		OTHER (to be authorised)			
ROUND SUM ALLOWANCES					
		TOTAL CLAIMED			£
GRAND TOTAL	£ 300	£	CAR MILEAGE	350	

Claimant's signature *O Switch*

Signature of authority *Ian Bennett*

Claimant's signature *O Switch*

Signature of authority *Ian Bennett*

First claim — Nov '00

Radio Gaga
EXPENSES CLAIM
PETROL, TELEPHONE BILLS & ROUND SUM ALLOWANCES

NAME Switch, O   MONTH Nov '00

	Amount (inc VAT) £	VAT (office use)
HOTEL	500	
BUSINESS ENTERTAINING		
ROUND SUM ALLOWANCES		
GRAND TOTAL	£ 500	£

Claimant's signature O Switch
Signature of authority Ian Bennett

MOTOR CAR EXPENSES	NET	VAT	TOTAL
Parking	£	£	£
Repairs/Service	£	£	£
Car Tax	£	£	£
Insurance	£	£	£
Taxis	£	£	£
Petrol	£	£	£
PROFESSIONAL SUBSCRIPTIONS			
Professional subscriptions	£	£	£
OTHER (to be authorised)			
TOTAL CLAIMED			£
CAR MILEAGE	350		

Claimant's signature O Switch
Signature of authority Ian Bennett

Second claim — Dec '00

Radio Gaga
EXPENSES CLAIM
PETROL, TELEPHONE BILLS & ROUND SUM ALLOWANCES

NAME Switch, O   MONTH Dec '00

	Amount (inc VAT) £	VAT (office use)
HOTEL	450	
BUSINESS ENTERTAINING		
ROUND SUM ALLOWANCES		
GRAND TOTAL	£ 450	£

Claimant's signature O Switch
Signature of authority Ian Bennett

MOTOR CAR EXPENSES	NET	VAT	TOTAL
Parking	£	£	£
Repairs/Service	£	£	£
Car Tax	£	£	£
Insurance	£	£	£
Taxis	£	£	£
Petrol	£	£	£
PROFESSIONAL SUBSCRIPTIONS			
Professional subscriptions	£	£	£
OTHER (to be authorised)			
TOTAL CLAIMED			£
CAR MILEAGE	250		

Claimant's signature O Switch
Signature of authority Ian Bennett

ʀadio Gaga

EXPENSES CLAIM
PETROL, TELEPHONE BILLS & ROUND SUM ALLOWANCES

NAME ___Switch, O___   MONTH ___Jan '01___

	Amount (inc VAT) £	VAT (office use)
HOTEL	250	
BUSINESS ENTERTAINING		
ROUND SUM ALLOWANCES		
GRAND TOTAL	£ 250	£

Claimant's signature   *O Switch*

Signature of authority   *Ian Bennett*

MOTOR CAR EXPENSES	NET	VAT	TOTAL
Parking	£	£	£
Repairs/Service	£	£	£
Car Tax	£	£	£
Insurance	£	£	£
Taxis	£	£	£
Petrol	£	£	£
PROFESSIONAL SUBSCRIPTIONS			
Professional subscriptions	£	£	£
OTHER (to be authorised)			
TOTAL CLAIMED			£
CAR MILEAGE	200		

Claimant's signature   *O Switch*

Signature of authority   *Ian Bennett*

ʀadio Gaga

EXPENSES CLAIM
PETROL, TELEPHONE BILLS & ROUND SUM ALLOWANCES

NAME ___Switch, O___   MONTH ___Feb '01___

	Amount (inc VAT) £	VAT (office use)
HOTEL	50	
BUSINESS ENTERTAINING		
ROUND SUM ALLOWANCES		
GRAND TOTAL	£ 50	£

Claimant's signature   *O Switch*

Signature of authority   *Ian Bennett*

MOTOR CAR EXPENSES	NET	VAT	TOTAL
Parking	£	£	£
Repairs/Service	£	£	£
Car Tax	£	£	£
Insurance	£	£	£
Taxis	£	£	£
Petrol	£	£	£
PROFESSIONAL SUBSCRIPTIONS			
Professional subscriptions	£	£	£
OTHER (to be authorised)			
TOTAL CLAIMED			£
CAR MILEAGE	50		

Claimant's signature   *O Switch*

Signature of authority   *Ian Bennett*

RADIO GAGA

'All you hear is Radio Gaga'

MEMORANDUM

To: Payroll
From: Managing Director
Date: February 7 2001

Orpheus Switch has left the employment of Radio Gaga Ltd as of today. He has accepted the month's pay in lieu of notice. For the week 1/2 - 7/2 calculate his salary due, on the basis of 261 days in the year. You will also need to work out his holiday pay.

Pay his expenses for February in his leaving cheque.

Pay his commission for February in the second week of March.

RADIO GAGA

'All you hear is Radio Gaga'

MEMORANDUM

To: Payroll
From: Sir Ian Bennett
Date: 1 September 2000

Orpheus Switch is to be given a company loan of £1,200 to be paid back at a rate of £100 per month, with the first repayment taken from his September pay packet. The loan is interest free. Any outstanding loan should be taken from his pay packet in the month he leaves the company.

The following is extracted from the company's monthly sales figures. They are calculated at the end of each month.

Sales booked by Orpheus Switch

	£
September 2000	10,560.00
October 2000	7,759.00
November 2000	16,832.00
December 2000	13,074.00
January 2001	9,365.00
February 2001	9,030.00

The Flashy Car Co

To: Radio Gaga Ltd
132 Marconi St
Valveton

30/8/00

FAO: Upton O'Good

SALES INVOICE

	£
1 Mikado 'Executive' 2L	14,936.00
VAT at 17.5%	2,613.80
	17,549.80

Approved Ian Bennett

Supplied to: Mr Orpheus Switch

VAT reg: 1234567

Form 1 (top)

Inland Revenue

Issued by
H.M. Inspector of Taxes

W MIDLANDS 4
WOLVERHAMPTON

PAYE - Notice to employer of employee's tax code (or amended code) and previous pay and tax

Date
14/1/01

Employer's PAYE reference
DDY/2422

Radio Gaga Ltd
132 Marconi St
Valveton
W Midlands DM1 AM2

Employee's name
O SWITCH

National Insurance number
(To be entered on the Deductions
Working Sheet and to be quoted
in any communication)
VH 123456H

Works/Payroll no., Branch etc.
345

Code:
The code of this employee is amended to
340 T

for the year to 5 April
2001

Please use this code from the next pay day after you receive
this form and follow the instructions in Part A overleaf.

Previous Pay and Tax

Where there is an entry here
please follow the instructions in
both Parts A and B overleaf.

Previous pay

Previous tax

P6 (T)

Form 2 (bottom)

Inland Revenue

Issued by
H.M. Inspector of Taxes

W MIDLANDS 4
WOLVERHAMPTON

PAYE - Notice to employer of employee's tax code (or amended code) and previous pay and tax

Date
1/10/00

Employer's PAYE reference
DDY/2422

Radio Gaga Ltd
132 Marconi St
Valveton
W Midlands DM1 AM2

Employee's name
O SWITCH

National Insurance number
(To be entered on the Deductions
Working Sheet and to be quoted
in any communication)
VH 123456H

Works/Payroll no., Branch etc.
345

Code:
The code of this employee is amended to
100 T

for the year to 5 April
2001

Please use this code from the next pay day after you receive
this form and follow the instructions in Part A overleaf.

Previous Pay and Tax

Where there is an entry here
please follow the instructions in
both Parts A and B overleaf.

Previous pay

Previous tax

P6 (T)

		New employee details **For completion by new employer**	**P45** **Part 3**

Inland **Revenue**

District number: W1 Reference number: B 004

1 Previous PAYE Reference

2 Employee's National Insurance number — VH 12 34 56 H

(Mr Mrs Miss Ms)

3 Surname — SWITCH — Mr

First name(s) — ORPHEUS

4 Date left previous employment — Day 28 Month 08 Year 20 00

5 Continue Student Loan Deductions (Y)

6 Tax Code at leaving date. 'x' in the box means Week 7 or Month 1 basis applies — Code 440 T — Week 1 or Month 1

7 Last entries on *Deductions Working Sheet (P11)*. If there is an 'X' at item 6, there will be no entries here

Week or Month number — Week / Month 5

Total pay to date — £ 8,750 00 p

Total tax to date — £ 1,444 63 p

To the new employer — Complete items 8 to 17 below and send this page of the form only to your Tax Office immediately.

8 New PAYE Reference

9 Date employment started (in figures) — Day Month Year 20

10 Tick here if you want these details to be shown on tax code notifications — Works/Payroll number, Department or branch if any

11 Enter P if employee will not be paid by you between date employment began and next 5 April

12 Enter code in use if different to code at item 6

13 If the tax figure you are entering on P11 differs from item 7 above (see CWG (1999) card 4) please enter your figure here — £

14 Employee's private address — Postcode

15 Employee's date of birth (if known)

16 Employee's job title or description

17 **Declaration.** I have prepared a *Deductions Working Sheet* (P11) in accordance with the details above.

Employer

Address — Postcode — Date

P45

Inland Revenue

Details of employee leaving work
Copy for Tax Office

P45 Part 1

1 PAYE Reference

District number   Reference number

2 Employee's National Insurance number

(Mr Mrs Miss Ms)

3 Surname (in capitals)

First name(s) (in capitals)

4 Leaving date (in figures)   Day   Month   Year   20

5 Continue Student Loan Deductions (Y)

6 Tax Code at leaving date. *If week 1 or Month 1 basis applies, write 'X' in the box marked Week 1 or Month 1*

Code   Week 1 or Month 1

7 Last entries on *Deductions Working Sheet* (P11) **Complete only if Tax Code is cumulative.** *Make no entry here if Week 1 or Month 1 basis applies. Go to item 7.*

Week or month number   Week   Month

Total pay to date   £   p

Total tax to date   £   p

8 This employment pay and tax. ■ *No entry needed if Tax Code is cumulative and amounts are same as item 6 entry.*

Total pay in this employment   £   p

Total tax in this employment   £   p

9 Works number/ Payroll number

10 Department or branch if any

11 Employee's private address and Postcode

12 I certify that the details entered above in items 1 to 9 are correct

Employer's name, address and Postcode

Date

To the employer   *Please complete with care* ★

For Tax Office use

- Complete this form following the 'Employee leaving' instructions in the *Employer's quick Guide to PAYE and NICs* (cards CWG1). ★ **Make sure the details are clear on all four parts of this form**. Make sure your name and address is shown on Parts 1 and 1A.

- Detach Part 1 and send it to your Tax Office immediately.

- Hand Parts 1A, 2 and 3 (unseparated) to your employee when he or she leaves

- If the employee has died, write 'D' in this box and send all three parts of this form (unseparated) to your Tax Office immediately.

P45

BMSD9/99

BPP PUBLISHING

Devolved assessment (data and tasks)

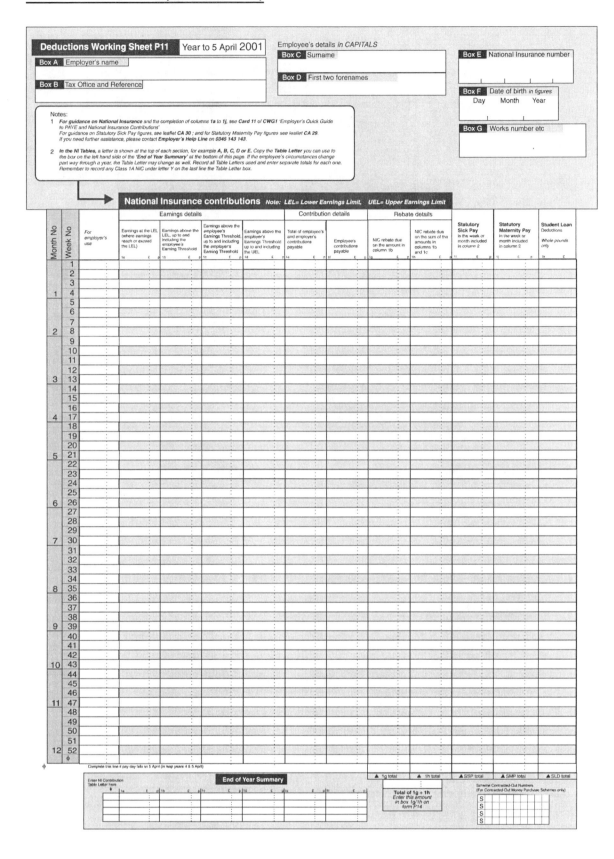

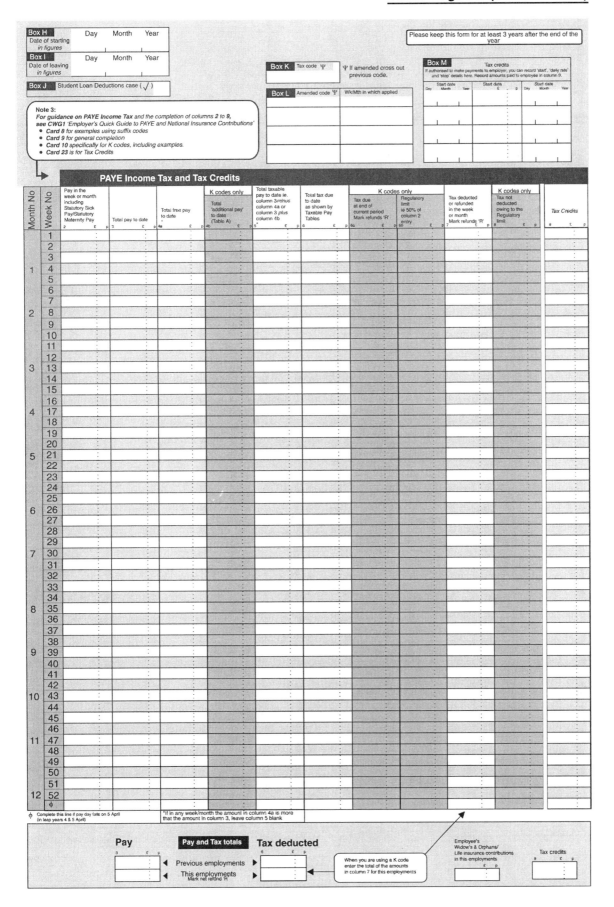

Complete in accordance with
CWG1 *Employer's Quick Guide to PAYE and NICs*

*Please write firmly to ensure your entries are clear on all three sheets.
£ spaces should be filled from the right-hand side.*

End of Year Summary P14

0 0 2

Tax Office number and Reference

Employer's name and address

Tax Office name

Tax Year to 5 April 2 0 0 1

For employer's use

Expenses payments and benefits paid to directors and employees:
Complete form P11D or P9D if appropriate and provide a copy of the information to the employee by 6 July.
See Employer's Guide for more details.

Employee's details

National Insurance number

Surname

First two forenames

Works/payroll no. etc

Date of birth in figures (if known)
Day Month Year

Sex
'M' if Male,
'F' if Female

Employee's private address (if known)

Postcode

National insurance contributions in this employment

(*Note: LEL = Lower Earnings Limit, UEL = Upper Earnings Limit*)

NIC table letter	Earnings at the LEL (where earnings reach or exceed the LEL) (whole £s only) From col.1a on P11 1a	Earnings above the LEL, up to and incl. the employer's Earnings Threshold (whole £s only) From col.1b on P11 1b	Earnings above the employee's Earnings Threshold, up to and incl. the employer's Earnings Threshold (whole £s only) From col.1c on P11 1c	Earnings above the employer's Earnings Threshold, up to and incl. the UEL (whole £s only) From col.1d on P11 1d	Total of employee's and employer's contributions payable From col.1e on P11 1e	Employee's contributions payable From col.1f on P11 1f

NIC rebate due
Total of cols.1g and 1h from P11
1g/1h £ p

Statutory Sick Pay
£ p

Statutory Maternity Pay
£ p

Scheme Contracted-out number
(for Contracted-out Money Purchase Schemes only)

Pay and income Tax details

	Pay £ p	Tax deducted £ p
In previous employment(s)		
In this employment		
Total for year		

Employee's Widows & Orphans/Life Assurance contributions in this employment
£ p

Student Loan Deductions
in this employment
From col.1k on P11
£

Tax Credits in this employment
From col.9 on P11
£ p

Enter 'R' in this box if net refund

Final tax code

Payment in Week 53: If included in Pay and Tax totals, enter 'X', '54' or '56' here
(see Employer's Guide)

Date of starting if during tax year shown above
Day Month Year

Date of leaving if during tax year shown above
Day Month Year

For official use

BxSSD 11/99

To Inland Revenue **National Insurance copy**

P14(Manual)(2000-01)

Please detach sheets and make separate bundles of National Insurance and Tax copies before despatch

Employee:		Staff No:			Employer:	RADIO GAGA LTD	
NI No:		Tax Code:	Pay By:		Date:	Tax Period:	
DESCRIPTION						AMOUNT	THIS YEAR
PAY							
DEDUCTIONS BEFORE TAX							
TOTAL PAY >>>							
OTHER DEDUCTIONS							
NET PAY >>>							
OTHER ITEMS							
ADD EXPENSES REIMBURSED							
PER CHEQUE >>>							
Employer's NICs £			To Date £				

Employee:		Staff No:			Employer:	RADIO GAGA LTD	
NI No:		Tax Code:	Pay By:		Date:	Tax Period:	
DESCRIPTION						AMOUNT	THIS YEAR
PAY							
DEDUCTIONS BEFORE TAX							
TOTAL PAY >>>							
OTHER DEDUCTIONS							
NET PAY >>>							
OTHER ITEMS							
ADD EXPENSES REIMBURSED							
PER CHEQUE >>>							
Employer's NICs £			To Date £				

BPP PUBLISHING

Employee:		Staff No:		Employer:	RADIO GAGA LTD	
NI No:	Tax Code:		Pay By:	Date:	Tax Period:	
DESCRIPTION					AMOUNT	THIS YEAR
PAY						
DEDUCTIONS BEFORE TAX						
		TOTAL	PAY >>>			
OTHER DEDUCTIONS						
		NET	PAY >>>			
OTHER ITEMS						
ADD EXPENSES REIMBURSED						
			PER CHEQUE >>>			
Employer's NICs £			To Date £			

Employee:		Staff No:		Employer:	RADIO GAGA LTD	
NI No:	Tax Code:		Pay By:	Date:	Tax Period:	
DESCRIPTION					AMOUNT	THIS YEAR
PAY						
DEDUCTIONS BEFORE TAX						
		TOTAL	PAY >>>			
OTHER DEDUCTIONS						
		NET	PAY >>>			
OTHER ITEMS						
ADD EXPENSES REIMBURSED						
			PER CHEQUE >>>			
Employer's NICs £			To Date £			

						AMOUNT	THIS YEAR
Employee:		Staff No:		Employer:	RADIO GAGA LTD		
NI No:	Tax Code:		Pay By:	Date:	Tax Period:		
DESCRIPTION						AMOUNT	THIS YEAR
PAY							
DEDUCTIONS BEFORE TAX							
		TOTAL	PAY	>>>			
OTHER DEDUCTIONS							
		NET	PAY	>>>			
OTHER ITEMS							
ADD EXPENSES REIMBURSED							
		PER CHEQUE	>>>				
Employer's NICs £			To Date £				

						AMOUNT	THIS YEAR
Employee:		Staff No:		Employer:	RADIO GAGA LTD		
NI No:	Tax Code:		Pay By:	Date:	Tax Period:		
DESCRIPTION						AMOUNT	THIS YEAR
PAY							
DEDUCTIONS BEFORE TAX							
		TOTAL	PAY	>>>			
OTHER DEDUCTIONS							
		NET	PAY	>>>			
OTHER ITEMS							
ADD EXPENSES REIMBURSED							
		PER CHEQUE	>>>				
Employer's NICs £			To Date £				

BPP PUBLISHING

Honor Switch
27 Cleaners Row
Hadeston
W Midlands
PL3 SS1

10 April 2001

Dear Sir or Madam,

Orpheus Switch

I should be grateful if you would let me know the amount of salary paid to my husband whilst he was in your employment.

I need this information to fill in my tax return.

Yours faithfully,

L Goal

M Honor Switch

RADIO GAGA

'All you hear is Radio Gaga'

INTERNAL MEMORANDUM

To: Payroll
From: Ian Bennett
Date: 11 April 2001
We are thinking of replacing Orpheus Switch. How much would this cost the company per annum if the new person received the same package as the one we gave Orpheus?

Specimen Central Assessment

SPECIMEN CENTRAL ASSESSMENT

NVQ/SVQ Level 2

UNIT 74
DETERMINE INDIVIDUAL AND AGGREGATE PAYMENTS

Time allowed - 2 hours
Plus 15 minutes' reading time
Answer **all** questions

**DO NOT OPEN THIS PAPER UNTIL YOU ARE READY TO START
UNDER TIMED CONDITIONS**

You are reminded that competence must be achieved in each section. You should therefore attempt and aim to complete EVERY task in EACH section.

All essential workings should be included within your answer, where appropriate.

You are advised to spend 60 minutes on Section 1 and 60 minutes on Section 2.

The Central Assessment is in two Sections.

Section 1   Operational Tasks. **Complete all four tasks**

Section 2   15 Short Answer Questions. **Answer all questions**

Sections 1 and 2 relate to the company described below.

Introduction

- Colin Fryer is the Managing Director of a jewellery-making business with 10 employees.
- The company trades under the name of Ruby 'n' Stone.
- You are employed by the company as a payroll administrator.
- The details shown on pages 91 and 92 are extracts from the payroll records and you will need them to complete this assessment.
- Assume today's date is 1 December 2000.

SOURCE INFORMATION

EMPLOYEE RECORD CARD

Name:	*Carol Jane Smith*	Start date: *07.07.97*
Address:	*3 High Road* *Compton* *West Midlands* *DY4 6JY*	Salary: *£16,800 per year*
Telephone No:	*01562 784571*	Voluntary deductions: *Pension 5%* *Trade Union £8 per month*
NI No:	*BS 26 88 44 D*	Holiday entitlement: *4 weeks pa*
Date of birth:	*16.05.68*	Status: *Jewellery Finisher*
Marital status:	*Married*	Tax code: *433L*

EMPLOYEE RECORD CARD

Name:	*Lionel Dyer*	Start date: *07.08.96*
Address:	*53 Knight Road* *Gornal* *West Midlands* *DY12 7AT*	Salary: *£35,400 per year*
Telephone No:	*01562 883342*	Voluntary deductions: *Pension 5%* *Payroll Giving £30 per month* *Trade Union £8 per month*
NI No:	*CT 18 15 22 C*	Holiday entitlement: *4 weeks pa*
Date of birth:	*10.05.71*	Status: *Workshop Manager*
Marital status:	*Married*	Tax code: *516H*

EMPLOYEE RECORD CARD

Name:	*Anna Benton*	Start date: *14.07.97*
Address:	*81 Knight Road* *Gornal* *West Midlands* *DY12 7AT*	Salary: *£14,400 per year*
Telephone No:	*01562 984512*	Voluntary deductions: *Pension 5%* *Payroll Giving £40 per month* *Trade Union £8 per month*
NI No:	*BL 71 05 06 B*	Holiday entitlement: *4 weeks pa*
Date of birth:	*10.07.61*	Status: *Jewellery Technician*
Marital status:	*Married*	Tax code: *440L*

2000/2001 Tax Bands and Rates

0 - £1,520	10%
£1,520 - £28,400	22%
Over £28,400	40%

Lionel,

As you know I am expecting a baby on 31 January and I wondered if you could find out what my SMP entitlement will be when I commence my maternity leave next week.

I started work with this company on 6 September 2000.

Janet Truman

01.12.00

November payroll

Gross wages	£25,000
PAYE deducted	£4,770
Employee's NIC	£2,220
Employer's NIC	£2,700
Trade Union Fees	£80
Payroll Giving	£160
Pension liability – employees	£1,250
Pension liability – employers	£1,250
Net pay	£16,520

CALENDAR FOR 2000/01

April

S	M	T	W	T	F	S
						1
2	3	4	5	6	7	8
9	10	11	12	13	14	15
16	17	18	19	20	21	22
23	24	25	26	27	28	29
30						

May

S	M	T	W	T	F	S
	1	2	3	4	5	6
7	8	9	10	11	12	13
14	15	16	17	18	19	20
21	22	23	24	25	26	27
28	29	30	31			

June

S	M	T	W	T	F	S
				1	2	3
4	5	6	7	8	9	10
11	12	13	14	15	16	17
18	19	20	21	22	23	24
25	26	27	28	29	30	

July

S	M	T	W	T	F	S
						1
2	3	4	5	6	7	8
9	10	11	12	13	14	15
16	17	18	19	20	21	22
23	24	25	26	27	28	29
30	31					

August

S	M	T	W	T	F	S
		1	2	3	4	5
6	7	8	9	10	11	12
13	14	15	16	17	18	19
20	21	22	23	24	25	26
27	28	29	30	31		

September

S	M	T	W	T	F	S
					1	2
3	4	5	6	7	8	9
10	11	12	13	14	15	16
17	18	19	20	21	22	23
24	25	26	27	28	29	30

October

S	M	T	W	T	F	S
1	2	3	4	5	6	7
8	9	10	11	12	13	14
15	16	17	18	19	20	21
22	23	24	25	26	27	28
29	30	31				

November

S	M	T	W	T	F	S
			1	2	3	4
5	6	7	8	9	10	11
12	13	14	15	16	17	18
19	20	21	22	23	24	25
26	27	28	29	30		

December

S	M	T	W	T	F	S
					1	2
3	4	5	6	7	8	9
10	11	12	13	14	15	16
17	18	19	20	21	22	23
24	25	26	27	28	29	30
31						

January

S	M	T	W	T	F	S
	1	2	3	4	5	6
7	8	9	10	11	12	13
14	15	16	17	18	19	20
21	22	23	24	25	26	27
28	29	30	31			

SECTION 1 – OPERATIONAL TASKS

(Suggested time allocation: 60 minutes)

COMPLETE ALL FOUR TASKS

Blank space for workings is available on page 99

Task 1.1　　Referring to the employee records and tax details on pages 91 and 92, calculate the income tax payable by each of the three employees, assuming each will work a full year from 6 April 2000 to 5 April 2001. Record your answer, showing workings to two decimal places, in the space provided on page 95.

Task 1.2　　Refer to the note on page 92 that an employee, Janet Truman, has sent to the Workshop Manager regarding Statutory Maternity Pay (SMP). There is a calendar available on page 93. Reply to the memo using the memo paper on page 96.

Task 1.3　　The accounting entries for the November payroll, shown on page 92, have been entered into the wages control account but corresponding entries have not been made in the other relevant accounts. Complete the double entry from the wages control account into the accounts shown on pages 97 – 98.

Task 1.4　　Refer to the partially designed pay advice slip on page 99 and, using your knowledge of the compulsory information required on a pay advice slip, insert your suggested headings for information which should be shown. Also, insert headings for any optional information you consider would be useful to the employee.

Task 1.1

NB You should work to two decimal places

You should assume the fourth figure digit of all tax codes is 9

Tax calculations for one year ended 05.04.01
Carol Jane Smith
Lionel Dyer
Anna Benton

BPP PUBLISHING

Task 1.2

MEMO	
To:	From:
Date:	Subject:

Task 1.3

GENERAL LEDGER

Wages Control Account

30.11.99	Bank	£16,520	30.11.99	Gross wages	£25,000
30.11.99	PAYE	£4,770	30.11.99	Employer's NIC	£2,700
30.11.99	Employee's NIC	£2,220	30.11.99	Employer's Pension	£1,250
30.11.99	Employer's NIC	£2,700			
30.11.99	Trade Union Fees	£80			
30.11.99	Payroll Giving	£160			
30.11.99	Pension-employee's	£1,250			
30.11.99	Pension-employer's	£1,250			

PAYE/NIC CREDITORS

Wages Account

Bank

Task 1.3, continued

Trade Union Fees Account

Payroll Giving Account

Pensions Account

Task 1.4

PAY ADVICE SLIP

Payments £	Deductions £	Year to date figures £
		Tax period:
Basic Pay:		
Total Gross Pay:	**Total Deductions:**	
Name:		

WORKINGS

SECTION 2 – SHORT ANSWER QUESTIONS

(Suggested time allocation: 60 minutes)

Write in the space provided OR circle the correct answers. Do not indicate your choice in any other way.

ANSWER ALL OF THE QUESTIONS ON PAGES 100 – 103.

2.1 An employee at Ruby 'n' Stone has a **BR** tax code. Briefly explain what you understand to be the meaning of this code.

....

....

....

....

2.2 An employee of Ruby 'n' Stone has asked if a friend can collect his wages at the end of the week as he will be on holiday. Name TWO precautions you will take before handing over the pay packet to the friend.

....

....

....

....

2.3 Anna Benton gives £40 per month to charity through GAYE payroll giving scheme. What is the *maximum* amount per year Anna would be able to donate through GAYE on which tax relief would be allowed?

....

2.4 The Inland Revenue issues two booklets to help in the calculation of PAYE: Pay Adjustment Tables and Taxable Pay Tables. What information do these tables give?

(a) **Pay Adjustment Tables**

....

....

(b) **Taxable Pay Tables**

....

....

2.5 An employee of Ruby 'n' Stone fell ill and was away from work from Monday 13 November to Wednesday 22 November inclusive. Qualifying days are Monday to Friday. How many days SSP would the employee be entitled to expect?

....

....

....

2.6 NIC's are payable by employees and employers. Show who is responsible for paying the following classes of National Insurance by *circling* the correct answer.

(a) Class 1

Employer /   Employee /   Both

(b) Class 1A

Employer /   Employee /   Both

2.7 Some computerised payroll systems are designed as stand alone systems, whilst others are integrated. What do you understand by the term 'integrated' in respect of a computerised payroll system?

....

....

....

....

2.8 One of the employees at Ruby 'n' Stone has an emergency tax code.

(a) What is the emergency tax code for the 2000/2001 tax year?

....

(b) What do you understand by the term emergency tax code?

....

....

....

....

2.9 Colin Fryer is concerned about the amount of office space being used to store records and he has asked you to dispose of all payroll records one month after the end of each tax year.

(a) Will you be able to comply with Colin's request? *Circle* the correct answer.

Yes   /   No

(b) Briefly explain the reason for your answer.

....

....

....

....

2.10 Colin Fryer is considering using an automated pay system for the payment of wages to employees. List TWO advantages of such a system to both employer and employee.

(a) Advantages to employer

....

....

(b) Advantages to employee

....

....

2.11 John Baker, an employee of Ruby 'n' Stone, will be made redundant on 31 December 2000, when he will be 36 years of age and will have 3 years' continuous service.

(a) Will John be entitled to a statutory redundancy payment? *Circle* the correct answer.

Yes / No

(b) Briefly explain the reason for your answer.

....

....

....

....

....

2.12 Name TWO precautions you would take to ensure the security and confidentiality of payroll information.

....

....

....

....

2.13 The weekly Lower earnings Limit (LEL) for National Insurance purposes for the tax year 2000/2001 is £67. What effect does this have on the employee's pay?

....

....

....

....

....

2.14 Briefly explain your understanding of the following terms in regard to occupational pension schemes.

    (a) Contributory pension.

....

....

....

....

    (b) Non-contributory pension

....

....

....

....

2.15 Colin Fryer is sometimes slow in providing employees with written terms and conditions of employment. What is the period of time, as set out by law, within which employees should be provided with written details of their contract of employment?

....

....

....

....

BPP
PUBLISHING

Answers to practice activities

Answer 1.1

Three years.

Answer 1.2

(a) Having self-employed status means a person is more favourably treated for tax and NIC purposes. On the other hand, a self-employed person has far fewer rights under employment protection legislation (eg on dismissal), and other benefits such as holiday pay.

(b) A contract of service is a contract of employment.

A contract for services is not a contract of employment, it is a contract with a self-employed person.

(c) The Inland Revenue will make up its own mind on the substance of the relationship, irrespective of its legal form. However, a number of possible criteria follows.

(i) Does Paula work from home or have her own place of business?
(ii) Does she use her own equipment?
(iii) Is she entitled to holiday pay or sick pay?
(iv) Does she, by and large, set her own work schedule?
(v) Can she refuse to accept particular tasks of work?
(vi) Does she work for more than one employer?

None of these is conclusive. However, Paula's regular pattern of work for the two companies may well make her an employee of both of them.

Answer 1.3

- Name and title
- Address
- Date of birth
- Sex
- Pensions status

- NI number and category
- Tax code
- Starting date
- Leaving date

Answer 1.4

As the employee is male, he can only change his name legally by deed poll. (A female can could decide to change her name on marriage, in which case you would need a copy of the marriage certificate.) Therefore you will need a copy of the registered deed poll before changing the records.

Answer 1.5

As there are only fifteen employees, the easiest way is to file their records in alphabetical order of surname.

Answer 1.6

Say that it is not in your power to determine if he is self-employed. Ultimately the Inland Revenue decides.

Say that the area is complex and there would have to be quite a significant change in the working relationship for self-employment to be accepted.

Tell him to talk to his Tax Office about the subject. You should supply the address and phone number, and give him his reference number.

Answer 2.1

Personnel should send you details of an employee's pay and this should be in the employee's records. You can also check the details to the contract of employment (eg overtime entitlement and rates, shift allowances, etc).

Answer 2.2

(a) The names of the employer and employee.
(b) The employee's job title (eg Payroll Assistant), or a description of duties.
(c) When the employee is to commence employment.
(d) How much the employee is to be paid (hourly rate, annual salary, overtime etc).
(e) When the employee is to be paid (eg weekly or monthly).
(f) Normal working hours (including requirement for overtime).
(g) Holiday entitlement, including any entitlement to accrued holiday pay.
(h) Notice period for leaving.
(i) Pension scheme details, if any.
(j) Disciplinary and grievance procedures.
(k) Injury and sickness terms.
(l) Place of work.

Answer 2.3

Implied terms

(a) On the employee:

    (i)   Fidelity
    (ii)   Obedience
    (iii) Diligence and care
    (iv) Honesty

(b) On the employer:

    (i)   To maintain a relationship of trust and confidence
    (ii)   To act fairly

Answer 2.4

Accounts is usually part of the financial department and so the code is F01.

Answer 2.5

Joe's original contract of employment, when he was employed in sales, will have altered on moving to accounts. Personnel should have told him of the revised terms (eg higher basic salary, but no commission) before he moved departments. Explain this to Joe and, if he is still not happy, refer him to the Personnel Department.

Answer 2.6

First check your in-tray and filing tray to ensure that the notification of change of bank account is not there. If you can find no evidence of a change in Joe's bank account, you should notify your supervisor, as it is possible that someone has committed a fraud. You will also need to speak to Joe to ensure that he has received his salary. If he has changed his bank account, ask him to complete the appropriate form.

Answer 2.7

Accuracy, timeliness, security, confidentiality.

Answer 3.1

Inland Revenue		**Details of employee leaving work** Copy for Tax Office	**P45** Part 1	

		District number	Reference number	
1	PAYE Reference	123	B1234	

2 Employee's National Insurance number   AB 22 55 18 C

3 Surname (in capitals)   WILSON   (Mr Mrs Miss Ms) Mr

First name(s) (in capitals)   ALAN

		Day	Month	Year			
4	Leaving date (in figures)	26	09	20 00	5	Continue Student Loan Deductions (Y)	

6 Tax Code at leaving date. *If week 1 or Month 1 basis applies, write 'X' in the box marked Week 1 or Month 1*

Code 547 H   Week 1 or Month 1

7 Last entries on *Deductions Working Sheet* (P11) **Complete only if Tax Code is cumulative.** *Make no entry here if Week 1 or Month 1 basis applies. Go to item 7.*

	Week	Month
Week or month number	25	
Total pay to date	£ 3,550	00 p
Total tax to date	£ 113	60 p

8 This employment pay and tax. ■ *No entry needed if Tax Code is cumulative and amounts are same as item 6 entry.*

Total pay in this employment	£	p
Total tax in this employment	£	p

9 Works number/ Payroll number

10 Department or branch if any

11 Employee's private address and Postcode

5 RIVER STREET
DUTTON
WORCS. DT13 9XX

12 I certify that the details entered above in items 1 to 9 are correct

Employer's name, address and Postcode

SHEPHERDS BRUSHES LTD
3 LONG ROAD
DUTTON, WORCS. DT2 3BP

Date   26.9.00

To the employer   *Please complete with care* ★

For Tax Office use

- Complete this form following the 'Employee leaving' instructions in the *Employer's quick Guide to PAYE and NICs* (cards CWG1). ★ **Make sure the details are clear on all four parts of this form**. Make sure your name and address is shown on Parts 1 and 1A.
- Detach Part 1 and send it to your Tax Office immediately.
- Hand Parts 1A, 2 and 3 (unseparated) to your employee when he or she leaves
- If the employee has died, write 'D' in this box and send all three parts of this form (unseparated) to your Tax Office immediately.

P45   BMSD9/99

Answer 3.2

A P45 should be prepared for all leavers. It is assumed here that Mr Ricketts's dismissal occurred on 21 July and that he is not due any more pay from the company.

	Details of employee leaving work Copy for Tax Office	P45 Part 1

Inland Revenue

		District number	Reference number
1	PAYE Reference	011	C2334

2	Employee's National Insurance number	DC 98 67 21 B

(Mr Mrs Miss Ms)

3	Surname (in capitals)	RICKETTS	Mr
	First name(s) (in capitals)	DAVID	

		Day	Month	Year
4	Leaving date (in figures)	21	07	2000

		Code		Week 1 or Month 1
5	Tax Code at leaving date. If week 1 or Month 1 basis applies, write 'X' in the box marked Week 1 or Month 1	350T		

			Week	Month
6	Last entries on Deductions Working Sheet (P11) **Complete only if Tax Code is cumulative** Make no entry here if Week 1 or Month 1 basis applies. Go to item 7	Week or month number	16	
		Total pay to date	£ 2,420	50 p
		Total tax to date	£ 248	19 p

7	This employment pay and tax. ■ No entry needed if Tax Code is cumulative and amounts are same as item 6 entry.	Total pay in this employment	£ 1,275	50 p
		Total tax in this employment	£ 116	70 p

8	Works number/ Payroll number		9	Department or branch if any	

10	Employee's private address and Postcode	17 RIVER MANSIONS HADERTON LANCS. HA12 1YP

11 I certify that the details entered above in items 1 to 9 are correct

Employer's name, address and Postcode	GUMM BOOTS LTD 7 WORPLE STREET HADERTON, LANCS. HA1 2YT
Date	24.7.00

To the employer

For Tax Office use

- Complete this form following the 'Employee leaving' instructions in the *Employer's Quick Guide to PAYE and NICs* (cards CWGI). Make sure the details are clear on all four parts of this form. Make sure your name and address is shown on Parts 1 and 1A.
- Detach part 1 and send it to your Tax Office immediately.
- Hand parts 1A, 2 and 3 (unseparated) to your employee when he or she leaves
- If the employee has died, write 'D' in this box and send all four parts of this form (unseparated) to your Tax Office immediately.

P45

A *point to note* is that total pay to date and total tax to date (item 6 above) includes pay and tax in previous employment: these are included in the P11 running totals for Week 16. Therefore in item 7 the amounts from his joining P45 need to be deducted from the P11 totals.

Part 1 of the form should be sent to the Tax Office immediately.

Parts 1A, 2 and 3 should be held until Mr Ricketts asks for them. Although the company has an address for him, it is possible that he no longer lives there, and it would be imprudent to send these parts of the P45 by post to that address.

Answer 3.3

(a)

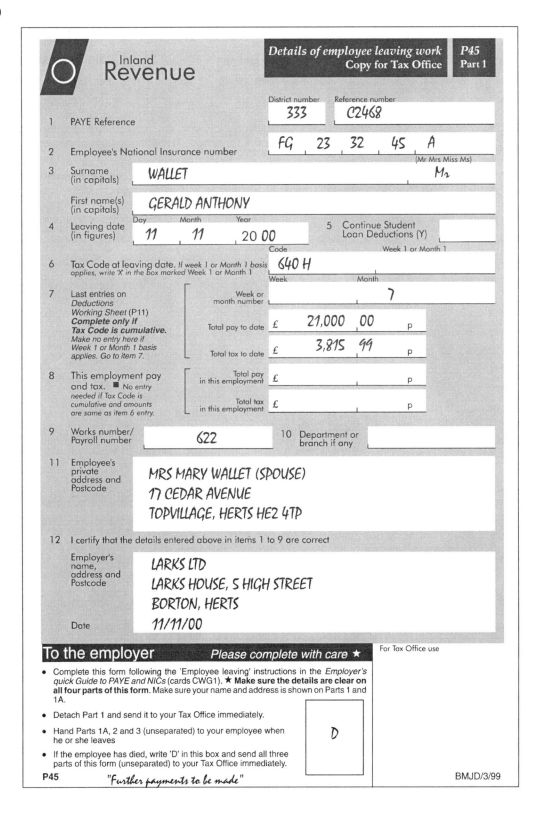

Note. Write D in the box provided and send all four parts to the Tax Office immediately you receive notification of the death. Since this is on 11 November, you do not wait until the end of Month 8 to complete the P45, and you should insert pay and tax details up to the latest known time, which is Month 7. You should write 'Further payment to be made' on the P45.

(b) You do not issue a revised or further form P45. Instead you should provide Mrs Wallet with a detailed payslip showing the deductions made. You should also write to your tax office with the details of the further payment and deductions made.

Answer 3.4

(a) Before any further action is taken, the details in item 6 of the P45s must be checked.

	Ms Williams	Mr Smith
	£	£
Tax due per tax tables	62.30	81.22
Per P45	(62.30)	(84.97)
Discrepancy	Nil	3.75

There is an incorrect entry for tax on Mr Smith's P45 and this should be noted on part 3 of his P45.

<table>
<tr><td></td><td></td><td>Inland
Revenue</td><td colspan="2">*New employee details*
For completion by new employer</td><td>**P45**
Part 3</td></tr>
</table>

	District number	Reference number
	152	C 3124

1 Previous PAYE Reference

2 Employee's National Insurance number   AB   23   45   67   C

     (Mr Mrs Miss Ms)

3 Surname   WILLIAMS   Ms

   First name(s)   KAREN ALICE

	Day	Month	Year		5 Continue Student Loan Deductions (Y)	
4 Date left previous employment	30	04	20 00			

                      Code   Week 1 or Month 1

6 Tax Code at leaving date. *'x' in the box means Week 7 or Month 1 basis applies*   379 L

7 Last entries on *Deductions Working Sheet (P11)*. *If there is an 'X' at item 6, there will be no entries here*	Week or Month number	Week 4	Month
	Total pay to date	£ 640 00 p	
	Total tax to date	£ 62 30 p	

To the new employer

Complete items 8 to 17 below and send this page of the form only to your Tax Office immediately.

8 New PAYE Reference   146/B 1323

	Day	Month	Year
9 Date employment started (in figures)	01	05	20 00

10 Tick here if you want these details to be shown on tax code notifications   ✓   Works/Payroll number   351

            Department or branch if any

11 Enter P if employee will not be paid by you between date employment began and next 5 April   12 Enter code in use if different to code at item 6

13 If the tax figure you are entering on P11 differs from item 7 above (see CWG (1999) card 4) please enter your figure here   £

14 Employee's private address	113A TOWN ST
	LITTLE SMELTINGS, GLOUCESTER Postcode G35 2HU

15 Employee's date of birth (if known)	12 12 1973	16 Employee's job title or description	QUALITY CONTROL CHECKER

17 **Declaration.** I have prepared a *Deductions Working Sheet (P11)* in accordance with the details above.

Employer	FRY & DICE LTD
Address	HOME WORKS, RUDDERTON ESTATE
	GLOUCESTER Postcode G99 1YY Date 1/5/00

P45

BPP PUBLISHING

Inland Revenue

New employee details
For completion by new employer

P45 Part 3

		District number	Reference number
1	Previous PAYE Reference	181	B 2697

2 Employee's National Insurance number LD 14 94 38 N

3 Surname SMITH (Mr Mrs Miss Ms) Mr

First name(s) BENJAMIN PETER

4 Date left previous employment
Day 30 Month 04 Year 20 00

5 Continue Student Loan Deductions (Y)

Week 1 or Month 1

6 Tax Code at leaving date. 'x' in the box means *Week 1 or Month 1 basis applies*
Code 502 H

7 Last entries on *Deductions Working Sheet (P11)*. If there is an 'X' at item 6, there will be no entries here

Week or Month number Week 4 Month

Total pay to date £ 820 00 p

Total tax to date £ 84 97 p

To the new employer

Complete items 8 to 17 below and send this page of the form only to your Tax Office immediately.

8 New PAYE Reference 146/ B 1323

9 Date employment started (in figures)
Day 01 Month 05 Year 20 00

10 Tick here if you want these details to be shown on tax code notifications ✓
Works/Payroll number 724
Department or branch if any

11 Enter P if employee will not be paid by you between date employment began and next 5 April

12 Enter code in use if different to code at item 6

13 If the tax figure you are entering on P11 differs from item 7 above (see CWG (1999) card 4) please enter your figure here
£ 81.22

14 Employee's private address 4 CONSTABLE DRIVE
GLOUCESTER Postcode G22 4PQ

15 Employee's date of birth (if known) 29 05 1980

16 Employee's job title or description PERSONNEL ASSISTANT

17 **Declaration.** I have prepared a *Deductions Working Sheet (P11)* in accordance with the details above.

Employer FRY & DICE LTD

Address HOMEWORKS, RUDDERTON ESTATE
GLOUCESTER Postcode G99 1YY Date 1/5/00

P45

(b)

	Tax code	Amended										
	502H	WK/mnth										
Week	Pay in the week 2	Total pay to date 3	Total free pay to date 4a	K codes Total additional pay to date 4b	Total taxable pay to date 5	Total tax due to date 6	K codes Tax due at end of current period 6a	K codes Regul. limit 6b	Tax deducted or refunded in the week 7	K codes Tax not deducted owing to the regul. limit 8	Tax credits 9
1											
2											
3											
4		820.00	386.88		433.12	81.22					

Answer 3.5

(a) This part of the activity is a straightforward test of your ability to fill in a P46. Three points to note are as follows.

  (i) Ms Carlyle will be taxed on Emergency Code to begin with. This is 438L for 2000/01. By ticking Statement A, she will be taxed on a cumulative basis, and so you should not put a cross in the Week 1 or Month 1 box near the bottom of the form.

  (ii) Use capital letters to complete the form.

PAYE Employer's notice to Inland Revenue Office

Send in on the first pay day for employees who
- do not have a form P45, or
- were previously paid below the PAYE threshold.

Section 1 - to be completed by the EMPLOYEE

Read each statement carefully. Tick **each one** that applies to you. **If none of them apply, do not sign the statement.**

Statement A
This is my first regular job since leaving full-time education. I have not claimed Jobseeker's Allowance, or income support paid because of unemployment since then. ✓

Statement B
This is my only or main job. ✓

Statement C
I receive a pension as well as the income from this job. ☐

I confirm that I have ticked the statements that apply to me.

Signed **R Carlyle**   Date **15 / 9 / 00**

Section 2 - to be completed by the EMPLOYER

Your employer's Quick Guide to PAYE and NICs (CWG1, Card 5) tells you how to complete this form.

Employee's details

National Insurance number: **YC 65 78 99 D**

Surname including title Mr/Mrs/Miss/Ms/Other **Mₐ CARLYLE**

First name(s) **ROBERTA JANE**

Address **15 CRESENT LANE**
WILLOWBY
BUCKS
Postcode **WLS 2TT**

Date of birth **19 / 08 / 1978**

Male/Female (enter M/F) **F**

Works/payroll number, if any

Department/Branch, if any **19**

Job title **RESEARCH OFFICER**

Date employment started **08 / 09 /2000**

P46

Coding information

Existing employee now above PAYE threshold ☐
(enter X in box if this applies)

New employee who has signed statement *(enter letter here)* **A,B**

New employee who has not signed a statement ☐

Code operated for this employee **438 L**

Enter X in box if code operated on week1/month 1 basis ☐

Employer's details

Employer's PAYE reference **186 DS432**

Name **HEALTH AUDIT AGENCY**

Address **MUSSEL HOUSE**
LYMM ROAD
LONDON
Postcode **ECSV 6QP**

Date this form was completed **15 / 09 / 2000**

Answer 3.6

The bonus would be assessed for NICs.

(a) As a monthly payment (because Olly was a monthly paid employee and the bonus was a regular payment, otherwise the weekly table would have been used).

(b) Using Table D, as the payment was within 6 weeks of his leaving (otherwise Table A would have been used).

(c) Using the rates at the time of payment.

Answer 4.1

Before any deductions for pension contributions can be made, the employee must be a member of the scheme. On joining the scheme, the employee should complete an instruction form enabling payroll to deduct the contribution from his or her pay. The form should be placed on the employee's personal file and details noted on the employee record.

Answer 4.2

	Month 1	*Amount deducted*
Net pay	800	
CSA order	(130)	130
Paid to Joe Johnson	670	

	Month 2	
Net pay	400	
CSA order	(130)	
	270	

As this is less than the minimum rate, only £50 is deducted this month
and £80 is carried forward. Joe Johnson is paid £350   50

	Month 3	
Net pay	600	
CSA order (130 + 80 b/f)	(210)	210
Paid to Joe Johnson	390	
		£390

Answer 4.3

You should have told Joe Johnson that the CSA can force employers to give details of an employee's pay, even when the employee has refused to co-operate with the CSA. When you receive the letter from the CSA, you must reply giving details of Joe's pay rise.

Answer 4.4

You can not deduct £2.00 per month from Marlene's pay without her permission. You need to send her a copy of the union letter, a copy of her authority form and a new authority form for her to sign. Advise her that it will save her having to sign a new authority every time the union rate changes, if she authorises payroll to deduct 'the current rate'. However if Marlene wants to specify the amount, and sign a new authority each time the note changes, that is her right.

Answer 5.1

Assuming that Joe normally works five days a week, than the self certification is sufficient for the first week. However, under the firm's rules, Joe needs to supply a doctor's certificate for the second week. You need to contact Joe to tell him that you can pay him sick pay for the first week, but you will need a doctor's certificate for the second week. If he does not provide a doctor's certificate for the second week, then he will not be paid for that week.

Answer 5.2

(a) The amount that you are authorised to pay ie £19,500 pa as stated in the personnel department's memorandum.

(b) In order to avoid future problems with Joe you should immediately send him a copy of personnel's memorandum. You should tell Joe that you are only authorised to pay him £19,500 pa not £20,000 pa. If he thinks that this is wrong, could he please speak to his supervisor to confirm his new rate. If it should be £20,000 pa, then perhaps both of them should go to see personnel to sort out the problem.

Answer 5.3

Not without confirming that the overtime was worked and is authorised. You would need to check Marlene's clock card or time sheet to check that the hours have been worked. The clock card or timesheet should also be signed by her supervisor to authorise payment of overtime and you should check the signature to the authorised signatories list.

Answer 5.4

(a) $40 \times £3.75 = £150$ per week

(b) $35 \times £4.00 = £140$ per week

Answer 6.1

		£
(a)	40 hours × £5 =	<u>200</u>
(b)	32 hours × £5 =	160
	8 hours × £10 =	<u>80</u>
		<u>240</u>
(c)	40 hours × £7.50 =	300
	4 hours × £7.50 =	<u>30</u>
		<u>330</u>

Answer 6.2

		£
(a)	50 widgets × £5 =	250
	Overtime 4 hours × £4 =	<u>16</u>
		<u>266</u>
(b)	Guaranteed minimum	<u>144</u>
(c)	29 widgets × £5 =	<u>145</u>
(d)	1st 60 widgets × £5 =	300
	Next 10 widgets × £6 =	60
	6 hours overtime × £4 =	<u>24</u>
		<u>384</u>

Answer 6.3

End of		£
January	£900 + (5% × £5,000) (December)	1,150
February	£900 + (5% × £5,000) (January)	1,150
March	£900 + (5% × £4,000) (February)	1,100
April	£900 + (5% × £3,000) (March) + £1,000 bonus (Total sales Jan-March of £12,000 exceed £10,000)	2,050
May	£900 + (5% × £2,000) (April)	1,000
June	£900 + (5% × £3,000) (May) (Total sales April to June of £9,000 do not exceed £10,000, so no bonus is payable in July)	1,050

Answer 7.1

	£
Basic salary £15,000/12	1,250.00
Overtime (175 – 156) × £10	190.00
Productivity bonus 5% × £1,250	62.50
	1,502.50
Back pay Jan – April (£15,000 – £12,000) × 4/12	1,000.00
	2,502.50

Answer 7.2

(a) and (b)

	£
Basic pay	150
Bonus	30
Staff suggestion award	20
Back pay	15
Overtime	20
= Gross pay	235
Income tax	(25)
National Insurance contribution	(10)
Net pay (as on pay cheque)	200

Answer 7.3

PAYROLL –20X1 WEEK 13 Employee	Staff number	Basic £ p	Saturday & overtime £ p	Total £ p
Ashdown P	071	208.00	104.00	312.00
Baker K	659	198.90	0.00	198.90
Blair T	660	184.00	92.00	276.00
Callaghan J	661	280.00	0.00	280.00
Clarke K	624	182.00	0.00	182.00
Delors J	010	300.00	90.00	390.00
Heath E	970	170.00	0.00	170.00
Heseltine M	664	208.00	7.80	215.80
Hurd D	663	230.00	43.13	273.13
King T	662	153.00	102.00	255.00
Kinnock N	992	260.00	61.75	321.75
Lamont N	666	166.40	0.00	166.40
Lilley P	665	208.00	0.00	208.00
Major J	990	175.00	80.00	255.00
Patten C	696	168.30	0.00	168.30
Rifkind M	621	163.20	81.60	244.80
Scargill A	917	230.00	17.25	247.25
Thatcher M	999	200.00	80.00	280.00
Waldegrave W	721	204.00	0.00	204.00
Wilson H	964	196.00	168.00	364.00
TOTAL		£4,084.80	£927.53	£5,012.33

Workings

1. Ashdown, P is an Underforeman, so is paid £6.50 per hour basic.

	£
32 hours at £6.50	208
8 hours at (£6.50 × 2) Saturday	104
	312

2. Baker, K is a Templateer, and so is paid £5.10 per hour basic. Baker has worked 39 hours this week. He has not worked on Saturday.

   Baker's pay is thus £5.10 × 39   £198.90

3. Blair, T is a Boilershutter, and so earns £5.75 an hour basic.

	£
32 × £5.75	184
8 × (£5.75 × 2) Saturday	92
	276

4. Callaghan, J is an Optical Fibre Twister, and so earns £7.00 an hour. For 40 hours (weekday) he earns £280.

5. Clarke, K is a Hopper Steerer, earning £5.20 per hour, which for 35 hours gives £182.00.

6. Delors, J the Foreman works for 48 hours. The basic rate is £7.50. Delors did not work on Saturday.

	£
40 × £7.50 basic	300
8 × (£7.50 × 1.5) overtime	90
	390

7. Heath, E is a Chargehand, at £5.00 per hour, which for 34 hours gives £170.

8. Heseltine, M is a Hopper Steerer, and so earns basic of £5.20 per hour.

	£
40 × £5.20 basic	208.00
1 × (£5.20 × 1.5) overtime	7.80
	215.80

9. Hurd, D is a Boilershutter who worked 45 hours at £5.75 basic.

	£
40 × £5.75 basic	230.00
5 × (£5.75 × 1.5) overtime	43.13
	273.13

10. King, T is a Templateer (£5.10 basic) who worked 40 hours, 10 on Saturday.

	£
30 × £5.10 basic	153
10 × (£5.10 × 2) Saturday	102
	255

11. Kinnock, N is an Underforeman, at £6.50 per hour basic.

	£
40 × £6.50 basic	260.00
1 × (£6.50 × 1.5) overtime	9.75
4 × (£6.50 × 2) Saturday	52.00
	321.75

12. Lamont, N is a Hopper Steerer at £5.20 per hour basic

    32 × £5.20 basic   £166.40

13. Lilley, P is a Hopper Steerer at £5.20 an hour.

    40 × £5.20 basic   £208

14. Major, J is a Chargehand at £5.00 an hour basic.

	£
35 × £5 basic	175
8 × (£5 × 2) Saturday	80
	255

15. Patten, C is a Templateer at £5.10 an hour basic.

    33 × £5.10   £168.30

16. Rifkind, M is a Templateer at £5.10 an hour basic.

	£
32 × £5.10	163.20
8 × (£5.10 × 2) Saturday	81.60
	244.80

17. Scargill, A is a Boilershutter at £5.75 an hour basic.

	£
40 × £5.75	230.00
2 × (£5.75 × 1.5) overtime	17.25
	247.25

18. Thatcher, M is a Chargehand at £5.00 an hour basic.

	£
40 × £5 basic	200.00
8 × (£5 × 2) Saturday	80.00
	280.00

19. Waldegrave, W is a Templateer at £5.10 an hour basic.

    40 × £5.10 basic   £204

20. Wilson, H is an Optical Fibre Twister at £7.00 an hour basic.

	£
28 × £7	196
12 × (£7 × 2) Saturday	168
	364

Answer 7.4

PAYROLL - 20X2 WEEK 20 Employee	Staff number	Basic £ p	Over-time £ p	Bonus £ p	Other £ p	Total £ p
Ashdown P	071	230.00	15.50	30.00	-	275.50
Baker K	659	180.00	25.20	30.00	-	235.20
Blair T	660	230.00	38.75	30.00	-	298.75
Callaghan J	661	285.00	46.50	30.00	-	361.50
Clarke K	624	180.00	6.30	30.00	-	216.30
Delors J	010	285.00	127.88	30.00	30.00	472.88
Heath E	970	180.00	6.30	30.00	-	216.30
Heseltine M	664	180.00	44.10	30.00	-	254.10
Hurd D	663	230.00	77.50	30.00	-	337.50
King T	662	180.00	44.10	30.00	-	254.10
Kinnock N	992	230.00	96.88	30.00	-	356.88
Lamont N	666	180.00	18.90	30.00	-	228.90
Lilley P	665	180.00	31.50	30.00	-	241.50
Major J	990	180.00	31.50	30.00	-	241.50
Patten C	696	180.00	12.60	30.00	-	222.60
Rifkind M	621	180.00	-	30.00	-	210.00
Scargill A	917	230.00	62.00	30.00	50.00	372.00
Thatcher M	999	180.00	37.80	30.00	-	247.80
Waldegrave W	721	180.00	37.80	30.00	-	247.80
Wilson H	964	285.00	9.30	30.00	-	324.30
TOTAL		4,165.00	770.41	600.00	80.00	5,615.41

Workings

(a) For the basic pay, just check the grades and write down the weekly standard for the grade.

(b) Overtime (hours × rate)

		£
1.	Ashdown, Grade B (37 – 35) × £7.75	15.50
2.	Baker, Grade C (39 – 35) × £6.30	25.20
3.	Blair, Grade B (40 – 35) × £7.75	38.75
4.	Callaghan, Grade A (40 – 35) × £9.30	46.50
5.	Clarke (C) (36 – 35) × £6.30	6.30
6.	Delors (A) ((48 – 45) × £9.30 × 1.25) + ((45 - 35) × £9.30)	127.88
7.	Heath (C) (36 – 35) × £6.30	6.30
8.	Heseltine (C) (42 – 35) × £6.30	44.10
9.	Hurd (B) (45 – 35) × £7.75	77.50
10.	King (C) (42 – 35) × £6.30	44.10
11.	Kinnock (B) ((47 – 45) × £7.75 × 1.25) + ((45 – 35) × £7.75)	96.88
12.	Lamont (C) (38 – 35) × £6.30	18.90
13.	Lilley (C) (40 – 35) × £6.30	31.50
14.	Major (C) (40 – 35) × £6.30	31.50
15.	Patten (C) (37 – 35) × £6.30	12.60
16.	Rifkind (C) (35 – 35) × £6.30	NIL
17.	Scargill (B) (43 – 35) × £7.75	62.00
18.	Thatcher (C) (41 – 35) × £6.30	37.80
19.	Waldegrave (C) (41 – 35) × £6.30	37.80
20.	Wilson (A) (36 – 35) × £9.30	9.30

(c) *Group bonus scheme*

The bonus per employee is ((1,120 – 1,000) × £5)/20 = £30 each

Answer 7.5

The *payroll proforma* needs to be redesigned. It needs a column showing the grade of each employee, a column for the number of basic hours, and a column for the number of hours at each overtime rate. The *timesheet summary* should also show the total number of hours at each rate for each employee as well as an overall total. In fact this company has enough employees for it to be cost effective to *computerise* the system, given the amount of calculation required and the potential for error.

Answer 8.1

George Ghost's taxable pay in Month 4 is as follows.

		£	£
(a)	Months 1 - 3 gross pay 3 × £1,000		3,000
	Gross pay in Month 4		1,500
	Total pay to date		4,500
	Less free pay Months 1 - 4		603
	Taxable pay to date		3,897
(b)	Total tax due		796.53
	Less tax paid to date		514.74
	Tax to be paid		281.79

Answer 8.2

A tax code tells you how much tax-free pay a person is entitled to. The Inland Revenue will send a Form P6(T) to advise an employer of an individual's tax code. They will also instruct employers to change employees' codes at the beginning of the tax year. The code is also noted down on the P45 which a new employee should give you.

Answer 8.3

The emergency code is a code giving only the personal allowance. It should be used in some cases where you do not know an employee's tax code. For the tax year 2000/01, the emergency code is 438L.

Answer 8.4

You look up the deduction for the Week or Month in the subtraction table, and deduct it from the amount calculated from Table B.

Answer 8.5

		8th April *Week 1*	*15th April* *Week 2*	*22nd April* *Week 3*
(a)	Tax code	472T	472T	472T
		£	£	£
	Pay in the week	240.60	290.30	260.00
	Total pay to date	240.60	530.90	790.90
	Free pay (Tables A) to date	90.95	181.90	272.85
	Taxable pay to date	149.65	349.00	518.05
	Use Table SR if pay does not exceed	£30	£59	£88
	Use Table B if pay does not exceed	£547	£1,093	£1,639
	Taxable Pay Table to use	B	B	B

BPP PUBLISHING

	£	£	£
Tax due to date per Table B			
On £100/£300/£500	22.00	66.00	110.00
On £49/£49/£18	10.78	10.78	3.96
	32.78	76.78	113.96
Starting rate rate relief	(3.51)	(7.02)	(10.53)
Cumulative tax due	29.27	69.76	103.43
Total tax deducted in the week	29.27	40.49	33.67

(b)

Tax code 472T	Amended WK/mnth		

W e e k	Pay in the week 2	Total pay to date 3	Total free pay to date 4a	K codes Total additional pay to date 4b	Total taxable pay to date 5	Total tax due to date 6	K codes Tax due at end of current period 6a	K codes Regul. limit 6b	Tax deducted or reduced in the week 7	K codes Tax not deducted owing to the regul. limit 8	Tax credit 9
1	240.60	240.60	90.95		149.65	29.27			29.27		
2	290.30	530.90	181.90		349.00	69.76			40.49		
3	260.00	790.90	272.85		518.05	103.43			33.67		

Answer 8.6

(a)

	End of April Month 1 £	*End of May Month 2* £
Pay in the month	3,000.00	3,000.00
Total pay to date	3,000.00	6,000.00
Tax free pay, Tables A		
Codes 5 + boxed 500	421.59 (4.92 + 416.67)	843.18 (9.84 + 833.34)
Taxable pay to date	2,578.41	5,156.82
Limitation on use of Table B	£2,367.00	£4,734.00
Taxable Pay Tables to use	C and D	C and D
	£	£
Taxable pay (ignoring pence)	2,578	5,156
Taxable at basic rate (Table C)	2,367	4,734
Taxable at higher rate (Table D)	211	422

		£		£		£
At basic rate, Table C	On £2,367/£4,734	505.59				1,011.19
Table D						
	On £200	80.00		On £400	160.00	
	On £11	4.40		On £22	8.80	
	On £211		84.40	On £422		168.80
Total tax to date			589.99			1,179.99
Tax due in month			£589.99			£590.00

Note that Table C already takes the starting rate relief into account.

(b)

Tax code	Amended
505H	WK/mnth

Month	Pay in the month 2	Total pay to date 3	Total free pay to date 4a	K codes Total additional pay to date 4b	Total taxable pay to date 5	Total tax due to date 6	K codes Tax due at end of current period 6a	K codes Regul. limit 6b	Tax deducted or reduced in the month 7	K codes Tax not deducted owing to the regul. limit 8	Tax credits 9
1	3,000.00	3,000.00	421.59		2,578.41	589.99			589.99		
2	3,000.00	6,000.00	843.18		5,156.82	1,179.99			590.00		

Answer 8.7

The most important point to remember is that enquiries about pay must be treated with the utmost courtesy. People do a job to earn money, and if they are worried about their pay, they will be unhappy at their work. When you have answered their query, they should feel comfortable with the idea of speaking to you again, if their problem has not been fully resolved.

Our answers are quite full ones: you need only have given the gist of what we say.

(a) *Ellen Priestley.* You need to tell her that, unfortunately, she is subject to PAYE income tax on her earnings, even though she is a pensioner. Her tax code will be higher because of her age so she pays less tax than a young person. It is the law that an employer should tax employees who are pensioners according to the appropriate tax code. (A pensioner is not required to pay National Insurance contributions, but that is not the subject of this activity.)

You should suggest to Ellen that she should get the Tax Office to check her tax coding. Give her the address and telephone number of the Tax Office, and suggest that she gets in touch with them.

(b) *Tina Rafferty.* You will obviously be sympathetic because the agency is not paying Tina on time. Unfortunately, you have to tell her that, because she is an agency worker, the agency is her 'official employer'. You can speak to your supervisor, who might be able to put some pressure on the agency to start paying Tina more promptly than in the past.

(c) *Bob Harkins.* A tax code BR means that all of Bob's pay will be taxable at the basic rate of 22%, and he will be entitled to no allowances at all on his pay (so there is no free pay) nor will he be eligible for Starting Rate relief. This is an unusual situation, as every individual is entitled to at least a personal allowance. It might be the case that Bob has another job, where the employer is giving him his allowances in his tax code. There could be other reasons why he should not be entitled to any allowances. He should be advised to telephone or write to his Tax Office. (You should give him the address and telephone number.)

(d) *Simone Michel*. Every employee should be subject to tax on income in one country or another (but not two!). When someone goes to work abroad, they might become subject to different treatment for tax purposes, but until you are told this officially by the Tax Office, Simone will still be subject to UK PAYE and National Insurance rules. Before she goes abroad, she should do the following.

(i) Write to the Tax Office notifying the Inland Revenue of her change of job location.

(ii) Speak to your supervisor about writing to the Tax Office on Simone's behalf.

(e) *Arthur Tildesley*. You must tell Arthur, as politely as possible, that you cannot treat him as a self-employed person if he is working for you regularly, even if only on a part-time basis, unless he can provide official confirmation of his new status from the Tax Office. He should be kept on the payroll, and PAYE income tax (and NI) deducted. You should advise him to write to the Tax Office if he is dissatisfied, and give him the address to write to (or number to telephone).

(f) *Alan Gorham*. Alan presumably doesn't understand about PAYE, and you might need to explain the system to him very carefully. Emergency code (438L for tax year 2000/01) is a code that gives the individual the allowances of a single person (no more and no less). He should write to the Tax Office and ask for a 'proper' coding. Emergency coding is temporary, and it is probable anyway that the Tax Office is in the process of re-coding him. If he gets a higher code eventually, he will benefit from a lower tax payment on the first pay day afterwards, or might even be entitled to a refund of tax previously paid.

'Emergency' is not really a very good word to use because it sounds so alarming. You might be able to reassure people by telling them that all it means is that a 'proper' code will emerge from the Tax Office in due course.

Answer 9.1

M o n t h	Pay in the month 2	Total pay to date 3	Total free pay to date 4a	K codes Total additional pay to date 4b	Total taxable pay to date 5	Total tax due to date 6	K codes Tax due at end of current period 6a	K codes Regul. limit 6b	Tax deducted or reduced in the month 7	K codes Tax not deducted owing to the regul. limit 8	Tax credits 9
1	1,250.00	1,250.00	361.59		888.41	180.15			180.15		
2	1,250.00	2,500.00	723.18		1,776.82	360.31			180.16		
3	1,250.00	3,750.00	1,084.77		2,665.23	540.70			180.39		
4	1,250.00	5,000.00	436.36		4,563.64	943.05			402.35		
5	1,250.00	6,250.00	545.45		5,704.55	1,178.87			235.82		
6	1,250.00	7,500.00	654.54		6,845.46	1,414.70			235.83		
7	1,250.00	8,750.00	763.63		7,986.37	1,650.50			235.81		
8	1,250.00	10,000.00	872.72		9,127.28	1,886.33			235.82		
9	1,250.00	11,250.00	981.81		10,268.19	2,122.16			235.83		
10	1,312.50	12,562.50	1,090.90		11,471.60	2,371.61			249.45		
11	1,312.50	13,875.00	1,199.99		12,675.01	2,621.29			249.68		
12	1,312.50	15,187.50	1,309.08		13,878.42	2,870.76			249.47		

Tax code: ~~433L~~ Amended: WK/mnth 130L 4

The most likely assumptions are that Maria is paid at the end of the month (which would be normal) and that the new tax code would be used in Month 4, and the first payment at the increased level would be on 31 January (in Month 10). You do not know this for certain, however, and you should make further enquiries to find out when pay day is and which tax month is the first in which the new tax code and the new rate of pay are to apply.

Answer 9.2

(a) (i) *Week 1/Month 1 basis*

	Month 1 £	Month 2 £
Gross pay	1,500.00	2,000.00
Free pay	(415.75)	(415.75)
Taxable pay	1,084.25	1,584.25

(ii) *Cumulative basis*

	Month 1 £	Month 2 £
Gross pay	1,500.00	3,500.00
Free pay	(415.75)	(831.50)
Taxable pay	1,084.25	2,668.50

(b) (i) *Week 1/Month 1 basis*

Tax for Month 1: (£1,084 × 22%) – £15.21 = £223.27

Tax for Month 2: (£1,584 × 22%) – £15.21 = £333.27

(ii) *Cumulative basis*

Tax for month 1 (£1,084 × 22%) – £15.21 = £223.27

Tax for month 2: (£2,668 × 22%) – £30.41 – £223.27 = £333.28

These figures can also be found using Table B and the Subtraction Tables.

Answer 9.3

Since John Rose is being taxed on a Week 1/Month 1 basis and earns a constant monthly salary, the tax computations for his pay will be the same every month (until his tax code changes in June).

(a) *For April and May*

	£
Total pay for the month	3,000.00
Tax free pay (code 608 = 108 + boxed 500)	
– Table A Month 1 £(90.75 + 416.67)	507.42
Taxable pay	2,492.58

Since the limitation on the use of Table B is £2,367, Tables C and D should be used. Taxable pay of £2,492 exceeds the Table B/Table C limit of £2,367 by £125.

	£	£
Taxable pay each month		
On first £2,367 (Table C)		505.59
On £125 (Table D)		50.00
Tax payable in each month		555.59

(b) *For June*

	£
Total pay to date (3 months)	9,000.00
Tax free pay (code 620 = 120 + boxed 500)	
– Table A Month 3 £(302.25 + 1,250.01)	1,552.26
Taxable pay	7,447.74

Tables C and D should be used.

	£
Taxable pay (ignoring the 74 pence)	7,447
Table C limit Month 3	7,100
Taxable at Table D rates	347

Tax payable in June

	£	£
On first £7,100 (Table C, Month 3)		1,516.40
Table D		
On £300	120.00	
On £47	18.80	
On £347		138.80
Total tax payable for the year to date		1,655.20

The tax payable in June is as follows.

	£
To date in June	1,655.20
To date in May (2 × £555.59)	1,111.18
	544.02

Tax code	Amended	620H	
~~608T m1~~	WK/mnth	3	

M o n t h	Pay in the month 2	Total pay to date 3	Total free pay to date 4a	K codes Total additional pay to date 4b	Total taxable pay to date 5	Total tax due to date 6	K codes Tax due at end of current period 6a	K codes Regul. limit 6b	Tax deducted or reduced in the month 7	K codes Tax not deducted owing to the regul. limit 8	Tax credits 9
1	3,000.00		507.42		2,492.58				555.59		
2	3,000.00	6,000.00	507.42		2,492.58	1,111.18			555.59		
3	3,000.00	9,000.00	1,552.26		7,447.74	1,655.20			544.02		

Note that the total pay to date and total tax to date (columns 3 and 6) are entered in the Month 2 row in Month 3, when John Rose changes to the cumulative basis.

Answer 9.4

In Week 53, compute free pay on a Week 1 basis, using the same tax code for the employee as before.

	Week 53 £
Pay for Week 53	300.00
Less free pay for Week 1	(63.45)
Taxable pay	236.55

	£
Table B applies	
On £200	44.00
On £36	7.92
	51.92
Less starting rate relief	(3.51)
Tax for Week 53	48.41

For Week 53, fill in column 7 of the P11 before you fill in column 6.

W e e k	Pay in the week 2	Total pay to date 3	Total free pay to date 4a	K codes Total additional pay to date 4b	Total taxable pay to date 5	Total tax due to date 6	K codes Tax due at end of current period 6a	K codes Regul. limit 6b	Tax deducted or reduced in the week 7	K codes Tax not deducted owing to the regul. limit 8	Tax credits 9
47	300.00	14,100.00	2,982.15		11,117.85	2,280.87			48.42		
48	300.00	14,400.00	3,045.60		11,354.40	2,329.51			48.64		
49	300.00	14,700.00	3,109.05		11,590.95	2,377.92			48.41		
50	300.00	15,000.00	3,172.50		11,827.50	2,426.55			48.63		
51	300.00	15,300.00	3,235.95		12,064.05	2,475.18			48.63		
52	300.00	15,600.00	3,299.40		12,300.60	2,523.60			48.42		
53	300.00	15,900.00	3,362.85		12,537.15	2,572.01			48.41		

Answer 9.5

(a) **Paul Rodgers**

He is on strike and is not paid in Week 2. You should not fill in the P11 for him for Week 2 or compute any refund.

Tax code 300T	Amended WK/mnth										

Week	Pay in the week 2	Total pay to date 3	Total free pay to date 4a	K codes Total additional pay to date 4b	Total taxable pay to date 5	Total tax due to date 6	K codes Tax due at end of current period 6a	K codes Regul. limit 6b	Tax deducted or reduced in the week 7	K codes Tax not deducted owing to the regul. limit 8	Tax credits 9
1	250.00	250.00	57.87		192.13	38.73			38.73		
2											

Richard Stout

Tax code 300T	Amended WK/mnth										

Week	Pay in the week 2	Total pay to date 3	Total free pay to date 4a	K codes Total additional pay to date 4b	Total taxable pay to date 5	Total tax due to date 6	K codes Tax due at end of current period 6a	K codes Regul. limit 6b	Tax deducted or reduced in the week 7	K codes Tax not deducted owing to the regul. limit 8	Tax credit 9
1	200.00	200.00	57.87		142.13	27.73			27.73		
2	50.00	250.00	115.74		134.26	22.46			(5.27) R		

(b) The refund should not be paid during the lay-off, but Richard Stout's P11 should be filled in.

The refund should be paid on the pay day following Richard Stout's eventual return to work. By that time, more refunds might be due.

Answer 9.6

(a) The Tax Office assigns K codes to people when their taxable benefits are greater than the allowances that they are entitled to.

(b)   **MEMO**

To: Carol Lewis
From: P Administrator
Subject: PAYE income tax
Date: 10 July 2000

Following our telephone conversation today I have looked into the sudden change in the amount of PAYE income tax deducted from your salary.

The calculations have been done correctly. The change is due to a change in your tax code which was notified to us last month. As these matters depend on personal circumstances, we are simply told what figures to use. The Tax Office should have notified you separately of this change and provided an explanation.

The tax code number determines the amount of adjustment to basic pay before calculating the tax due, both to give credit for personal tax allowances and to ensure that tax is collected on taxable benefits such as company cars. You have been given a code K321. This means that, according to the Inland Revenue's records, the amount of your taxable benefits exceeds the amount of your allowances by about £3,215.

Unless we are notified of a further change, this means that in future income tax will be payable on an amount in addition to your basic salary each month. However, the maximum amount of income tax that can be deducted each month is 50% of your gross pay (ie your pay excluding benefits in kind).

Please contact me again if I can be of further assistance. If you need to contact the Tax Office about this, their address (and your reference, which you should quote in any correspondence) is as follows:

> Address of Tax Office
>
> Employee's reference number

(c) You should certainly not leave the memo anywhere where it can be read by other people because this is a confidential matter. You should institute whatever procedure is used to deliver confidential messages in your organisation - perhaps use a sealed envelope and mark it 'Private and Confidential'.

(d) It is bad practice to leave any task unfinished, because you might forget to come back to it. In any case, since the information is to hand and fresh in your mind, now is the best time to deal with it.

Answer 9.7

Tax code	Amended		
K149	WK/mnth		

M o n t h	Pay in the month 2	Total pay to date 3	Total free pay to date 4a	K codes Total additional pay to date 4b	Total taxable pay to date 5	Total tax due to date 6	K codes Tax due at end of current period 6a	K codes Regul. limit 6b	Tax deducted or reduced in the month 7	K codes Tax not deducted owing to the regul. limit 8	Tax credits 9
1	3,000.00	3,000.00		124.92	3,124.92	808.39	808.39	1,500.00	808.39		
2	3,000.00	6,000.00		249.84	6,249.84	1,617.19	808.80	1,500.00	808.80		
3	3,000.00	9,000.00		374.76	9,374.76	2,426.00	808.81	1,500.00	808.81		

Answer 9.8

(a)

Tax code	Amended		
K491	WK/mnth		

M o n t h	Pay in the month 2	Total pay to date 3	Total free pay to date 4a	K codes Total additional pay to date 4b	Total taxable pay to date 5	Total tax due to date 6	K codes Tax due at end of current period 6a	K codes Regul. limit 6b	Tax deducted or reduced in the month 7	K codes Tax not deducted owing to the regul. limit 8	Tax credits 9
1	125.00	125.00		409.92	534.92	102.27	102.27	62.50	62.50	39.77	
2	125.00	250.00		819.84	1,069.84	204.77	142.27	62.50	62.50	79.77	

BPP PUBLISHING

Answers to practice activities

(b)

	Tax code K491 Mth1	Amended WK/mnth										
M o n t h	**Pay in the month** 2	**Total pay to date** 3	**Total free pay to date** 4a	**K codes** Total additional pay to date 4b	**Total taxable pay to date** 5	**Total tax due to date** 6	**K codes** Tax due at end of current period 6a	**K codes** Regul. limit 6b	**Tax deducted or reduced in the month** 7	**K codes** Tax not deducted owing to the regul. limit 8	**Tax credits** 9
1	125.00			409.92	534.92		102.27	62.50	62.50		
2	125.00			409.92	534.92		102.27	62.50	62.50		

No entry is made in Column 8.

Answer 10.1

(a) None. People aged under 16 do not pay NICs, nor do their employers.
(b) Table C, CA38
(c) Table D.
(d) Table A.

Answer 10.2

(a) The upper earnings limit less the lower earnings limit: £535 – £67 = £468.
(b) All earnings over the earnings threshold: £550 – £84 = £466.

Answer 10.3

False. There may be occasions when items are assessable for NICs but are not taxable, and vice versa.

Answer 10.4

Employees pay NICs when earnings are paid.

Employees' NICs collected by the employer are paid to the Inland Revenue's Collector of Taxes, with a few exceptions, 14 days after the end of each tax month.

Answer 10.5

NICs are not payable by persons under 16. His sixteenth birthday has no significance for tax purposes as he can be taxed at any age. (However, his income of £80 a week is probably too small to be taxed, as the personal allowance of £4,385/52 gives him free pay each week of £84.33 per week.)

Answer 10.6

To: Harold Childe
From: Payroll Administrator

From the age of 16 you must pay National Insurance Contributions (NICs) on your pay, if your pay is at least as high as the lower earnings limit (£67 a week for the tax year 2000/01). Although the deduction is nil, until you reach £76 a week.

Your employer is required by law to deduct NICs. These are worked out using Tables supplied to us by the Inland Revenue.

For pay of £80 a week, we are required to deduct £0.45 a week from your pay.

Your National Insurance Contributions are used to fund a number of social benefits. If you are ill, for example, then you can be paid Statutory Sick Pay. This is more than the benefit you would receive if you had not contributed.

Answer 10.7 _____

To: Harold Childe
From: Payroll Administrator

Contracting out

It is true that some people are entitled to contract out of paying full National Insurance Contributions.

Contracting out means that you pay NICs at a lower rate because you are not participating in the State Earnings Related Pension Scheme (SERPS). You are only allowed to contract out if the employer runs a contracted-out occupational pension scheme of which you are a member. This usually means, of course, that you have to pay pension contributions as well as NICs.

I hope this clarifies the matter for you.

Answer 10.8 _____

Notes to the solution

(i)   Did you remember to fill in the NI contribution table letter at the bottom?

(ii) Did you remember the procedure? Look up the employee's gross earnings in the appropriate table. If there is no exact match, take the nearest lower amount.

(a) *Diane Geness*

We use Table A to work out the NICs of £2,200, go to the next lowest figure of £2,199.

(b) *Horace Inkley*

Horace's Table changes during the year.

For his payments up to, but not including, Week 7 he pays contributions under Table A. Once he has reached pension age he goes to Table C. He pays nothing, but Churne Orvill Ltd still contributes.

You can fill in the totals for letter A at the bottom of the P11.

(c) *Maggie Knox*

For Maggie Knox go to Table A and read off the figures from the next lower figure to £305 which is £303.

(d) *Silas Izewell*

Silas Izewell, being over pension age, pays no employee's contribution. The employer, however, is still liable on all Silas Izewell's salary. This is over the upper earnings limit in Month 3. Go to Table C. The fact that he gives his bonuses to charity has no effect on his NIC liability. The Month 3 bonus is not treated as having been paid in Month 2.

	Month 3
	£
Total earnings	2,350.00
Maximum earnings shown in Table C	2,319.00
	31.00

Per 'additional gross pay table'
Employer's contributions
On £31   3.78

Per Table C
On £2,319   238.39
                                                                       242.17

(*Tutorial note.* Try applying the exact percentage method (12.2% of earnings above the earnings threshold) and see if you prefer this method!)

Answers to practice activities

Diane Geness

National Insurance contributions *Note:*   **LEL = Lower Earnings Limit,   UEL = Upper Earnings Limit**

Week No	Month No	1a Earnings at the LEL (where earnings reach or exceed the LEL) £ p	1b Earnings above the LEL, up to and including the employee's Earnings Threshold £ p	1c Earnings above the employee's threshold, up to and including the employer's Earnings Threshold £ p	1d Earnings above the employer's Earnings Threshold, up to and including the UEL £ p	1e Total of employee's and employer's contributions payable £ p	1f Employee's contribution payable £ p	1g NIC rebate due on amount in 1b £ p	1h NIC rebate due on the sum of the amounts in 1b and 1c £ p	1i Statutory Sick Pay in the week or month included in column 2 £ p	1j Statutory Maternity Pay in the week or month included in column 2 £ p	1k Student loan £ p
4	1	291	38	36	1,210	272.66	124.80					
8	2	291	38	36	1,834	411.19	187.20					
13	3	291	38	36	1,834	411.19	187.20					

Enter NIC Contribution Table letter here

End of Year Summary

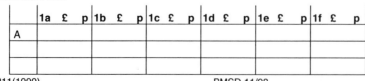

	1a £ p	1b £ p	1c £ p	1d £ p	1e £ p	1f £ p
A						

P11(1999)   BMSD 11/98

Horace Inkley

National Insurance contributions *Note:*   LEL = Lower Earnings Limit,   UEL = Upper Earnings Limit

WEEK NO	MONTH NO	Earnings details 1a £ p — Earnings at the LEL (where earnings reach or exceed the LEL)	1b £ p — Earnings above the LEL, up to and including the employee's Earnings Threshold	1c £ p — Earnings above the employee's threshold, up to and including the employer's Earnings Threshold	1d £ p — Earnings above the employer's Earnings Threshold, up to and including the UEL	Contribution details 1e £ p — Total of employee's and employer's contributions payable	1f £ p — Employee's contribution payable	Rebate details 1g £ p — NIC rebate due on amount in 1b	1h £ p — NIC rebate due on the sum of the amounts in 1b and 1c	1i £ p — Statutory Sick Pay in the week or month included in column 2	1j £ p — Statutory Maternity Pay in the week or month included in column 2	1k £ p — Student loan
1		67	9	8	96	22.22	10.45					
2		67	9	8	96	22.22	10.45					
3		67	9	8	96	22.22	10.45					
4	1	67	9	8	96	22.22	10.45					
5		67	9	8	96	22.22	10.45					
6		67	9	8	96	22.22	10.45					
7		67	9	8	96	11.77	-					
8	2	67	9	8	96	11.77	-					
9		67	9	8	96	11.77	-					
10		67	9	8	96	11.77	-					
11		67	9	8	96	11.77	-					
12		67	9	8	96	11.77	-					
13	3	67	9	8	96	11.77	-					

For employer's use only

Enter NIC Contribution Table letter here   **End of Year Summary**

	1a £ p	1b £ p	1c £ p	1d £ p	1e £ p	1f £ p
A	402	54	48	576	133.32	62.70
C						

P11(1999)   BMSD 11/98

Maggie Knox

National Insurance contributions *Note:*   LEL = Lower Earnings Limit,   UEL = Upper Earnings Limit

		Earnings details				Contribution details		Rebate details				
For employer's use only	Earnings at the LEL (where earnings reach or exceed the LEL) 1a £ p	Earnings above the LEL, up to and including the employee's Earnings Threshold 1b £ p	Earnings above the employee's threshold, up to and including the employer's Earnings Threshold 1c £ p	Earnings above the employer's Earnings Threshold, up to and including the UEL 1d £ p	Total of employee's and employer's contributions payable 1e £ p	Employee's contribution payable 1f £ p	NIC rebate due on amount in 1b 1g £ p	NIC rebate due on the sum of the amounts in 1b and 1c 1h £ p	Statutory Sick Pay in the week or month included in column 2 1i £ p	Statutory Maternity Pay in the week or month included in column 2 1j £ p	Student loan 1k £ p
WEEK NO 1	291	12									
2											
3											
MONTH NO 1 — 4	291	12	–	–	–	–					
5 — 8											
MONTH NO 2 — 8	291	12	–	–	–	–					
9 — 12											
MONTH NO 3 — 13	291	12	–	–	–	–					

Enter NIC Contribution Table letter here

End of Year Summary

	1a £ p	1b £ p	1c £ p	1d £ p	1e £ p	1f £ p
A						

P11(1999)   BMSD 11/98

Silas Izewell

National Insurance contributions *Note:* LEL = Lower Earnings Limit, UEL = Upper Earnings Limit

Week No	Month No	For employer's use only	Earnings details				Contribution details		Rebate details				
			1a £ p — Earnings at the LEL (where earnings reach or exceed the LEL)	1b £ p — Earnings above the LEL, up to and including the employee's Earnings Threshold	1c £ p — Earnings above the employee's Earnings threshold, up to and including the employer's Earnings Threshold	1d £ p — Earnings above the employer's Threshold, up to and including the UEL	1e £ p — Total of employee's and employer's contributions payable	1f £ p — Employee's contribution payable	1g £ p — NIC rebate due on amount in 1b	1h £ p — NIC rebate due on the sum of the amounts in 1b and 1c	1i £ p — Statutory Sick Pay in the week or month included in column 2	1j £ p — Statutory Maternity Pay in the week or month included in column 2	1k £ p — Student loan
1													
2													
3													
4	1		291	38	36	1,934	236.19	-					
5													
6													
7													
8	2		291	38	36	1,634	199.59	-					
9													
10													
11													
12													
13	3		291	38	36	1,954	242.17	-					

Enter NIC Contribution Table letter here **End of Year Summary**

	1a £ p	1b £ p	1c £ p	1d £ p	1e £ p	1f £ p
C						

P11(1999) BMSD 11/98

Answer 10.9

(a) (i) *Morris* - Table A (£2,000 a month)

	£
Employee's contribution (£2,000 – 329) × 10%	<u>167.10</u>
Employer's contribution: (£2,000 – £365) × 12.2%	<u>199.47</u>

(ii) *Jones* - Table A (£150 a week)

	£
Employee's contribution (£150 – £76) × 10%	7.40
Employer's contribution (£150 – £84) × 12.2%	8.05

(iii) *Sanders* – Table A (£80 a week)

	£
Employee's contribution (£80 – £76) × 10%	0.40
Employer's contribution not required; earnings below threshold	Nil

(iv) *Jellicoe* – Table A (£552.45 a week)

	£
Employee's contribution: (£535 – £76) × 10%	45.90
Employer's contribution (£552.45 – £84) × 12.2%	57.15

★ Amounts of exactly 0.5p are always rounded *down*. Otherwise round to the nearest penny.

(v) *Majid* - Table B (£90 a week)

Employee's contribution (£90 – £76) × 3.85%	<u>£0.54</u>
Employer's contribution (£90 – £84) × 12.2%	<u>£0.73</u>

(b)

Name	Column 1a £	Column 1b £	Column 1c £	Column 1d £	Column 1e £	Column 1f £
P Morris	291	38	36	1,635	336.57	167.10
B Jones	67	9	8	66	15.45	7.40
F Sanders	67	9	4	-	0.40	0.40
J Jellicoe	67	9	8	451	103.05	45.90
F Majid	67	9	8	6	1.27	0.54

Answer 10.10

Although Penny does not have to pay tax on her pension contribution, the amount she contributes is still included in gross pay for NIC purposes.

Contracting out means that earnings between the lower earnings limit (LEL) and upper earnings limit (UEL) are assessed for reduced employee's contributions.

The employer reverts to the normal rate beyond the UEL but pays a reduced rate on earnings between the earnings threshold and the UEL. The employer also gets a rebate on earnings between the LEL and the earnings threshold to compensate for increases in NIC rates introduced in the 2000 budget.

Working

Employer's contributions

	£	£
On earnings between ET and UEL: (£2,319 – £365) × 9.2%		179.77
On earnings above UEL (£2,400 – £2,319) × 12.2%		9.88
		189.65

Employee's contributions
(£2,319 – £329) × 8.4%   167.16

Total of employee's and employer's contributions   356.81

Column 1g (rebate): (Employee's ET – LEL) × 1.6% = (£329 – £291) × 1.6% = £0.61

Column 1h: (Employer's ET – LEL) × 3% = (365 – 291) × 3% = £2.22

National Insurance contributions *Note:*   LEL = Lower Earnings Limit,   UEL = Upper Earnings Limit

MONTH or WEEK NO	For employer's use only	Earnings details				Contribution details		Rebate details		Statutory Sick Pay in the week or month included in column 2	Statutory Maternity Pay in the week or month included in column 2	Student loan
		Earnings at the LEL (where earnings reach or exceed the LEL)	Earnings above the LEL, up to and including the employee's Earnings Threshold	Earnings above the employee's threshold, up to and including the employer's Earnings Threshold	Earnings above the employer's Earnings Threshold, up to and including the UEL	Total of employee's and employer's contributions payable	Employee's contribution payable	NIC rebate due on amount in 1b	NIC rebate due on the sum of the amounts in 1b and 1c			
		1a £ p	1b £ p	1c £ p	1d £ p	1e £ p	1f £ p	1g £ p	1h £ p	1i £ p	1j £ p	1k £ p
1		291	38	36	1954	356.81	167.16	0.61	2.22			
2												
3												
4												

Answer 10.11

(a) Tom is a weekly paid employee. In Weeks 2 - 52 neither he nor his employer will pay NICs because his earnings are below the lower earnings limit. In Week 1 NICs will be payable as follows.

(It should be appreciated that the Inland Revenue could make an order for the NICs to be assessed differently as this arrangement appears to be so unusual.)

Employee's: upper earnings limit £535 – employee's earnings threshold £76 at 10% = £45.90.

Employer's: £36,634.51 – earnings threshold £84.00 = £36,550.51 × 12.2% = £4,459.16.

(b) (i) Tom is now a director and so special rules apply.

Week 1

Earnings to date/52 = £36,634.51/52 = £704.51. This notional weekly figure exceeds the weekly UEL. Employee's NICs due to date will be payable as calculated above then multiplied by 52.

$$52 \times £45.90 = £2,386.80$$

Employer's NIC's are (£704.51 – £84) × 12.2% × 52 = £3,936.52 (slightly different answers are possible, depending upon rounding).

No NICs have been paid to date and so these two amounts must be paid.

Week 2

$$\frac{£36,634.51 + £65.99}{52} = £705.78$$

Again employee's NICs due to date are payable up to the upper earnings limit and come to £2,386.80 as calculated above. Employer's NICs are (£705.78 – £84) × 12.2% × 52 = £3,944.57.

	Employee's £	Employer's £
Due to date Week 2	2,386.80	3,944.57
Paid to date	2,386.80	3,936.52
	Nil	8.05

(ii) Employee's NICs for the year are due as follows: (£535 – £67) × 10% × 52 = £2,386.80

This is the amount paid in Week 1, as shown in (b) (i).

Employer's NICs are due at 12.2% on the total salary for the year less the annual earnings threshold: (£40,000 – £4,385) × 12.2% = £4,345.03.

The first £3,936.52 is paid in Week 1 as shown above. The balance (£408.51) will be paid off in weeks 2 to 52.

	£
Weeks 2 to 51: 50 × £8.05	402.50
Week 52: remainder, lower due to rounding	6.01
	408.51

Answer 11.1

MEMO

To: Gilberta Sullivan
From: A Payroll Clerk   Date:
Subject: Gross and net pay

Gross pay is all the income you have earned for the work you have done, or what you have been given by the company. Gross pay comprises basic pay, overtime, bonuses, commission, holiday pay, statutory sick pay and statutory maternity pay. Net pay is gross pay minus deductions, like income tax, NICs, pension contributions, season ticket loan repayments and advances of pay.

Tax and NICs are calculated on gross pay following rules laid down by the Inland Revenue. Some deductions from gross pay (like GAYE Give As You Earn and pension contributions) reduce the amount of tax due.

A deduction from pay after tax reduces the amount of your pay cheque, but does not affect the tax computation. Loan repayments fall into this category.

Answer 11.2

(a) Charles Kingsley does not need a P11 for the following reasons.

    (i)   He is too young (under 16) for NICs.

    (ii)   He earns less than the basic level at which NICs and income tax are payable. The Employee's Earnings Threshold for NICs is £76 per week. The PAYE threshold is £84.

    Note down his name, NI number and earnings, and send in the details at the end of the year. Keep his P46 and ensure that he signs it as a school leaver. He will need a P11 after the age of 16, at his earnings exceed the LEL of £67 per week.

(b) Freddie Scullion should be given form P38(S) to sign to state that he is a student in full time education and that his income for the year to the following 5 April will be less than the personal allowance.

    However, NICs are still relevant for Freddie. As his weekly earnings (£70) are above the lower earnings limit (£67), a P11 will have to be prepared, but no contributions are due until his salary exceeds the employee's threshold of £76.

(c) Oliver Spend works for one evening a week during term time. In this case, his status as a student is irrelevant. Tax and NICs must be deducted if he earns enough. He does not at the moment, so just note down his pay and earnings.

Answer 11.3

(a) See the form on the next page.

(b) (i) Elizabeth Windsor is obviously a higher rate tax payer so each month she is saving:

       £15 × 40% = £6

   (ii) Elizabeth Windsor saves nothing in NICs, as GAYE is only deducted from earnings for tax purposes, *not* for NIC purposes.

INSTRUCTIONS FOR SUBMITTING DONATIONS

1. Quote your CONTRACT NUMBER and PAYROLL NAME on all documentation.

2. Check that the Employee identification number on each Charity Choice Form is correct.

3. Check that the Employee identification number which you quote on your monthly deduction list is also the same on the Charity Choice form.

4. Send us the completed TOP SECTION of the Charity Choice form AND keep a copy or the yellow carbonated copy on your file for future reference.

5. Please arrange for your monthly lists to be in this format or PHOTOCOPY FREELY and write or type the information required.

6. Please arrange for your monthly lists to show the MONTH OF DEDUCTION where possible.

7. Please submit donations by cheque. Other means of payment should be agreed with Give As You Earn prior to any change.

8. Please arrange for all Give As You Earn documentation to come to us in one monthly packet.

9. Use this as an example of the format needed for computer printouts.

10. It will help us if we could have both these numbers. If this poses a problem, please submit one or the other (see * overleaf).

GIVE AS YOU EARN EMPLOYEE DONATIONS

PAYLISTING/DEDUCTION STATEMENT

CONTRACT NUMBER: _ _ _9752 _ _ _ _ _
MONTH OF DEDUCTION: _ March 2001_
PAYROLL NAME/ID/CODE: _ N/A _ _ _ _ _ _ _ _ _

EMPLOYER NAME: _ _ _ GILL, TEE (91) _ _ _ _ _ _ _
EMPLOYER ADDRESS: _ Workhouse Buildings _ _ _ _
_ Almshouse Lane _ _ _ _ _ _
_ Workington _ _ _ _ _ _ _ _ _

NI NUMBER AND PAYROLL NUMBER		DONATION	NAME	STARTER/ LEAVER
QE201649C	02	15	Windsor, E.	——
AJ999999D	07	15	Ayre, M.	——
KE777777B	03	20	Croesus, R.S.I.	——
ON222222A	33	20	Pope, J.P.	——

PAGE TOTAL	70	
OPTIONAL 5% ADMIN	——	
REMITTANCE ENCLOSED	70	MUST AGREE WITH ENCLOSED CHEQUE

PTO....

Answer 11.4

(a) *See workings*

National Insurance contributions *Note:*   LEL = Lower Earnings Limit,   UEL = Upper Earnings Limit

MONTH or WEEK NO	For employer's use only	Earnings details				Contribution details		Rebate details		Statutory Sick Pay in the week or month included in column 2	Statutory Maternity Pay in the week or month included in column 2	Student loan
		Earnings at the LEL (where earnings reach or exceed the LEL)	Earnings above the LEL, up to and including the employee's Earnings Threshold	Earnings above the employee's threshold, up to and including the employer's Earnings Threshold	Earnings above the employer's Threshold, up to and including the UEL	Total of employee's and employer's contributions payable	Employee's contribution payable	NIC rebate due on amount in 1b	NIC rebate due on the sum of the amounts in 1b and 1c			
		1a £ p	1b £ p	1c £ p	1d £ p	1e £ p	1f £ p	1g £ p	1h £ p	1i £ p	1j £ p	1k £ p
1		67	9	8	53	12.68	6.15					
2		67	9	8	11	3.35	1.95					
3		67	9	8	11	3.35	1.95					

W e e k	Pay in the week 2	Total pay to date 3	Total free pay to date 4a	K codes Total additional pay to date 4b	Total taxable pay to date 5	Total tax due to date 6	K codes Tax due at end of current period 6a	K codes Regul. limit 6b	Tax deducted or reduced in the week 7	K codes Tax not deducted owing to the regul. limit 8	Tax credits 9
1	137.00	137.00	80.75		56.25	8.81			8.81		
2											
3	190.00	327.00	242.25		84.75	8.40			(0.41)R		

Workings

NICs are recorded on a payment by payment basis; that is, even though the holiday pay is for the future it is being paid *now*. Pretend that the holiday pay is being paid at the right time, and so look up each week separately.

				NICs	
		Gross pay		*Total*	*Employee*
	£			£	£
Wk 1	137	Earnings		12.68	6.15
Wk 2	95	Holiday pay		3.35	1.95
Wk 3	95	Holiday pay		3.35	1.95
	327			19.38	10.05

Income tax PAYE

Here the situation is a little different. Income tax is cumulative.

Work out the tax on the holiday pay as if it had been received at the end of Week 3, and note down the amounts at the end of Week 3 on the P11. Table SR should be used for week 3!

		£
(b)	Gross pay (ie £137 + £95 + £95)	327.00
	Less employee's NICs	(10.05)
	Less tax due to date (£8.81 on week 1 less £0.41 refund for weeks 2 and 3)	(8.40)
	Amount actually paid	308.55

Note that this covers Week 1 to Week 3.

Answer 11.5

All are eligible *except the following.*

A Foot has not been in permanent full-time employment for long enough. This employee was a temporary worker (perhaps sent by an agency) for three months.

B Quiet has only been working for the company for 5 months so is not yet eligible.

Note. Although R Dworkin has left the company scheme, there is no harm in suggesting rejoining. The company scheme might offer greater security or benefits than the personal pension plan.

Answer 11.6

(a) Employee name
   Date employment commenced with employer
   Date joined scheme

Date left employer
Expected date of retirement
Date of reaching state retirement age
Employee NI number
Date of birth
Marital status
Sex
Amounts transferred into scheme from another scheme
Next of kin
Salary, and all increases
Contracted percentage contribution for employer and employee
Actual employee's and employer's pension contributions
AVCs
Whether or not employee is contracted out of SERPS

(b)

NAME: A. HOPEFUL		NI NO: WC963123X		A/C: H0943
SEX: M/F M		BIRTHDATE: 3/6/1965		
DATE JOINED COMPANY: 15/6/1999		DATE JOINED SCHEME: 1/1/2000		
ESTIMATED DATE OF RETIREMENT: 3/6/2030		DATE LEFT SCHEME:		

YEARS (cross off)

1,2,3,4,5,6,7,8,9,10,11,12,13,14,15,16,17,18,19,20,21,22,23,24,25,26,27,28,29,30,31,32,33,34,35,36,37,38,39,40

YEAR	PENSIONABLE EARNINGS (from 1/1)	YEAR	PENSIONABLE EARNINGS (from 1/1)	YEAR	PENSIONABLE EARNINGS (from 1/1)	YEAR	PENSIONABLE EARNINGS (from 1/1)
1	£22,000	11		21		31	
2	£27,500	12		22		32	
3		13		23		33	
4		14		24		34	
5		15		25		35	
6		16		26		36	
7		17		27		37	
8		18		28		38	
9		19		29		39	
10		20		30		40	

Pensionable earnings are earnings at 1 January of each year

Notes

Pensionable earnings are those at 1 January.

Year 1 (2000) Earnings at 1 January 2000 are £22,000, so these are pensionable earnings.

		£
Year 2 (2001)	Basic pay at 1 January 2000 is	14,500
	Commission earned in 2000	13,000
	Pensionable earnings 2001	27,500

(c) £22,000 × 6% = £1,320 pa or £110 per month

(d) £27,500 × 10% = £2,750 pa or £229.17 per month

(e)

	Pensionable earnings £	Employee (6%) £	Employer (10%) £	Total (16%) £
2000	22,000	1,320	2,200	3,520
2001	27,500	1,650	2,750	4,400
		2,970	4,950	7,920

Answer 11.7

(a)

NAME:	*Jill Kernot*	ACCOUNT:	K002

YEAR	B/F	JAN (W1)	FEB	MAR (W2)	APR	MAY	JUNE	JULY	AUG	SEP (W3)	OCT (W3)	NOV	DEC	C/F
EMP'EE	....	62.50	62.50	68.68	62.50	62.50	62.50	62.50	62.50	74.33	79.24	70.83	70.83	801.41
EMP'ER	....	125.00	125.00	137.36	125.00	125.00	125.00	125.00	125.00	148.67	158.48	141.67	141.67	1602.85
EMP'EE	801.41	70.83	70.83	70.83	70.83	70.83	70.83	70.83	70.83	87.50	99.68	87.50	87.50	1730.23
EMP'ER	1602.85	141.67	141.67	141.67	141.67	141.67	141.67	141.67	141.67	175.00	199.22	175.00	175.00	3460.43
EMP'EE										(W4)	(W5)			

Workings

1 Contributions in months when no overtime is worked January to August 2000

£15,000/12 × 5% = £62.50
£15,000/12 × 10% = £125.00

2 *March 2000.* 10 hours overtime is paid at time and a half

$\dfrac{£15,000}{(35 \times 52)} \times 1.5$ = £12.36 per hour

10 × £12.36 = £123.60

 5% × £123.60 = £6.18
10% × £123.60 = £12.36

These amounts are added to the basic contributions (W1).

3 *September and October 2000.*

£17,000/12 × 5% = £70.83
£17,000/12 × 10% = £141.67

Overtime hours affect the contributions in September (5 hours) and October (12 hours).

$$\frac{£17,000}{(35 \times 52)} \times 1.5 = £14.01 \text{ per hour}$$

September 2000		*October 2000*	
5 × £14.01 = £70.05		12 × £14.01 = £168.12	
5% × £70.05 = £3.50		5% × £168.12 = £8.41	
10% × £70.05 = £7.00		10% × £168.12 = £16.81	

These amounts are added to the basic calculation above (£70.83 and £141.67).

4   £21,000/12 × 5% =   £87.50 (£175 for employer)

5    $\frac{£21,000}{(35 \times 52)} \times 1.5 \times 5\% = £0.87$ per hour (£1.73 for employer) to be added to contributions per W4 (so £12.18 employee's and £24.22 employer's)

(b) Jill would receive back the contributions she had paid, less 20% tax. She would receive nothing in respect of the employer's contributions.

	£
Contributions	801.41
Tax deducted	(160.28)
	641.13

(c) The contributions would be frozen. They would be used to give Jill some small pension when she retired.

Alternatively, they could be transferred to another scheme.

(d) **MEMO**

To: Jill Kernot
From: A Clerk   Date:
Subject: Additional pension contributions

If you want to increase your pension above what is already provided in your company scheme you have a number of choices.

Additional Voluntary Contributions (AVCs)

These can be paid to the company pension fund. You will receive tax relief on them at source. They form part of your contribution record to the company scheme, so should you leave they would make up part of the frozen pension, or transfer value to another scheme.

Free Standing AVCs (FSAVCs)

In this case an arrangement, outside the company pension scheme, is made by you with another pension provider. The provider receives the tax relief on your behalf.

FSAVCs do not form part of your contribution record to the company scheme, and so will not go to make up a transfer value or frozen pension should you leave.

You should note that there is a limit on the proportion of your pensionable earnings that you can set aside as pension contributions eligible for tax relief.

Answer 11.8

		£
Per payroll	employees	18,000
	employer	30,000
	total deductions	48,000
Reimburse Dr Watson		(100)
Registration fee 500 × 10p		(50)
AVC - from employee		78
Tax relief on AVC		22
Per contribution record		47,950

Answer 12.1

(a) Put the packet in the safe.

(b) Call her over the PA system.

(c) Phone her home.

(d) 'Do you have a letter from Miss Humbert and some means of identification?'

(e) Lolita's letter has not been signed by her, and so it should be returned to her for her signature. Moreover the procedures manual requires that the representative's address on the identification is correct as well as the name, so you should ask Mr Nabokov for some other means of identification to verify the address given in Lolita's letter.

You might phone Lolita at home again, just to check the situation. If in doubt consult your supervisor.

Answer 12.2

(Note. You should have remembered that as the balance is cleared every September, on September 30 the balance on Abigail's expense account should be nil. Consequently the reimbursement of her expenses should be limited to the outstanding balance of £518.36 owing to her on the account.)

Employee: AMI, S Staff No: 012		Employer: ASTRAL FOODS LTD		
NI No: TH123456E Tax Code: 270T Pay By: CHEQUE		Date: 30/9/00 Tax Period: 6		
DESCRIPTION			AMOUNT	THIS YEAR
PAY	BASIC		1,000.00	5,900.00
	BONUS		100.00	100.00
DEDUCTIONS BEFORE TAX GAYE			- 20.00	- 120.00
	TOTAL PAY >>>		1,080.00	5,880.00
OTHER DEDUCTIONS	INCOME TAX		141.22	904.30
	NATIONAL INSURANCE		77.20	424.20
	SEASON TICKET		75.00	
	NET PAY >>>		786.58	
OTHER ITEMS				
ADD EXPENSES REIMBURSED			————	
	PER CHEQUE >>>		786.58	
Employer's NICs £ 89.79				

Employee: EEL, V Staff No: 015 Pay By: CHEQUE	Employer: ASTRAL FOODS	
NI No: SP123456I Tax Code: 320T	Date: 30/9/00 Tax Period: 6	
DESCRIPTION	**AMOUNT**	**THIS YEAR**
PAY BASIC	600.00	3,500.00
BONUS	60.00	60.00
DEDUCTIONS BEFORE TAX GAYE	- 20.00	- 120.00
TOTAL PAY >>>	640.00	3,440.00
OTHER DEDUCTIONS INCOME TAX	57.49	312.50
NATIONAL INSURANCE	33.20	180.20
NET PAY >>>	549.31	
OTHER ITEMS		
ADD EXPENSES REIMBURSED	——	
PER CHEQUE >>>	549.31	
Employer's NICs £ 36.11		

Employee: TOWER, A Staff No: 031 Pay By: CHEQUE	Employer: ASTRAL FOODS LTD	
NI No: WA123456N Tax Code: 400T	Date: 30/9/00 Tax Period: 6	
DESCRIPTION	**AMOUNT**	**THIS YEAR**
PAY BASIC	2,000.00	11,900.00
BONUS	150.00	150.00
DEDUCTIONS BEFORE TAX GAYE	- 20.00	- 120.00
TOTAL PAY >>>	2,130.00	11,930.00
OTHER DEDUCTIONS INCOME TAX	303.88	2,092.30
NATIONAL INSURANCE	182.00	1,029.00
NET PAY >>>	1,644.12	
OTHER ITEMS		
ADD EXPENSES REIMBURSED	518.36	
PER CHEQUE >>>	2,162.48	
Employer's NICs £ 217.65		

Answer 12.3

(a) Cash payments

Denom-ination	Mr Barnet	Mrs Bromley	Mr Ealing	Mr Kensington	Mrs Wandsworth	Mr Westminster	Total	Total
	(no)	(no)	(no)	(no)	(no)	(no)	(no)	£
£50	3	4	2	4	2	3	18	900.00
£20	1	-	1	1	2	-	5	100.00
£10	-	1	1	1	-	-	3	30.00
£5	1	-	-	-	1	1	3	15.00
£2	-	1	1	1	1	2	6	12.00
£1	-	1	-	-	1	-	2	2.00
50p	1	-	-	1	-	1	3	1.50
20p	2	2	-	2	-	2	8	1.60
10p	-	-	1	-	-	-	1	0.10
5p	-	-	-	-	-	-	-	
2p	-	1	-	-	2	-	3	0.06
1p	1	1	-	1	-	1	4	0.04
Total	175.91	213.43	132.10	232.91	148.04	159.91		1,062.30

(b)

			£
Cash			1,062.30
Cheque	10855	Mr Camden	141.32
	10856	Mrs Enfield	241.53
	10857	Mr Hackney	113.95
	10858	Mrs Hammersmith	204.11
	10859	Mr Haringey	123.45
	10860	Mrs Islington	67.89
	10861	Mrs Lambeth	184.32
	10862	Mr Redditch	166.66
	10863	Mr Southwark	297.43
	Per payroll		2,602.96

Answer 12.4

MEMO

To: A N Employee
From: A Clerk
Date: X/X/XX
Subject: Payment of wages by Direct Credit

Thank you for getting in touch with the payroll department about Direct Credit. I hope the following sets your mind at rest.

Direct Credit is a system which enables us to make wages payments by electronic transfer from our bank account directly into our employees' bank or building society accounts. It is operated by BACS, the UK's authorised payments clearing service which is owned by the major banks and building societies.

There is a minimum of paperwork. The information detailing net pay for each employee is sent to BACS via a telephone line so it can be input directly to the BACS system.

The advantages of direct credit over cash or cheques are as follows.

(a) It is much cheaper, as all the payroll department has to do is press a button, and the banks charge less for direct credit than they do for processing cheques.

(b) It is much safer, as there is no chance of cash or cheques being stolen.

(c) It is quicker, as the money does not have to be counted, nor does each cheque have to be signed, if you are paid by cheque.

If you wish, you can open a building society account instead of a bank account.

The company is paying £50 (before tax and national insurance) to every employee who switches over to the BACS system. The company is also happy to help you in your arrangements for opening a bank or building society account.

Answer to practice devolved assessment

ANSWER TO PRACTICE DEVOLVED ASSESSMENT RADIO GAGA LTD

(a)   The contract is legally valid on the date it was signed (23 July 2000), not the date Orpheus is supposed to start work.

(b) - (g)

Workings for these tasks and completed documents are shown below.

Month 5

Free pay Month 5 Code 440 is £1,837.10

		£
Taxable pay is:	pay to date	8,750.00
	less free pay to date	(1,837.10)
		6,912.90

		£	£
Per Table B	Tax on	6,900	1,518.00
	Tax on	12	2.64
Less starting rate relief		-	(76.01)
		6,912	1,444.63

This agrees to the P45.

Month 6 onwards

Income tax: use Table B. The tax code changes in Months 7 and 10.

National Insurance: use Table A. The employee's contributions are only calculated on earnings up to the limit of £2,319 a month. Employer's contributions are needed on all earnings.

Month 11

Some further complications are:

(a)   Orpheus' pay for February (up to 7 February).
(b)   his pay in lieu of notice.
(c)   holiday pay owing to him.

His pay in lieu of notice is mentioned in the employment contract, so is taxable and subject to NICs.

Let's work these out in turn.

	£
Week 1/2 to 7/2, includes 5 working days	
5/261 × £18,000 = amount for February	344.82
Basic pay for a month, in lieu of notice	1,500.00
	1,844.82
Holiday pay (see below)	114.94
Total due	1,959.76

The holiday year is January 1 to December 31. It is accrued at the rate of $1^2/_3$ days per completed calendar month, in this case, January. Orpheus' entitlement, then, is:

$1^2/_3$ days × (1/261 × £18,000) = holiday pay = £114.94.

No unused entitlement from the previous calendar year can be brought forward.

Do the PAYE and NIC calculations in the normal way and remember to fill in the P45. Remember to add together the January expenses and the February expenses (£250 + £50 = £300). Orpheus has repaid £500 of the £1,200 loan, so £700 is still outstanding.

Month 12

Orpheus' commission income is 10% × £9,030. It is paid after he has left and after the P45 has been drawn up for him. Deduct tax at the basic rate (22%) and change the code to BR.

NICs are calculated on the commission at the same rate as the final pay. The commission is a regular payment, and so NICs are calculated at the monthly rate.

Inland Revenue

New employee details
For completion by new employer

P45 Part 3

		District number	Reference number
1	Previous PAYE Reference	W1	B 004

2 Employee's National Insurance number VH 12 34 56 H

(Mr Mrs Miss Ms)

3 Surname SWITCH Mr

First name(s) ORPHEUS

4 Date left previous employment — Day 28 Month 08 Year 20 00

5 Continue Student Loan Deductions (Y)

6 Tax Code at leaving date. 'x' in the box means Week 7 or Month 1 basis applies Code 440 T Week 1 or Month 1

7 Last entries on Deductions Working Sheet (P11). If there is an 'X' at item 6, there will be no entries here

Week or Month number Week / Month 5

Total pay to date £ 8,750 00 p

Total tax to date £ 1,444 63 p

To the new employer

Complete items 8 to 17 below and send this page of the form only to your Tax Office immediately.

8 New PAYE Reference DDY/2422

9 Date employment started (in figures) Day 01 Month 09 Year 20 00

10 Tick here if you want these details to be shown on tax code notifications ✓ Works/Payroll number 345 Department or branch if any

11 Enter P if employee will not be paid by you between date employment began and next 5 April

12 Enter code in use if different to code at item 6

13 If the tax figure you are entering on P11 differs from item 7 above (see CWG (1999) card 4) please enter your figure here £

14 Employee's private address 13 LYRE STREET HADESTON

W MIDLANDS Postcode PL2 TUO

15 Employee's date of birth (if known) 21 01 1955

16 Employee's job title or description SALES MANAGER

17 **Declaration.** I have prepared a *Deductions Working Sheet* (P11) in accordance with the details above.

Employer RADIO GAGA

Address 132 MARCONI STREET, VALVETON

W MIDLANDS Postcode PM1 AM2 Date 01/09/00

P45

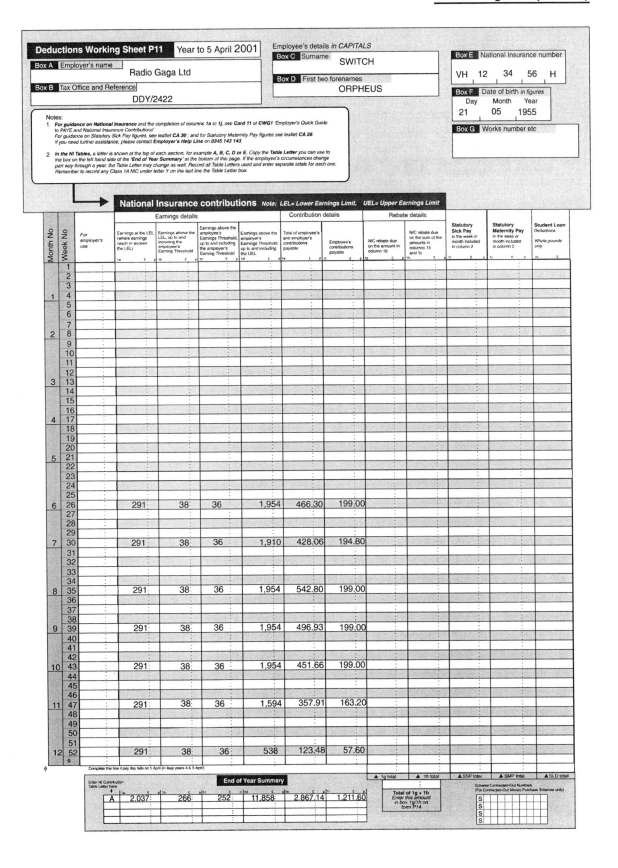

Month No	Week No	For employer's use	Earnings at the LEL (where earnings reach or exceed the LEL) 1a	Earnings above the LEL, up to and including the employee's Earnings Threshold 1b	Earnings above the employee's Earnings Threshold up to and including the employer's Earning Threshold 1c	Earnings above the employer's Earnings Threshold up to and including the UEL 1d	Total of employee's and employer's contributions payable 1e	Employee's contributions payable 1f	NIC rebate due on the amount in column 1b 1g	NIC rebate due on the sum of the amounts in columns 1b and 1c 1h	Statutory Sick Pay in the week or month included in column 2 1i	Statutory Maternity Pay in the week or month included in column 2 1j	Student Loan Deductions Whole pounds only 1k
	1												
	2												
	3												
1	4												
	5												
	6												
	7												
2	8												
	9												
	10												
	11												
	12												
3	13												
	14												
	15												
	16												
4	17												
	18												
	19												
	20												
5	21												
	22												
	23												
	24												
	25												
6	26		291	38	36	1,954	466.30	199.00					
	27												
	28												
	29												
7	30		291	38	36	1,910	428.06	194.80					
	31												
	32												
	33												
	34												
8	35		291	38	36	1,954	542.80	199.00					
	36												
	37												
	38												
9	39		291	38	36	1,954	496.93	199.00					
	40												
	41												
	42												
10	43		291	38	36	1,954	451.66	199.00					
	44												
	45												
	46												
11	47		291	38	36	1,594	357.91	163.20					
	48												
	49												
	50												
	51												
12	52		291	38	36	538	123.48	57.60					

Deductions Working Sheet P11 — Year to 5 April 2001
Box A Employer's name: Radio Gaga Ltd
Box B Tax Office and Reference: DDY/2422
Box C Surname: SWITCH
Box D First two forenames: ORPHEUS
Box E National Insurance number: VH 12 34 56 H
Box F Date of birth in figures: Day 21 Month 05 Year 1955
Box G Works number etc

End of Year Summary

Enter NI Contribution Table Letter here	1a	1b	1c	1d	1e	1f
A	2,037	266	252	11,858	2,867.14	1,211.60

Total of 1g + 1h Enter this amount in box 1g/1h on form P14

BPP PUBLISHING

Answer to practice devolved assessment

Box H	Day	Month	Year
Date of starting in figures	01	09	00

Box I	Day	Month	Year
Date of leaving in figures	07	02	01

Box J Student Loan Deductions case (✓)

Please keep this form for at least 3 years after the end of the year

Box K Tax code Ψ
440T

Ψ If amended cross out previous code.

Box L Amended code Ψ Wk/Mth in which applied

100T	7
340T	10
BR	12

Box M Tax credits
If authorised to make payments to employer, you can record 'start', 'daily rate' and 'stop' details here. Record amounts paid to employee in column 9.

Note 3:
For guidance on **PAYE Income Tax** and the completion of columns **2 to 9**, see **CWG1** 'Employer's Quick Guide to PAYE and National Insurance Contributions'
- **Card 8** for examples using suffix codes
- **Card 9** for general completion
- **Card 10** specifically for K codes, including examples.
- **Card 23** is for Tax Credits

PAYE Income Tax and Tax Credits

Month No	Week No	Pay in the week or month including Statutory Sick Pay/Statutory Maternity Pay 2	Total pay to date 3	Total free pay to date 4a	K codes only Total 'additional pay' to date (Table A) 4b	Total taxable pay to date ie. column 3 minus column 4a or column 3 plus column 4b 5	Total tax due to date as shown by Taxable Pay Tables 6	K codes only Tax due at end of current period Mark refunds 'R' 6a	K codes only Regulatory limit ie 50% of column 2 entry 6b	Tax deducted or refunded in the week or month Mark refunds 'R' 7	K codes only Tax not deducted owing to the Regulatory limit 8	Tax Credits 9
	1											
	2											
	3											
1	4											
	5											
	6											
	7											
2	8											
	9											
	10											
	11											
	12											
3	13											
	14											
	15											
	16											
4	17											
	18											
	19											
	20											
5	21		8,750.00	1,837.10		6,912.90	1,444.63					
	22											
	23											
	24											
	25											
6	26	2,556	11,306.00	2,204.52		9,101.48	1,911.02			466.39		
	27											
	28											
	29											
7	30	2,275.90	13,581.90	588.63		12,993.27	2,752.05			841.03		
	31											
	32											
	33											
	34											
8	35	3,183.20	16,765.10	672.72		16,902.38	3,378.63			626.58		
	36											
	37											
	38											
9	39	2,807.40	19,572.50	756.81		18,815.69	4,002.50			623.87		
	40											
	41											
	42											
10	43	2,436.50	22,009.00	2,840.90		19,168.10	4,064.95			62.45		
	44											
	45											
	46											
11	47	1,959.76	23,968.76	3,124.99		20,843.77	4,418.25			353.30		
	48											
	49											
	50											
	51											
12	52	903.00	24,871.76				4,616.69			198.44		
	φ											

φ Complete this line if pay day falls on 5 April (in leap years 4 & 5 April)

*If in any week/month the amount in column 4a is more that the amount in column 3, leave column 5 blank

	Pay £ p	Pay and Tax totals	Tax deducted £ p
	8,750.00 ◄	Previous employments ►	1,444.63
	16,121.76 ◄	This employments Mark net refund 'R' ►	3,172.06 ◄

When you are using a K code enter the total of the amounts in column 7 for this employments

Employee's Widow's & Orphans/ Life insurance contributions in this employments

Tax credits

| Employee: Orpheus Switch Staff No: 345 | | Employer: RADIO GAGA LTD | | |
| NI No: VH123456H Tax Code: 440T Pay By: CHQ | | Date: 30/9/2000 Tax Period: Mth 6 | | |
DESCRIPTION			AMOUNT	THIS YEAR
PAY	Basic		1,500.00	1,500.00
	Commission		1,056.00	1,056.00
DEDUCTIONS BEFORE TAX				
	TOTAL PAY >>>		2,556.00	2,556.00
OTHER DEDUCTIONS	Tax		466.39	466.39
	NICs		199.00	199.00
	NET PAY >>>		1,890.61	
OTHER ITEMS Company loan			-100.00	
ADD EXPENSES REIMBURSED				
	PER CHEQUE >>>		1,790.61	
Employer's NICs £ 267.30 To Date £ 267.30				

| Employee: Orpheus Switch Staff No: 345 | | Employer: RADIO GAGA LTD | | |
| NI No: VH123456H Tax Code: 100T Pay By: CHQ | | Date: 30/10/2000 Tax Period: Mth 7 | | |
DESCRIPTION			AMOUNT	THIS YEAR
PAY	Basic		1,500.00	3,000.00
	Commission		775.90	1,831.90
DEDUCTIONS BEFORE TAX				
	TOTAL PAY >>>		2,275.90	4,831.90
OTHER DEDUCTIONS	Tax		841.03	1,307.42
	NICs		194.80	393.80
	NET PAY >>>		1,240.07	
OTHER ITEMS Company loan			-100.00	
ADD EXPENSES REIMBURSED			50.00	
	PER CHEQUE >>>		1,190.07	
Employer's NICs £ 233.26 To Date £ 500.56				

Answer to practice devolved assessment

Employee: Orpheus Switch Staff No: 345	Employer: RADIO GAGA LTD		
NI No: VH123456H Tax Code: 100T Pay By: CHQ	Date: 30/11/2000 Tax Period: Mth 8		
DESCRIPTION		AMOUNT	THIS YEAR
PAY Basic		1,500.00	4,500.00
Commission		1,683.20	3,515.10
DEDUCTIONS BEFORE TAX			
TOTAL PAY >>>		3,183.20	8,015.10
OTHER DEDUCTIONS Tax		626.58	1,934.00
NICs		199.00	592.80
NET PAY >>>		2,357.62	
OTHER ITEMS Company loan		-100.00	
ADD EXPENSES REIMBURSED		300.00	
PER CHEQUE >>>		2,557.62	
Employer's NICs £ 343.80 To Date £ 844.36			

Employee: Orpheus Switch Staff No: 345	Employer: RADIO GAGA LTD		
NI No: VH123456H Tax Code: 100T Pay By: CHQ	Date: 31/12/2000 Tax Period: Mth 9		
DESCRIPTION		AMOUNT	THIS YEAR
PAY Basic		1,500.00	6,000.00
Commission		1,307.40	4,822.50
DEDUCTIONS BEFORE TAX			
TOTAL PAY >>>		2,807.40	10,822.50
OTHER DEDUCTIONS Tax		623.87	2,557.87
NICs		199.00	791.80
NET PAY >>>		1,984.53	
OTHER ITEMS Company loan		-100.00	
ADD EXPENSES REIMBURSED		500.00	
PER CHEQUE >>>		2,384.53	
Employer's NICs £ 297.93 To Date £ 1,142.29			

Employee: Orpheus Switch Staff No: 345		Employer: RADIO GAGA LTD	
NI No: VH123456H Tax Code: 340T Pay By: CHQ		Date: 31/1/2001 Tax Period: Mth 10	
DESCRIPTION		AMOUNT	THIS YEAR
PAY Basic		1,500.00	7,500.00
Commission		936.50	5,759.00
DEDUCTIONS BEFORE TAX			
TOTAL PAY >>>		2,436.50	13,259.00
OTHER DEDUCTIONS Tax		62.45	2,620.32
NICs		199.00	990.80
NET PAY >>>		2,175.05	
OTHER ITEMS Company loan		-100.00	
ADD EXPENSES REIMBURSED		450.00	
PER CHEQUE >>>		2,525.05	
Employer's NICs £ 252.66 To Date £ 1,394.95			

Employee: Orpheus Switch Staff No: 345		Employer: RADIO GAGA LTD	
NI No: VH123456H Tax Code: 340T Pay By: CHQ		Date: 7/2/001 Tax Period: Mth 11	
DESCRIPTION		AMOUNT	THIS YEAR
PAY Basic		344.82	7,844.82
In lieu of notice		1,500.00	
Holiday pay		114.94	
Commission		-	5,759.00
DEDUCTIONS BEFORE TAX			
TOTAL PAY >>>		1,959.76	15,218.76
OTHER DEDUCTIONS Tax		353.30	2,973.62
NICs		163.20	1,154.00
NET PAY >>>		1,424.26	
OTHER ITEMS Company loan		-700.00	
ADD EXPENSES REIMBURSED		300.00	
PER CHEQUE >>>		1,043.26	
Employer's NICs £194.71 To Date £ 1,589.66			

	Inland **Revenue**	Details of employee leaving work Copy for Tax Office	P45 Part 1

		District number	Reference number
1	PAYE Reference	DDY	2422

2 Employee's National Insurance number   VH 12 34 56 H

3 Surname (in capitals)   **SWITCH**   (Mr Mrs Miss Ms) **Mr**

First name(s) (in capitals)   **ORPHEUS**

4 Leaving date (in figures)   Day **07** Month **02** Year 20**01**   5 Continue Student Loan Deductions (Y)

6 Tax Code at leaving date. *If week 1 or Month 1 basis applies, write 'X' in the box marked Week 1 or Month 1*   Code **340 T**   Week 1 or Month 1

7 Last entries on *Deductions Working Sheet* (P11) **Complete only if Tax Code is cumulative.** *Make no entry here if Week 1 or Month 1 basis applies. Go to item 7.*

	Week	Month
Week or month number		**11**
Total pay to date	£ **23,968** **76** p	
Total tax to date	£ **4,418** **25** p	

8 This employment pay and tax. ■ *No entry needed if Tax Code is cumulative and amounts are same as item 6 entry.*

Total pay in this employment £ **15,218 76** p
Total tax in this employment £ **2,973 62** p

9 Works number/ Payroll number   **345**

10 Department or branch if any

11 Employee's private address and Postcode   **13 LYRE STREET HADESTON W MIDLANDS PL2 WTO**

12 I certify that the details entered above in items 1 to 9 are correct

Employer's name, address and Postcode   **RADIO GAGA LTD 132 MARCONI STREET, VALVETON W MIDLANDS PM1 AM2**

Date   **7 2 00**

To the employer   *Please complete with care* ★

For Tax Office use

- Complete this form following the 'Employee leaving' instructions in the *Employer's quick Guide to PAYE and NICs* (cards CWG1). ★ **Make sure the details are clear on all four parts of this form**. Make sure your name and address is shown on Parts 1 and 1A.
- Detach Part 1 and send it to your Tax Office immediately.
- Hand Parts 1A, 2 and 3 (unseparated) to your employee when he or she leaves
- If the employee has died, write 'D' in this box and send all three parts of this form (unseparated) to your Tax Office immediately.

P45   BMSD9/99

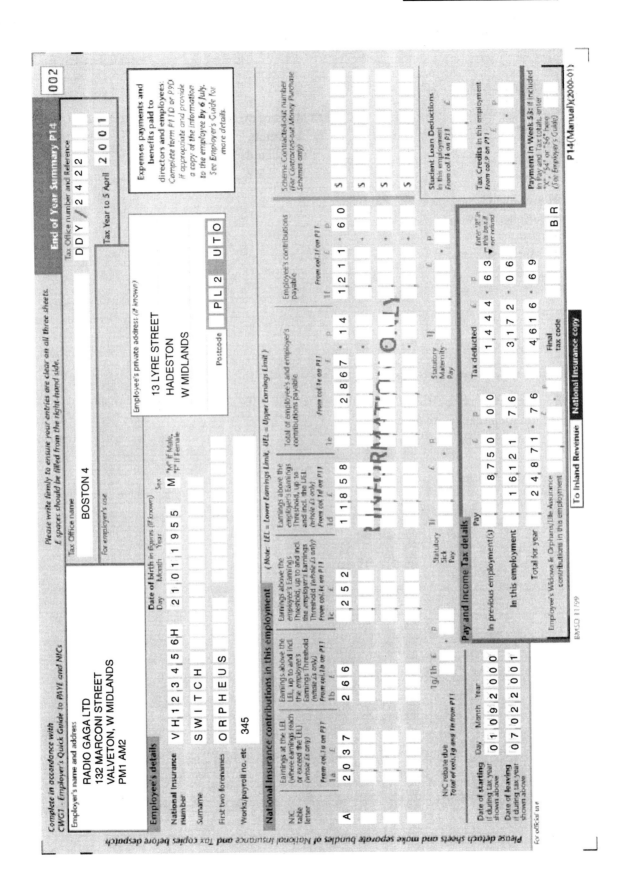

RADIO GAGA

132 Marconi Street
Valveton
W Midlands
PM1 AM2

Honor Switch
27 Cleaners Row
Hadeston
W Midlands
PL3 SS1

12 April 2001

Dear Mrs Switch,

I refer to your letter of 10 April.

I regret that all payroll information is confidential, therefore I am unable to supply the information that you request.

Yours sincerely,

V Discreet

V Discreet
Payroll assistant

RADIO GAGA

'All you hear is Radio Gaga'

INTERNAL MEMORANDUM

To: Sir Ian Bennett
From: A Payroll-Clarke
Date: 12 April 2001

Replacement for Orpheus Switch

Orpheus Switch was paid a starting salary of £18,000 increasing to £21,000 after six months probation. He also received commission of 10% of all fees earned personally.

Mr Switch earned a total of £6,662 in commission during the six months that he was with the company. Taking this as average the annual cost of such an employee may be estimated as follows.

	£
Salary (6/12 × £18,000 + 6/12 × £21,000)	19,500
Commission (2 × say £6,500)	13,000
	32,500
Employer's National Insurance (12.2% × (£32,500 – £4,385))	3,430
	35,930

There are also other costs that could be considered relevant depending on the circumstances. For example, the cost of owning and running a company car might be taken into account if such a car is not otherwise needed. Likewise the cost of expenses incurred (£1,600 by Orpheus Switch, and therefore perhaps £3,000 or so during a whole year) should be taken into account if they will not otherwise be incurred.

Answers to specimen central assessment

SECTION 1

Task 1.1

Carol Jane Smith	**£**
Annual salary	16,800
less pension	(840)
Gross pay	15,960
Free pay	(4,339)
Taxable pay	11,621

Tax due for year	
£1,520 @ 10%	152.00
£10,101 @ 22%	2,222.22
£11,621	£2,374.22

Lionel Dyer	**£**	**£**
Annual salary		35,400
Less pension	1,770	
payroll giving	360	(2,130)
Gross pay		33,270
Free pay		(5,169)
Taxable pay		28,101

Tax due for year	
£1,520 @ 10%	152.00
£26,581 @ 22%	5,847.82
£28,101	£5,999.82

Anna Benton	**£**	**£**
Annual salary		14,400
Less pension	720	
payroll giving	480	(1,200)
Gross pay		13,200
Free pay		(4,409)
Taxable pay		8,791

Tax due for year	
£1,520 @ 10%	152.00
£7,271 @ 22%	1,599.62
£8,791	£1,751.62

Task 1.2

	MEMO	
To: Janet Truman	From: Payroll clerk	
Date: 1 December 2000	Subject: SMP	

I have been given the note that you sent to Lionel concerning your SMP entitlement.

SMP can only be paid if you have been continuously employed by the company for 26 weeks, including the Qualifying Week. The Qualifying Week is the 15th week before the Expected Week of Confinement.

Your Qualifying Week, therefore, starts on 16 October 2000. As you only joined on 6 September 2000, I regret that you are not entitled to SMP.

BPP PUBLISHING

Task 1.3

Wages Control Account

30.11.99	Bank	£16,520	30.11.99	Gross wages	£25,000
30.11.99	PAYE	£4,770	30.11.99	Employer's NIC	£2,700
30.11.99	Employee's NIC	£2,220	30.11.99	Employer's Pension	£1,250
30.11.99	Employer's NIC	£2,700			
30.11.99	Trade Union Fees	£80			
30.11.99	Payroll Giving	£160			
30.11.99	Pension-employee's	£1,250			
30.11.99	Pension-employer's	£1,250			

PAYE/NIC Creditors

		30.11.99	Wages control	
			- PAYE	4,770
			- Employees' NIC	2,220
			- Employers' NIC	2,700

Wages Account

30.11.99	Wages control		
	- Gross wages	25,000	
	- Employers' NIC	2,700	
	- Employers' pension	1,250	

Bank

		30.11.99	Wages control	16,250

Trade Union Fees Account

	30.11.99	Wages control	80

Payroll Giving Account

	30.11.99	Wages control	160

Pensions Account

	30.11.99	Wages control	
		- Employees' pension	1,250
		- Employers' pension	1,250

Task 1.4

PAY ADVICE SLIP

Payments £	Deductions £	Year to date figures £
Basic Pay:	*Income Tax:*	*Gross pay:*
Shift pay:		
Overtime:	*NIC:*	*Taxable pay:*
Commission:	*Pension:*	*Tax paid:*
Bonus:	*Payroll giving:*	*NIC:*
SSP:		
SMP:	*Trade Union:*	*Pension:*
Other:	*Other:*	*Payroll giving:*
Total Gross Pay:	**Total Deductions:**	**Net pay:**
Name:	*Tax code:* *NI Number:*	*Paid by:*

Employer's name: *Employee number:*   *Tax period:*

Section 2

2.1   A BR code means that all pay will be taxed at the basic rate of 22% (2000/01). No allowances or starting rate are available.

2.2   (a)   Written authorisation from the employee, including the name and address of the friend.

        (b)   The friend has proof of identification eg a driving licence.

2.3   For tax year 2000/01, there is no limit. (For 1999/00, the limit was £1,200 pa.)

2.4   (a)   Pay adjustment tables give the amount of tax free pay that the employee can earn. With K codes, the pay adjustment tables give the additional pay for tax purposes.

        (b)   Taxable pay tables show the amount of tax due on taxable pay.

2.5 The employee was away for 8 working days. The first three days are waiting days, so the employee would be entitled to 5 days SSP.

2.6 (a) Both
    (b) Employer

2.7 An integrated computerised payroll system will not only calculate the payroll, but will transfer information to and from other parts of the computer system eg accounts, personnel, employee records, pension records.

2.8 (a) 438L

    (b) An emergency tax code is used when a new employee does not have a tax code, as an interim measure until a proper code is obtained from the tax office. The code gives a single person's allowance and is often applied on a non-cumulative (wk1/mth1) basis.

2.9 (a) No

    (b) By law, payroll records have to be kept for at least three years after the end of the tax year.

2.10 (a) Any two of the following.

    (i) No need to work out cash in advance, to order it from the bank.

    (ii) No security problems with cash on the premises.

    (iii) Reduced handling costs as less staff needed than with cash.

    (iv) Reduced bank transaction costs over cheques.

    (v) Easier to account for as only one bank transaction as compared to many with cheques.

    (b) Any two of the following.

    (i) Money is in the bank on pay day.

    (ii) No delays with having to pay the cheque in and wait for it to clear.

    (iii) Money available even if absent on pay day eg sick, on holiday.

    (iv) No need to obtain holiday money in advance, as money will be paid in while away.

    (v) No need to send a friend to collect wages when away.

2.11 (a) Yes

    (b) Any employee over the age of 18 and with two years' continuous service is entitled to statutory redundancy pay.

2.12 Any two of the following.

    (a) Information given to third parties only with employee's authorisation.

    (b) Do not leave records lying around.

    (c) Do not leave computer system on when away from your desk, or password protect your screen saver.

    (d) Password protect computer systems and ensure only authorised people have access to the password.

    (e) Manual records kept locked away when not in use.

2.13 No NIC is payable on earnings below the LEL. In addition, for 2000/01, no NIC is payable on earnings between the LEL and the employees' earnings threshold (EET). (The distinction is important as anyone earning below the LEL will not be entitled to benefits like SSP and SMP. If they earn between the LEL and EET, they will be entitled to those benefits even though they do not pay NIC).

2.14 (a) With a contributory pension, the employee pays contributions to the scheme as well as the employer.

(b) With a non-contributory pension, only the employer contributes to the scheme.

2.15 Eight weeks from commencement of employment.

Appendix I:
Taxable pay tables

Appendix I: Taxable pay tables

If you do not use the correct tables your employees may pay the wrong amount of tax.

Annual Bands

Tax Rates				
Starting Rate	10%	up to	£1520	
Basic Rate	22%	from	£1521	to £28400
Higher Rate	40%	over	£28400	

Using these Tables

Working out taxable pay
Before you can use these Tables, you must work out the employee's taxable pay. Follow the instructions on CWG1 **Card 6**.

 Help
If you need help using these Tables, please call the Employer's Helpline on **0845 7 143 143** for advice.

Suggestions
Any suggestions for improving these Tables should be sent to: Inland Revenue, BMSD Operational Policy, 4th Floor, South West Wing, Bush House, Strand, London, WC2B 4RD.

Finding out which Table to use

Code BR, always use **Table B** on pages 8 and 9.   **For Code D0, always** use **Table D** on page 11.

Other codes

Use the charts below and on page 3 to find out which Tables to use.

- Look on the reverse of CWG1 Card 2 to find out the month or week.

- Find the month (see below) or week (see page 3) for which you are working out the tax due. Columns 1 and 2 show the **highest** amount of total taxable pay for which each Table can be used for the month or week shown. For Week 1/Month 1 Codes, always refer to the amounts shown in the columns for Week 1 or Month 1.

- Look across the columns in turn, starting with column 1. When you find an amount beside the month or week number which is **the same as or more** than the employee's total taxable pay, look at the column heading and use the Table shown under the column heading.

If the employee's total taxable pay is _more_ than the amount shown in column 2, use Tables C and D.

Month	Column 1 Use Table SR on page 5 £	Column 2 Use Tables B on pages 8 and 9 £
1	127	2367
2	254	4734
3	380	7100
4	507	9467
5	634	11834
6	760	14200
7	887	16567
8	1014	18934
9	1140	21300
10	1267	23667
11	1394	26034
12	1520	28400

2

Week	Column 1 Use Table SR on page 5 (£)	Column 2 Use Tables B on pages 8 and 9 (£)
1	30	547
2	59	1093
3	88	1639
4	117	2185
5	147	2731
6	176	3277
7	205	3824
8	234	4370
9	264	4916
10	293	5462
11	322	6008
12	351	6554
13	380	7100
14	410	7647
15	439	8193
16	468	8739
17	497	9285
18	527	9831
19	556	10377
20	585	10924
21	614	11470
22	644	12016
23	673	12562
24	702	13108
25	731	13654
26	760	14200
27	790	14747
28	819	15293
29	848	15839
30	877	16385
31	907	16931
32	936	17477
33	965	18024
34	994	18570
35	1024	19116
36	1053	19662
37	1082	20208
38	1111	20754
39	1140	21300
40	1170	21847
41	1199	22393
42	1228	22939
43	1257	23485
44	1287	24031
45	1316	24577
46	1345	25124
47	1374	25670
48	1404	26216
49	1433	26762
50	1462	27308
51	1491	27854
52	1520	28400

Columns 1 and 2 show the **highest** amount of total **taxable** pay for which each Table can be used for the week shown.

If the employee's total **taxable** pay is **more** than the amount shown in column 2, use Tables C and D.

For Code BR always use Table B on pages 8 and 9.

For Code D0 always use Table D on page 11.

Table SR to work out tax at 10%

Pages 2 and 3 tell you when to use this table

Where the exact amount of taxable pay is not shown, add together the figures for two (or more) entries to make up the amount of taxable pay to the nearest £1 below.

Tax Due on Taxable Pay from £100 to £1500		Tax Due on Taxable Pay from £1 to £99			
Total TAXABLE PAY to date	Total TAX DUE to date	Total TAXABLE PAY to date	Total TAX DUE to date	Total TAXABLE PAY to date	Total TAX DUE to date
£	£	£	£	£	£
100	10.00	1	0.10	50	5.00
200	20.00	2	0.20	51	5.10
300	30.00	3	0.30	52	5.20
400	40.00	4	0.40	53	5.30
500	50.00	5	0.50	54	5.40
600	60.00	6	0.60	55	5.50
700	70.00	7	0.70	56	5.60
800	80.00	8	0.80	57	5.70
900	90.00	9	0.90	58	5.80
1000	100.00	10	1.00	59	5.90
1100	110.00	11	1.10	60	6.00
1200	120.00	12	1.20	61	6.10
1300	130.00	13	1.30	62	6.20
1400	140.00	14	1.40	63	6.30
1500	150.00	15	1.50	64	6.40
		16	1.60	65	6.50
		17	1.70	66	6.60
		18	1.80	67	6.70
		19	1.90	68	6.80
		20	2.00	69	6.90
		21	2.10	70	7.00
		22	2.20	71	7.10
		23	2.30	72	7.20
		24	2.40	73	7.30
		25	2.50	74	7.40
		26	2.60	75	7.50
		27	2.70	76	7.60
		28	2.80	77	7.70
		29	2.90	78	7.80
		30	3.00	79	7.90
		31	3.10	80	8.00
		32	3.20	81	8.10
		33	3.30	82	8.20
		34	3.40	83	8.30
		35	3.50	84	8.40
		36	3.60	85	8.50
		37	3.70	86	8.60
		38	3.80	87	8.70
		39	3.90	88	8.80
		40	4.00	89	8.90
		41	4.10	90	9.00
		42	4.20	91	9.10
		43	4.30	92	9.20
		44	4.40	93	9.30
		45	4.50	94	9.40
		46	4.60	95	9.50
		47	4.70	96	9.60
		48	4.80	97	9.70
		49	4.90	98	9.80
				99	9.90

Remember to use the green Subtraction Table on page 9 after working out tax at 22% to give Starting Rate Relief.

Tables B Tax at 22%

Pages 2 and 3 tell you when to use these tables.

Tax Due on Taxable Pay from £100 to £28400

Total TAXABLE PAY to date	Total TAX DUE to date	Total TAXABLE PAY to date	Total TAX DUE to date	Total TAXABLE PAY to date	Total TAX DUE to date	Total TAXABLE PAY to date	Total TAX DUE to date	Total TAXABLE PAY to date	Total TAX DUE to date	Total TAXABLE PAY to date	Total TAX DUE to date
£	£	£	£	£	£	£	£	£	£	£	£
100	22.00	5100	1122.00	10100	2222.00	15100	3322.00	20100	4422.00	25100	5522.00
200	44.00	5200	1144.00	10200	2244.00	15200	3344.00	20200	4444.00	25200	5544.00
300	66.00	5300	1166.00	10300	2266.00	15300	3366.00	20300	4466.00	25300	5566.00
400	88.00	5400	1188.00	10400	2288.00	15400	3388.00	20400	4488.00	25400	5588.00
500	110.00	5500	1210.00	10500	2310.00	15500	3410.00	20500	4510.00	25500	5610.00
600	132.00	5600	1232.00	10600	2332.00	15600	3432.00	20600	4532.00	25600	5632.00
700	154.00	5700	1254.00	10700	2354.00	15700	3454.00	20700	4554.00	25700	5654.00
800	176.00	5800	1276.00	10800	2376.00	15800	3476.00	20800	4576.00	25800	5676.00
900	198.00	5900	1298.00	10900	2398.00	15900	3498.00	20900	4598.00	25900	5698.00
1000	220.00	6000	1320.00	11000	2420.00	16000	3520.00	21000	4620.00	26000	5720.00
1100	242.00	6100	1342.00	11100	2442.00	16100	3542.00	21100	4642.00	26100	5742.00
1200	264.00	6200	1364.00	11200	2464.00	16200	3564.00	21200	4664.00	26200	5764.00
1300	286.00	6300	1386.00	11300	2486.00	16300	3586.00	21300	4686.00	26300	5786.00
1400	308.00	6400	1408.00	11400	2508.00	16400	3608.00	21400	4708.00	26400	5808.00
1500	330.00	6500	1430.00	11500	2530.00	16500	3630.00	21500	4730.00	26500	5830.00
1600	352.00	6600	1452.00	11600	2552.00	16600	3652.00	21600	4752.00	26600	5852.00
1700	374.00	6700	1474.00	11700	2574.00	16700	3674.00	21700	4774.00	26700	5874.00
1800	396.00	6800	1496.00	11800	2596.00	16800	3696.00	21800	4796.00	26800	5896.00
1900	418.00	6900	1518.00	11900	2618.00	16900	3718.00	21900	4818.00	26900	5918.00
2000	440.00	7000	1540.00	12000	2640.00	17000	3740.00	22000	4840.00	27000	5940.00
2100	462.00	7100	1562.00	12100	2662.00	17100	3762.00	22100	4862.00	27100	5962.00
2200	484.00	7200	1584.00	12200	2684.00	17200	3784.00	22200	4884.00	27200	5984.00
2300	506.00	7300	1606.00	12300	2706.00	17300	3806.00	22300	4906.00	27300	6006.00
2400	528.00	7400	1628.00	12400	2728.00	17400	3828.00	22400	4928.00	27400	6028.00
2500	550.00	7500	1650.00	12500	2750.00	17500	3850.00	22500	4950.00	27500	6050.00
2600	572.00	7600	1672.00	12600	2772.00	17600	3872.00	22600	4972.00	27600	6072.00
2700	594.00	7700	1694.00	12700	2794.00	17700	3894.00	22700	4994.00	27700	6094.00
2800	616.00	7800	1716.00	12800	2816.00	17800	3916.00	22800	5016.00	27800	6116.00
2900	638.00	7900	1738.00	12900	2838.00	17900	3938.00	22900	5038.00	27900	6138.00
3000	660.00	8000	1760.00	13000	2860.00	18000	3960.00	23000	5060.00	28000	6160.00
3100	682.00	8100	1782.00	13100	2882.00	18100	3982.00	23100	5082.00	28100	6182.00
3200	704.00	8200	1804.00	13200	2904.00	18200	4004.00	23200	5104.00	28200	6204.00
3300	726.00	8300	1826.00	13300	2926.00	18300	4026.00	23300	5126.00	28300	6226.00
3400	748.00	8400	1848.00	13400	2948.00	18400	4048.00	23400	5148.00	28400	6248.00
3500	770.00	8500	1870.00	13500	2970.00	18500	4070.00	23500	5170.00		
3600	792.00	8600	1892.00	13600	2992.00	18600	4092.00	23600	5192.00		
3700	814.00	8700	1914.00	13700	3014.00	18700	4114.00	23700	5214.00		
3800	836.00	8800	1936.00	13800	3036.00	18800	4136.00	23800	5236.00		
3900	858.00	8900	1958.00	13900	3058.00	18900	4158.00	23900	5258.00		
4000	880.00	9000	1980.00	14000	3080.00	19000	4180.00	24000	5280.00		
4100	902.00	9100	2002.00	14100	3102.00	19100	4202.00	24100	5302.00		
4200	924.00	9200	2024.00	14200	3124.00	19200	4224.00	24200	5324.00		
4300	946.00	9300	2046.00	14300	3146.00	19300	4246.00	24300	5346.00		
4400	968.00	9400	2068.00	14400	3168.00	19400	4268.00	24400	5368.00		
4500	990.00	9500	2090.00	14500	3190.00	19500	4290.00	24500	5390.00		
4600	1012.00	9600	2112.00	14600	3212.00	19600	4312.00	24600	5412.00		
4700	1034.00	9700	2134.00	14700	3234.00	19700	4334.00	24700	5434.00		
4800	1056.00	9800	2156.00	14800	3256.00	19800	4356.00	24800	5456.00		
4900	1078.00	9900	2178.00	14900	3278.00	19900	4378.00	24900	5478.00		
5000	1100.00	10000	2200.00	15000	3300.00	20000	4400.00	25000	5500.00		

Tables B Tax at 22%

Total TAXABLE PAY to date £	Total TAX DUE to date £	Total TAXABLE PAY to date £	Total TAX DUE to date £
1	0.22	51	11.22
2	0.44	52	11.44
3	0.66	53	11.66
4	0.88	54	11.88
5	1.10	55	12.10
6	1.32	56	12.32
7	1.54	57	12.54
8	1.76	58	12.76
9	1.98	59	12.98
10	2.20	60	13.20
11	2.42	61	13.42
12	2.64	62	13.64
13	2.86	63	13.86
14	3.08	64	14.08
15	3.30	65	14.30
16	3.52	66	14.52
17	3.74	67	14.74
18	3.96	68	14.96
19	4.18	69	15.18
20	4.40	70	15.40
21	4.62	71	15.62
22	4.84	72	15.84
23	5.06	73	16.06
24	5.28	74	16.28
25	5.50	75	16.50
26	5.72	76	16.72
27	5.94	77	16.94
28	6.16	78	17.16
29	6.38	79	17.38
30	6.60	80	17.60
31	6.82	81	17.82
32	7.04	82	18.04
33	7.26	83	18.26
34	7.48	84	18.48
35	7.70	85	18.70
36	7.92	86	18.92
37	8.14	87	19.14
38	8.36	88	19.36
39	8.58	89	19.58
40	8.80	90	19.80
41	9.02	91	20.02
42	9.24	92	20.24
43	9.46	93	20.46
44	9.68	94	20.68
45	9.90	95	20.90
46	10.12	96	21.12
47	10.34	97	21.34
48	10.56	98	21.56
49	10.78	99	21.78
50	11.00		

Tax Due on Taxable Pay from £1 to £99

Tables B Subtraction Tables to give
Starting Rate Relief at 10%

After you have used Tables B to work out the tax at 22% use the green Tables below to give your employee the benefit of the 10% rate band.

Do not use the Subtraction Tables for codes BR and D0.

Find the month or week in which the pay day falls and **subtract** the amount shown to arrive at the tax due. For Week 1/Month 1 codes subtract the amount shown for Week 1 or Month 1.

Employee paid at Monthly rates

Month No.	Amount to subtract £
1	15.21
2	30.41
3	45.60
4	60.81
5	76.01
6	91.20
7	106.41
8	121.61
9	136.80
10	152.01
11	167.21
12	182.40

Employee paid at Weekly rates

Week No.	Amount to subtract £
1	3.51
2	7.02
3	10.53
4	14.04
5	17.54
6	21.05
7	24.56
8	28.07
9	31.57
10	35.08
11	38.59
12	42.10
13	45.60
14	49.11
15	52.62
16	56.13
17	59.64
18	63.14
19	66.65
20	70.16
21	73.67
22	77.17
23	80.68
24	84.19
25	87.70
26	91.20
27	94.71
28	98.22
29	101.73
30	105.24
31	108.74
32	112.25
33	115.76
34	119.27
35	122.77
36	126.28
37	129.79
38	133.30
39	136.80
40	140.31
41	143.82
42	147.33
43	150.84
44	154.34
45	157.85
46	161.36
47	164.87
48	168.37
49	171.88
50	175.39
51	178.90
52	182.40

Table C

Pages 2 and 3 tell you when to use this Table

How to use Table C

Example

Employee's code is **438L**
The payment is made in **Week 10**

	£
Pay in the week	700
Previous pay to date	6300
Total pay to date	7000
Less free pay in Week 10 (Table A)	844.10
Total taxable pay to date	**6155.90**

Subtract amount in Col 1 (for Week 10)
£5462 tax due per Col 2   **1166.64**

Excess (£6155 – £5462) £693
therefore tax due per Table D = **277.20**

Total tax due to date   **1443.84**

Employee paid at Weekly rates

Week No.	If total taxable pay to date exceeds	Total tax due to date	
	Col. 1 £	Col. 2 £	
1	547	116.98	
2	1093	233.56	
3	1639	350.15	
4	2185	466.73	
5	2731	583.32	
6	3277	699.90	
7	3824	816.89	
8	4370	933.47	
9	4916	1050.06	
10	5462	1166.64	
11	6008	1283.23	
12	6554	1399.81	
13	7100	1516.40	
14	7647	1633.38	
15	8193	1749.96	
16	8739	1866.55	
17	9285	1983.13	
18	9831	2099.72	
19	10377	2216.30	
20	10924	2333.29	
21	11470	2449.87	
22	12016	2566.46	Add tax at 40% as shown in Table D on the amount by which the total Taxable Pay to date exceeds the figure in Col. 1
23	12562	2683.04	
24	13108	2799.63	
25	13654	2916.21	
26	14200	3032.80	
27	14747	3149.78	
28	15293	3266.36	
29	15839	3382.95	
30	16385	3499.53	
31	16931	3616.12	
32	17477	3732.70	
33	18024	3849.69	
34	18570	3966.27	
35	19116	4082.86	
36	19662	4199.44	
37	20208	4316.03	
38	20754	4432.61	
39	21300	4549.20	
40	21847	4666.18	
41	22393	4782.76	
42	22939	4899.35	
43	23485	5015.93	
44	24031	5132.52	
45	24577	5249.10	
46	25124	5366.09	
47	25670	5482.67	
48	26216	5599.26	
49	26762	5715.84	
50	27308	5832.43	
51	27854	5949.01	
52	28400	6065.60	

Employee paid at Monthly rates

Month No.	If total taxable pay to date exceeds	Total tax due to date	
	Col. 1 £	Col. 2 £	
1	2367	505.59	
2	4734	1011.19	Add tax at 40% as shown in Table D on the amount by which the total Taxable Pay to date exceeds the figure in Col. 1
3	7100	1516.40	
4	9467	2021.99	
5	11834	2527.59	
6	14200	3032.80	
7	16567	3538.39	
8	18934	4043.99	
9	21300	4549.20	
10	23667	5054.79	
11	26034	5560.39	
12	28400	6065.60	

BPP
PUBLISHING

Table D

Pages 2 and 3 tell you when to use this Table

Tax at 40%   **Also to be used for code D0**

Taxable Pay	Tax	Taxable Pay	Tax	Taxable Pay	Tax	Taxable Pay	Tax
£	£	£	£	£	£	£	£
1	0.40	50	20.00	100	40.00	6100	2440.00
2	0.80	51	20.40	200	80.00	6200	2480.00
3	1.20	52	20.80	300	120.00	6300	2520.00
4	1.60	53	21.20	400	160.00	6400	2560.00
5	2.00	54	21.60	500	200.00	6500	2600.00
6	2.40	55	22.00	600	240.00	6600	2640.00
7	2.80	56	22.40	700	280.00	6700	2680.00
8	3.20	57	22.80	800	320.00	6800	2720.00
9	3.60	58	23.20	900	360.00	6900	2760.00
10	4.00	59	23.60	1000	400.00	7000	2800.00
11	4.40	60	24.00	1100	440.00	7100	2840.00
12	4.80	61	24.40	1200	480.00	7200	2880.00
13	5.20	62	24.80	1300	520.00	7300	2920.00
14	5.60	63	25.20	1400	560.00	7400	2960.00
15	6.00	64	25.60	1500	600.00	7500	3000.00
16	6.40	65	26.00	1600	640.00	7600	3040.00
17	6.80	66	26.40	1700	680.00	7700	3080.00
18	7.20	67	26.80	1800	720.00	7800	3120.00
19	7.60	68	27.20	1900	760.00	7900	3160.00
20	8.00	69	27.60	2000	800.00	8000	3200.00
21	8.40	70	28.00	2100	840.00	8100	3240.00
22	8.80	71	28.40	2200	880.00	8200	3280.00
23	9.20	72	28.80	2300	920.00	8300	3320.00
24	9.60	73	29.20	2400	960.00	8400	3360.00
25	10.00	74	29.60	2500	1000.00	8500	3400.00
26	10.40	75	30.00	2600	1040.00	8600	3440.00
27	10.80	76	30.40	2700	1080.00	8700	3480.00
28	11.20	77	30.80	2800	1120.00	8800	3520.00
29	11.60	78	31.20	2900	1160.00	8900	3560.00
30	12.00	79	31.60	3000	1200.00	9000	3600.00
31	12.40	80	32.00	3100	1240.00	9100	3640.00
32	12.80	81	32.40	3200	1280.00	9200	3680.00
33	13.20	82	32.80	3300	1320.00	9300	3720.00
34	13.60	83	33.20	3400	1360.00	9400	3760.00
35	14.00	84	33.60	3500	1400.00	9500	3800.00
36	14.40	85	34.00	3600	1440.00	9600	3840.00
37	14.80	86	34.40	3700	1480.00	9700	3880.00
38	15.20	87	34.80	3800	1520.00	9800	3920.00
39	15.60	88	35.20	3900	1560.00	9900	3960.00
40	16.00	89	35.60	4000	1600.00	10000	4000.00
41	16.40	90	36.00	4100	1640.00	20000	8000.00
42	16.80	91	36.40	4200	1680.00	30000	12000.00
43	17.20	92	36.80	4300	1720.00	40000	16000.00
44	17.60	93	37.20	4400	1760.00	50000	20000.00
45	18.00	94	37.60	4500	1800.00	60000	24000.00
46	18.40	95	38.00	4600	1840.00	70000	28000.00
47	18.80	96	38.40	4700	1880.00	80000	32000.00
48	19.20	97	38.80	4800	1920.00	90000	36000.00
49	19.60	98	39.20	4900	1960.00	100000	40000.00
		99	39.60	5000	2000.00	200000	80000.00
				5100	2040.00	300000	120000.00
				5200	2080.00	400000	160000.00
				5300	2120.00	500000	200000.00
				5400	2160.00	600000	240000.00
				5500	2200.00	700000	280000.00
				5600	2240.00	800000	320000.00
				5700	2280.00	900000	360000.00
				5800	2320.00	1000000	400000.00
				5900	2360.00		
				6000	2400.00		

Where the exact amount of taxable pay is not shown, add together the figures for two (or more) entries to make up the amount of taxable pay to the nearest £1 below

Monthly paid – Calculator Tables

Read first		Table SR	Tables B			Table D	Table C
		Work out tax at 10% only if Total Taxable Pay does not exceed	**Step 1** Work out tax at 22% if Total Taxable Pay exceeds	but is not more than	**Step 2** deduct Starting Rate Relief	**Step 1** Work out tax at 40% on amount by which Total Taxable Pay exceeds	**Step 2** add the figure below
For Code BR work out tax at 22% on Total Taxable Pay.	Month	£	£	£	£	£	£
	1	127	127	2367	less 15.21	2367	plus 505.59
For Code D0 work out tax at 40% on Total Taxable Pay.	2	254	254	4734	less 30.41	4734	plus 1011.19
	3	380	380	7100	less 45.60	7100	plus 1516.40
	4	507	507	9467	less 60.81	9467	plus 2021.99
For all other codes find the taxable pay for the month and follow the steps at the top of the column.	5	634	634	11834	less 76.01	11834	plus 2527.59
	6	760	760	14200	less 91.20	14200	plus 3032.80
	7	887	887	16567	less 106.41	16567	plus 3538.39
	8	1014	1014	18934	less 121.61	18934	plus 4043.99
If the code is on a Month 1 basis, use the Month 1 figures for each calculation.	9	1140	1140	21300	less 136.80	21300	plus 4549.20
	10	1267	1267	23667	less 152.01	23667	plus 5054.79
	11	1394	1394	26034	less 167.21	26034	plus 5560.39
	12	1520	1520	28400	less 182.40	28400	plus 6065.60

Weekly paid – Calculator Tables

Read first

For Code BR work out tax at 22% on Total Taxable Pay.

For Code D0 work out tax at 40% on Total Taxable Pay.

For all other codes find the taxable pay for the week and follow the steps at the top of the column.

If the code is on a Week 1 basis, use the Week 1 figures for each calculation.

	Table SR	Tables B		Table D	Table C
		Step 1	**Step 2**	**Step 1**	**Step 2**
	Work out tax at 10% only if Total Taxable Pay does not exceed	Work out tax at 22% if Total Taxable Pay	deduct starting rate relief	Work out tax at 40% on amount by which Total Taxable Pay exceeds	add the figure below
Week	£	exceeds £	but is not more than £	less £	£	plus £
1	30	30	547	less 3.51	547	plus 116.98
2	59	59	1093	less 7.02	1093	plus 233.56
3	88	88	1639	less 10.53	1639	plus 350.15
4	117	117	2185	less 14.04	2185	plus 466.73
5	147	147	2731	less 17.54	2731	plus 583.32
6	176	176	3277	less 21.05	3277	plus 699.90
7	205	205	3824	less 24.56	3824	plus 816.89
8	234	234	4370	less 28.07	4370	plus 933.47
9	264	264	4916	less 31.57	4916	plus 1050.06
10	293	293	5462	less 35.08	5462	plus 1166.64
11	322	322	6008	less 38.59	6008	plus 1283.23
12	351	351	6554	less 42.10	6554	plus 1399.81
13	380	380	7100	less 45.60	7100	plus 1516.40
14	410	410	7647	less 49.11	7647	plus 1633.38
15	439	439	8193	less 52.62	8193	plus 1749.96
16	468	468	8739	less 56.13	8739	plus 1866.55
17	497	497	9285	less 59.64	9285	plus 1983.13
18	527	527	9831	less 63.14	9831	plus 2099.72
19	556	556	10377	less 66.65	10377	plus 2216.30
20	585	585	10924	less 70.16	10924	plus 2333.29
21	614	614	11470	less 73.67	11470	plus 2449.87
22	644	644	12016	less 77.17	12016	plus 2566.46
23	673	673	12562	less 80.68	12562	plus 2683.04
24	702	702	13108	less 84.19	13108	plus 2799.63
25	731	731	13654	less 87.70	13654	plus 2916.21
26	760	760	14200	less 91.20	14200	plus 3032.80
27	790	790	14747	less 94.71	14747	plus 3149.78
28	819	819	15293	less 98.22	15293	plus 3266.36
29	848	848	15839	less 101.73	15839	plus 3382.95
30	877	877	16385	less 105.24	16385	plus 3499.53
31	907	907	16931	less 108.74	16931	plus 3616.12
32	936	936	17477	less 112.25	17477	plus 3732.70
33	965	965	18024	less 115.76	18024	plus 3849.69
34	994	994	18570	less 119.27	18570	plus 3966.27
35	1024	1024	19116	less 122.77	19116	plus 4082.86
36	1053	1053	19662	less 126.28	19662	plus 4199.44
37	1082	1082	20208	less 129.79	20208	plus 4316.03
38	1111	1111	20754	less 133.30	20754	plus 4432.61
39	1140	1140	21300	less 136.80	21300	plus 4549.20
40	1170	1170	21847	less 140.31	21847	plus 4666.18
41	1199	1199	22393	less 143.82	22393	plus 4782.76
42	1228	1228	22939	less 147.33	22939	plus 4899.35
43	1257	1257	23485	less 150.84	23485	plus 5015.93
44	1287	1287	24031	less 154.34	24031	plus 5132.52
45	1316	1316	24577	less 157.85	24577	plus 5249.10
46	1345	1345	25124	less 161.36	25124	plus 5366.09
47	1374	1374	25670	less 164.87	25670	plus 5482.67
48	1404	1404	26216	less 168.37	26216	plus 5599.26
49	1433	1433	26762	less 171.88	26762	plus 5715.84
50	1462	1462	27308	less 175.39	27308	plus 5832.43
51	1491	1491	27854	less 178.90	27854	plus 5949.01
52	1520	1520	28400	less 182.40	28400	plus 6065.60

Appendix II:
Extracts from National Insurance Tables

Earnings limits and National Insurance contribution rates

Earnings limits	Employee's contribution			Employer's contribution
	Contribution Table letter A	Contribution Table letter B	Contribution Table letter C	Table letters A, B and C
Below £67.00 weekly or Below £291.00 monthly or Below £3484.00 yearly	Nil	Nil	Nil	Nil
£67.00 to £76.00 weekly or £291.00 to £329.00 monthly or £3484.00 to £3952.00 yearly	0%	0%	Nil	0%
£76.01 to £84.00 weekly or £329.01 to £365.00 monthly or £3952.01 to £4385.00 yearly	10% on earnings above the Employee's Earnings Threshold	3.85% on earnings above the Employee's Earnings Threshold	Nil	0%
£84.01 to £535.00 weekly or £365.01 to £2319.00 monthly or £4385.01 to £27820.00 yearly			Nil	12.2% on earnings above the Employer's Earnings Threshold
Over £535.00 weekly or over £2319.00 monthly or over £27820.00 yearly	10% on earnings above the Employee's Earnings Threshold, up to and including the UEL then **NIL** on earnings above the UEL	3.85% on earnings above the Employee's Earnings Threshold, up to and including the UEL then **NIL** on earnings above the UEL	Nil	12.2% on all earnings above the Employer's Earnings Threshold

5

2000-2001

Weekly table for not contracted-out standard rate contributions for use from 6 April 2000 to 5 April 2001

Contribution table letter

A

Use this table for:

- employees who are age 16 or over and under State pension age (65 for men, 60 for women)
- employees who have an Appropriate Personal Pension.

Do not use this table for:

- married women or widows who have the right to pay reduced rate employee's contributions, see Table B
- employees who are State pension age or over, see Table C
- employees for whom you hold form CA2700, see Table C.

Completing Deductions Working Sheet, form P11 or substitute:

- enter 'A' in the space provided in the 'End of Year Summary' box of form P11
- copy the figures in columns 1a-1f of the table to columns 1a-1f of form P11 on the line next to the tax week in which the employee is paid.

If the exact gross pay is not shown in the table, use the next smaller figure shown.

The figures in the left hand column of each table show steps between the Lower Earnings Limit and the Upper Earnings Limit. The National Insurance contributions liability for each step is calculated at the mid-point of the steps so you and your employee may pay slightly more or less than if you used the exact percentage method.

▼ Employee's Earnings up to and including the UEL	Earnings at the LEL (Where earnings reach or exceed the LEL)	Earnings above the LEL, up to and including the employee's Earnings Threshold	Earnings above the employee's Earnings Threshold, up to and including the employer's Earnings Threshold	Earnings above the employer's Earnings Threshold, up to and including the UEL	Total of employee's and employer's contributions payable	Employee's contributions payable	▼ Employer's contributions
	1a	1b	1c	1d	1e	1f	
£	£	£	£	£	£ P	£ P	£ P
Up to and including 66.99			No NIC Liability, make no entries on forms P11 and P14				
67	67	0	0	0	0.00	0.00	0.00
68	67	1	0	0	0.00	0.00	0.00
69	67	2	0	0	0.00	0.00	0.00
70	67	3	0	0	0.00	0.00	0.00
71	67	4	0	0	0.00	0.00	0.00
72	67	5	0	0	0.00	0.00	0.00
73	67	6	0	0	0.00	0.00	0.00
74	67	7	0	0	0.00	0.00	0.00
75	67	8	0	0	0.00	0.00	0.00
76	67	9	0	0	0.00	0.00	0.00
77	67	9	1	0	0.15	0.15	0.00
78	67	9	2	0	0.25	0.25	0.00
79	67	9	3	0	0.35	0.35	0.00
80	67	9	4	0	0.45	0.45	0.00
81	67	9	5	0	0.55	0.55	0.00
82	67	9	6	0	0.65	0.65	0.00
83	67	9	7	0	0.75	0.75	0.00
84	67	9	8	0	0.85	0.85	0.00
85	67	9	8	1	1.13	0.95	0.18
86	67	9	8	2	1.35	1.05	0.30
87	67	9	8	3	1.58	1.15	0.43
88	67	9	8	4	1.80	1.25	0.55
89	67	9	8	5	2.02	1.35	0.67
90	67	9	8	6	2.24	1.45	0.79
91	67	9	8	7	2.46	1.55	0.91
92	67	9	8	8	2.69	1.65	1.04
93	67	9	8	9	2.91	1.75	1.16
94	67	9	8	10	3.13	1.85	1.28
95	67	9	8	11	3.35	1.95	1.40
96	67	9	8	12	3.57	2.05	1.52

▼ for information only - do not enter on Deductions Working Sheet, form P11

7

2000-2001

BPP PUBLISHING

A Contribution table letter

Weekly table

Employee's Earnings up to and including the UEL	Earnings at the LEL (Where earnings reach or exceed the LEL) 1a	Earnings above the LEL, up to and including the employee's Earnings Threshold 1b	Earnings above the employee's Earnings Threshold, up to and including the employer's Earnings Threshold 1c	Earnings above the employer's Earnings Threshold, up to and including the UEL 1d	Total of employee's and employer's contributions payable 1e	Employee's contributions payable 1f	Employer's contributions
£	£	£	£	£	£ P	£ P	£ P
97	67	9	8	13	3.80	2.15	1.65
98	67	9	8	14	4.02	2.25	1.77
99	67	9	8	15	4.24	2.35	1.89
100	67	9	8	16	4.46	2.45	2.01
101	67	9	8	17	4.68	2.55	2.13
102	67	9	8	18	4.91	2.65	2.26
103	67	9	8	19	5.13	2.75	2.38
104	67	9	8	20	5.35	2.85	2.50
105	67	9	8	21	5.57	2.95	2.62
106	67	9	8	22	5.79	3.05	2.74
107	67	9	8	23	6.02	3.15	2.87
108	67	9	8	24	6.24	3.25	2.99
109	67	9	8	25	6.46	3.35	3.11
110	67	9	8	26	6.68	3.45	3.23
111	67	9	8	27	6.90	3.55	3.35
112	67	9	8	28	7.13	3.65	3.48
113	67	9	8	29	7.35	3.75	3.60
114	67	9	8	30	7.57	3.85	3.72
115	67	9	8	31	7.79	3.95	3.84
116	67	9	8	32	8.01	4.05	3.96
117	67	9	8	33	8.24	4.15	4.09
118	67	9	8	34	8.46	4.25	4.21
119	67	9	8	35	8.68	4.35	4.33
120	67	9	8	36	8.90	4.45	4.45
121	67	9	8	37	9.12	4.55	4.57
122	67	9	8	38	9.35	4.65	4.70
123	67	9	8	39	9.57	4.75	4.82
124	67	9	8	40	9.79	4.85	4.94
125	67	9	8	41	10.01	4.95	5.06
126	67	9	8	42	10.23	5.05	5.18
127	67	9	8	43	10.46	5.15	5.31
128	67	9	8	44	10.68	5.25	5.43
129	67	9	8	45	10.90	5.35	5.55
130	67	9	8	46	11.12	5.45	5.67
131	67	9	8	47	11.34	5.55	5.79
132	67	9	8	48	11.57	5.65	5.92
133	67	9	8	49	11.79	5.75	6.04
134	67	9	8	50	12.01	5.85	6.16
135	67	9	8	51	12.23	5.95	6.28
136	67	9	8	52	12.45	6.05	6.40
137	67	9	8	53	12.68	6.15	6.53
138	67	9	8	54	12.90	6.25	6.65
139	67	9	8	55	13.12	6.35	6.77
140	67	9	8	56	13.34	6.45	6.89
141	67	9	8	57	13.56	6.55	7.01
142	67	9	8	58	13.79	6.65	7.14
143	67	9	8	59	14.01	6.75	7.26
144	67	9	8	60	14.23	6.85	7.38
145	67	9	8	61	14.45	6.95	7.50
146	67	9	8	62	14.67	7.05	7.62
147	67	9	8	63	14.90	7.15	7.75
148	67	9	8	64	15.12	7.25	7.87
149	67	9	8	65	15.34	7.35	7.99
150	67	9	8	66	15.56	7.45	8.11
151	67	9	8	67	15.78	7.55	8.23
152	67	9	8	68	16.01	7.65	8.36
153	67	9	8	69	16.23	7.75	8.48
154	67	9	8	70	16.45	7.85	8.60
155	67	9	8	71	16.67	7.95	8.72
156	67	9	8	72	16.89	8.05	8.84

2000-2001

▼ for information only - do not enter on Deductions Working Sheet, form P11

8

Weekly table

▼ Employee's Earnings up to and including the UEL	Earnings at the LEL (Where earnings reach or exceed the LEL)	Earnings above the LEL, up to and including the *employee's* Earnings Threshold	Earnings above the *employee's* Earnings Threshold, up to and including the *employer's* Earnings Threshold	Earnings above the *employer's* Earnings Threshold, up to and including the UEL	Total of employee's and employer's contributions payable	Employee's contributions payable	▼ Employer's contributions
	1a	**1b**	**1c**	**1d**	**1e**	**1f**	
£	£	£	£	£	£ P	£ P	£ P
157	67	9	8	73	17.12	8.15	8.97
158	67	9	8	74	17.34	8.25	9.09
159	67	9	8	75	17.56	8.35	9.21
160	67	9	8	76	17.78	8.45	9.33
161	67	9	8	77	18.00	8.55	9.45
162	67	9	8	78	18.23	8.65	9.58
163	67	9	8	79	18.45	8.75	9.70
164	67	9	8	80	18.67	8.85	9.82
165	67	9	8	81	18.89	8.95	9.94
166	67	9	8	82	19.11	9.05	10.06
167	67	9	8	83	19.34	9.15	10.19
168	67	9	8	84	19.56	9.25	10.31
169	67	9	8	85	19.78	9.35	10.43
170	67	9	8	86	20.00	9.45	10.55
171	67	9	8	87	20.22	9.55	10.67
172	67	9	8	88	20.45	9.65	10.80
173	67	9	8	89	20.67	9.75	10.92
174	67	9	8	90	20.89	9.85	11.04
175	67	9	8	91	21.11	9.95	11.16
176	67	9	8	92	21.33	10.05	11.28
177	67	9	8	93	21.56	10.15	11.41
178	67	9	8	94	21.78	10.25	11.53
179	67	9	8	95	22.00	10.35	11.65
180	67	9	8	96	22.22	10.45	11.77
181	67	9	8	97	22.44	10.55	11.89
182	67	9	8	98	22.67	10.65	12.02
183	67	9	8	99	22.89	10.75	12.14
184	67	9	8	100	23.11	10.85	12.26
185	67	9	8	101	23.33	10.95	12.38
186	67	9	8	102	23.55	11.05	12.50
187	67	9	8	103	23.78	11.15	12.63
188	67	9	8	104	24.00	11.25	12.75
189	67	9	8	105	24.22	11.35	12.87
190	67	9	8	106	24.44	11.45	12.99
191	67	9	8	107	24.66	11.55	13.11
192	67	9	8	108	24.89	11.65	13.24
193	67	9	8	109	25.11	11.75	13.36
194	67	9	8	110	25.33	11.85	13.48
195	67	9	8	111	25.55	11.95	13.60
196	67	9	8	112	25.77	12.05	13.72
197	67	9	8	113	26.00	12.15	13.85
198	67	9	8	114	26.22	12.25	13.97
199	67	9	8	115	26.44	12.35	14.09
200	67	9	8	116	26.66	12.45	14.21
201	67	9	8	117	26.88	12.55	14.33
202	67	9	8	118	27.11	12.65	14.46
203	67	9	8	119	27.33	12.75	14.58
204	67	9	8	120	27.55	12.85	14.70
205	67	9	8	121	27.77	12.95	14.82
206	67	9	8	122	27.99	13.05	14.94
207	67	9	8	123	28.22	13.15	15.07
208	67	9	8	124	28.44	13.25	15.19
209	67	9	8	125	28.66	13.35	15.31
210	67	9	8	126	28.88	13.45	15.43
211	67	9	8	127	29.10	13.55	15.55
212	67	9	8	128	29.33	13.65	15.68
213	67	9	8	129	29.55	13.75	15.80
214	67	9	8	130	29.77	13.85	15.92
215	67	9	8	131	29.99	13.95	16.04
216	67	9	8	132	30.21	14.05	16.16

▼ for information only - do not enter on Deductions Working Sheet, form P11

9

2000-2001

Weekly table

▼ Employee's Earnings up to and including the UEL	Earnings at the LEL (Where earnings reach or exceed the LEL)	Earnings above the LEL, up to and including the employee's Earnings Threshold	Earnings above the employee's Earnings Threshold, up to and including the employer's Earnings Threshold	Earnings above the employer's Earnings Threshold, up to and including the UEL	Total of employee's and employer's contributions payable	Employee's contributions payable	▼ Employer's contributions
	1a	**1b**	**1c**	**1d**	**1e**	**1f**	
£	£	£	£	£	£ P	£ P	£ P
517	67	9	8	433	97.04	44.15	52.89
518	67	9	8	434	97.26	44.25	53.01
519	67	9	8	435	97.48	44.35	53.13
520	67	9	8	436	97.70	44.45	53.25
521	67	9	8	437	97.92	44.55	53.37
522	67	9	8	438	98.15	44.65	53.50
523	67	9	8	439	98.37	44.75	53.62
524	67	9	8	440	98.59	44.85	53.74
525	67	9	8	441	98.81	44.95	53.86
526	67	9	8	442	99.03	45.05	53.98
527	67	9	8	443	99.26	45.15	54.11
528	67	9	8	444	99.48	45.25	54.23
529	67	9	8	445	99.70	45.35	54.35
530	67	9	8	446	99.92	45.45	54.47
531	67	9	8	447	100.14	45.55	54.59
532	67	9	8	448	100.37	45.65	54.72
533	67	9	8	449	100.59	45.75	54.84
534	67	9	8	450	100.81	45.85	54.96
535	67	9	8	451	100.92	45.90	55.02

If the employee's gross pay is over £535, go to page 61

▼ for information only - do not enter on Deductions Working Sheet, form P11

2000-2001

Monthly table for not contracted-out standard rate contributions for use from 6 April 2000 to 5 April 2001

A *Contribution table letter*

Use this table for:

- employees who are age 16 or over and under State pension age (65 for men, 60 for women)
- employees who have an Appropriate Personal Pension.

Do not use this table for:

- married women or widows who have the right to pay reduced rate employee's contributions, see Table B
- employees who are State pension age or over, see Table C
- employees for whom you hold form CA2700, see Table C.

Completing Deductions Working Sheet, form P11 or substitute:

- enter 'A' in the space provided in the 'End of Year Summary' box of form P11
- copy the figures in columns 1a-1f of the table to columns 1a-1f of form P11 on a line appropriate to the tax month in which the employee is paid.

If the exact gross pay is not shown in the table, use the next smaller figure shown.

The figures in the left hand column of each table show steps between the Lower Earnings Limit and the Upper Earnings Limit. The National Insurance contributions liability for each step is calculated at the mid-point of the steps so you and your employee may pay slightly more or less than if you used the exact percentage method.

▼ Employee's Earnings up to and including the UEL	Earnings at the LEL (Where earnings reach or exceed the LEL) 1a	Earnings above the LEL, up to and including the employee's Earnings Threshold 1b	Earnings above the employee's Earnings Threshold, up to and including the employer's Earnings Threshold 1c	Earnings above the employer's Earnings Threshold, up to and including the UEL 1d	Total of employee's and employer's contributions payable 1e	Employee's contributions payable 1f	▼ Employer's contributions
£	£	£	£	£	£ P	£ P	£ P
Up to and including 290.99	No NIC liability, make no entries on form P11 and P						
291	291	0	0	0	0.00	0.00	0.00
295	291	4	0	0	0.00	0.00	0.00
299	291	8	0	0	0.00	0.00	0.00
303	291	12	0	0	0.00	0.00	0.00
307	291	16	0	0	0.00	0.00	0.00
311	291	20	0	0	0.00	0.00	0.00
315	291	24	0	0	0.00	0.00	0.00
319	291	28	0	0	0.00	0.00	0.00
323	291	32	0	0	0.00	0.00	0.00
327	291	36	0	0	0.00	0.00	0.00
329	291	38	0	0	0.00	0.00	0.00
331	291	38	2	0	0.40	0.40	0.00
335	291	38	6	0	0.80	0.80	0.00
339	291	38	10	0	1.20	1.20	0.00
343	291	38	14	0	1.60	1.60	0.00
347	291	38	18	0	2.00	2.00	0.00
351	291	38	22	0	2.40	2.40	0.00
355	291	38	26	0	2.80	2.80	0.00
359	291	38	30	0	3.20	3.20	0.00
363	291	38	34	0	3.50	3.50	0.00
365	291	38	36	0	3.70	3.70	0.00
367	291	38	36	2	4.49	4.00	0.49
371	291	38	36	6	5.38	4.40	0.98
375	291	38	36	10	6.26	4.80	1.46
379	291	38	36	14	7.15	5.20	1.95
383	291	38	36	18	8.04	5.60	2.44
387	291	38	36	22	8.93	6.00	2.93
391	291	38	36	26	9.82	6.40	3.42
395	291	38	36	30	10.70	6.80	3.90
399	291	38	36	34	11.59	7.20	4.39

▼ for information only - do not enter on Deductions Working Sheet, form P11

16

Monthly table

Contribution table letter **A**

▼ Employee's Earnings up to and including the UEL	Earnings at the LEL (Where earnings reach or exceed the LEL)	Earnings above the LEL, up to and including the *employee's* Earnings Threshold	Earnings above the *employee's* Earnings Threshold, up to and including the *employer's* Earnings Threshold	Earnings above the *employer's* Earnings Threshold, up to and including the UEL	Total of employee's and employer's contributions payable	Employee's contributions payable	▼ Employer's contributions
	1a	**1b**	**1c**	**1d**	**1e**	**1f**	
£	£	£	£	£	£ P	£ P	£ P
883	291	38	36	518	119.04	55.60	63.44
887	291	38	36	522	119.93	56.00	63.93
891	291	38	36	526	120.82	56.40	64.42
895	291	38	36	530	121.70	56.80	64.90
899	291	38	36	534	122.59	57.20	65.39
903	291	38	36	538	123.48	57.60	65.88
907	291	38	36	542	124.37	58.00	66.37
911	291	38	36	546	125.26	58.40	66.86
915	291	38	36	550	126.14	58.80	67.34
919	291	38	36	554	127.03	59.20	67.83
923	291	38	36	558	127.92	59.60	68.32
927	291	38	36	562	128.81	60.00	68.81
931	291	38	36	566	129.70	60.40	69.30
935	291	38	36	570	130.58	60.80	69.78
939	291	38	36	574	131.47	61.20	70.27
943	291	38	36	578	132.36	61.60	70.76
947	291	38	36	582	133.25	62.00	71.25
951	291	38	36	586	134.14	62.40	71.74
955	291	38	36	590	135.02	62.80	72.22
959	291	38	36	594	135.91	63.20	72.71
963	291	38	36	598	136.80	63.60	73.20
967	291	38	36	602	137.69	64.00	73.69
971	291	38	36	606	138.58	64.40	74.18
975	291	38	36	610	139.46	64.80	74.66
979	291	38	36	614	140.35	65.20	75.15
983	291	38	36	618	141.24	65.60	75.64
987	291	38	36	622	142.13	66.00	76.13
991	291	38	36	626	143.02	66.40	76.62
995	291	38	36	630	143.90	66.80	77.10
999	291	38	36	634	144.79	67.20	77.59
1003	291	38	36	638	145.68	67.60	78.08
1007	291	38	36	642	146.57	68.00	78.57
1011	291	38	36	646	147.46	68.40	79.06
1015	291	38	36	650	148.34	68.80	79.54
1019	291	38	36	654	149.23	69.20	80.03
1023	291	38	36	658	150.12	69.60	80.52
1027	291	38	36	662	151.01	70.00	81.01
1031	291	38	36	666	151.90	70.40	81.50
1035	291	38	36	670	152.78	70.80	81.98
1039	291	38	36	674	153.67	71.20	82.47
1043	291	38	36	678	154.56	71.60	82.96
1047	291	38	36	682	155.45	72.00	83.45
1051	291	38	36	686	156.34	72.40	83.94
1055	291	38	36	690	157.22	72.80	84.42
1059	291	38	36	694	158.11	73.20	84.91
1063	291	38	36	698	159.00	73.60	85.40
1067	291	38	36	702	159.89	74.00	85.89
1071	291	38	36	706	160.78	74.40	86.38
1075	291	38	36	710	161.66	74.80	86.86
1079	291	38	36	714	162.55	75.20	87.35
1083	291	38	36	718	163.44	75.60	87.84
1087	291	38	36	722	164.33	76.00	88.33
1091	291	38	36	726	165.22	76.40	88.82
1095	291	38	36	730	166.10	76.80	89.30
1099	291	38	36	734	166.99	77.20	89.79
1103	291	38	36	738	167.88	77.60	90.28
1107	291	38	36	742	168.77	78.00	90.77
1111	291	38	36	746	169.66	78.40	91.26
1115	291	38	36	750	170.54	78.80	91.74
1119	291	38	36	754	171.43	79.20	92.23

▼ for information only - do not enter on Deductions Working Sheet, form P11

19

2000-2001

Monthly table

Employee's Earnings up to and including the UEL	Earnings at the LEL (Where earnings reach or exceed the LEL) 1a	Earnings above the LEL, up to and including the employee's Earnings Threshold 1b	Earnings above the employee's Earnings Threshold, up to and including the employer's Earnings Threshold 1c	Earnings above the employer's Earnings Threshold, up to and including the UEL 1d	Total of employee's and employer's contributions payable 1e	Employee's contributions payable 1f	Employer's contributions
£	£	£	£	£	£ P	£ P	£ P
1363	291	38	36	998	225.60	103.60	122.00
1367	291	38	36	1002	226.49	104.00	122.49
1371	291	38	36	1006	227.38	104.40	122.98
1375	291	38	36	1010	228.26	104.80	123.46
1379	291	38	36	1014	229.15	105.20	123.95
1383	291	38	36	1018	230.04	105.60	124.44
1387	291	38	36	1022	230.93	106.00	124.93
1391	291	38	36	1026	231.82	106.40	125.42
1395	291	38	36	1030	232.70	106.80	125.90
1399	291	38	36	1034	233.59	107.20	126.39
1403	291	38	36	1038	234.48	107.60	126.88
1407	291	38	36	1042	235.37	108.00	127.37
1411	291	38	36	1046	236.26	108.40	127.86
1415	291	38	36	1050	237.14	108.80	128.34
1419	291	38	36	1054	238.03	109.20	128.83
1423	291	38	36	1058	238.92	109.60	129.32
1427	291	38	36	1062	239.81	110.00	129.81
1431	291	38	36	1066	240.70	110.40	130.30
1435	291	38	36	1070	241.58	110.80	130.78
1439	291	38	36	1074	242.47	111.20	131.27
1443	291	38	36	1078	243.36	111.60	131.76
1447	291	38	36	1082	244.25	112.00	132.25
1451	291	38	36	1086	245.14	112.40	132.74
1455	291	38	36	1090	246.02	112.80	133.22
1459	291	38	36	1094	246.91	113.20	133.71
1463	291	38	36	1098	247.80	113.60	134.20
1467	291	38	36	1102	248.69	114.00	134.69
1471	291	38	36	1106	249.58	114.40	135.18
1475	291	38	36	1110	250.46	114.80	135.66
1479	291	38	36	1114	251.35	115.20	136.15
1483	291	38	36	1118	252.24	115.60	136.64
1487	291	38	36	1122	253.13	116.00	137.13
1491	291	38	36	1126	254.02	116.40	137.62
1495	291	38	36	1130	254.90	116.80	138.10
1499	291	38	36	1134	255.79	117.20	138.59
1503	291	38	36	1138	256.68	117.60	139.08
1507	291	38	36	1142	257.57	118.00	139.57
1511	291	38	36	1146	258.46	118.40	140.06
1515	291	38	36	1150	259.34	118.80	140.54
1519	291	38	36	1154	260.23	119.20	141.03
1523	291	38	36	1158	261.12	119.60	141.52
1527	291	38	36	1162	262.01	120.00	142.01
1531	291	38	36	1166	262.90	120.40	142.50
1535	291	38	36	1170	263.78	120.80	142.98
1539	291	38	36	1174	264.67	121.20	143.47
1543	291	38	36	1178	265.56	121.60	143.96
1547	291	38	36	1182	266.45	122.00	144.45
1551	291	38	36	1186	267.34	122.40	144.94
1555	291	38	36	1190	268.22	122.80	145.42
1559	291	38	36	1194	269.11	123.20	145.91
1563	291	38	36	1198	270.00	123.60	146.40
1567	291	38	36	1202	270.89	124.00	146.89
1571	291	38	36	1206	271.78	124.40	147.38
1575	291	38	36	1210	272.66	124.80	147.86
1579	291	38	36	1214	273.55	125.20	148.35
1583	291	38	36	1218	274.44	125.60	148.84
1587	291	38	36	1222	275.33	126.00	149.33
1591	291	38	36	1226	276.22	126.40	149.82
1595	291	38	36	1230	277.10	126.80	150.30
1599	291	38	36	1234	277.99	127.20	150.79

▼ for information only - do not enter on Deductions Working Sheet, form P11

2000-2001

BPP PUBLISHING

Monthly table

Employee's Earnings up to and including the UEL	Earnings at the LEL (Where earnings reach or exceed the LEL) 1a	Earnings above the LEL, up to and including the *employee's* Earnings Threshold 1b	Earnings above the *employee's* Earnings Threshold, up to and including the *employer's* Earnings Threshold 1c	Earnings above the *employer's* Earnings Threshold, up to and including the UEL 1d	Total of employee's and employer's contributions payable 1e	Employee's contributions payable 1f	Employer's contributions
£	£	£	£	£	£ P	£ P	£ P
1843	291	38	36	1478	332.16	151.60	180.56
1847	291	38	36	1482	333.05	152.00	181.05
1851	291	38	36	1486	333.94	152.40	181.54
1855	291	38	36	1490	334.82	152.80	182.02
1859	291	38	36	1494	335.71	153.20	182.51
1863	291	38	36	1498	336.60	153.60	183.00
1867	291	38	36	1502	337.49	154.00	183.49
1871	291	38	36	1506	338.38	154.40	183.98
1875	291	38	36	1510	339.26	154.80	184.46
1879	291	38	36	1514	340.15	155.20	184.95
1883	291	38	36	1518	341.04	155.60	185.44
1887	291	38	36	1522	341.93	156.00	185.93
1891	291	38	36	1526	342.82	156.40	186.42
1895	291	38	36	1530	343.70	156.80	186.90
1899	291	38	36	1534	344.59	157.20	187.39
1903	291	38	36	1538	345.48	157.60	187.88
1907	291	38	36	1542	346.37	158.00	188.37
1911	291	38	36	1546	347.26	158.40	188.86
1915	291	38	36	1550	348.14	158.80	189.34
1919	291	38	36	1554	349.03	159.20	189.83
1923	291	38	36	1558	349.92	159.60	190.32
1927	291	38	36	1562	350.81	160.00	190.81
1931	291	38	36	1566	351.70	160.40	191.30
1935	291	38	36	1570	352.58	160.80	191.78
1939	291	38	36	1574	353.47	161.20	192.27
1943	291	38	36	1578	354.36	161.60	192.76
1947	291	38	36	1582	355.25	162.00	193.25
1951	291	38	36	1586	356.14	162.40	193.74
1955	291	38	36	1590	357.02	162.80	194.22
1959	291	38	36	1594	357.91	163.20	194.71
1963	291	38	36	1598	358.80	163.60	195.20
1967	291	38	36	1602	359.69	164.00	195.69
1971	291	38	36	1606	360.58	164.40	196.18
1975	291	38	36	1610	361.46	164.80	196.66
1979	291	38	36	1614	362.35	165.20	197.15
1983	291	38	36	1618	363.24	165.60	197.64
1987	291	38	36	1622	364.13	166.00	198.13
1991	291	38	36	1626	365.02	166.40	198.62
1995	291	38	36	1630	365.90	166.80	199.10
1999	291	38	36	1634	366.79	167.20	199.59
2003	291	38	36	1638	367.68	167.60	200.08
2007	291	38	36	1642	368.57	168.00	200.57
2011	291	38	36	1646	369.46	168.40	201.06
2015	291	38	36	1650	370.34	168.80	201.54
2019	291	38	36	1654	371.23	169.20	202.03
2023	291	38	36	1658	372.12	169.60	202.52
2027	291	38	36	1662	373.01	170.00	203.01
2031	291	38	36	1666	373.90	170.40	203.50
2035	291	38	36	1670	374.78	170.80	203.98
2039	291	38	36	1674	375.67	171.20	204.47
2043	291	38	36	1678	376.56	171.60	204.96
2047	291	38	36	1682	377.45	172.00	205.45
2051	291	38	36	1686	378.34	172.40	205.94
2055	291	38	36	1690	379.22	172.80	206.42
2059	291	38	36	1694	380.11	173.20	206.91
2063	291	38	36	1698	381.00	173.60	207.40
2067	291	38	36	1702	381.89	174.00	207.89
2071	291	38	36	1706	382.78	174.40	208.38
2075	291	38	36	1710	383.66	174.80	208.86
2079	291	38	36	1714	384.55	175.20	209.35

▼ for information only - do not enter on Deductions Working Sheet, form P11

2000-2001

Monthly table

Contribution table letter

Employee's Earnings up to and including the UEL	Earnings at the LEL (Where earnings reach or exceed the LEL)	Earnings above the LEL, up to and including the *employee's* Earnings Threshold	Earnings above the *employee's* Earnings Threshold, up to and including the *employer's* Earnings Threshold	Earnings above the *employer's* Earnings Threshold, up to and including the UEL	Total of employee's and employer's contributions payable	Employee's contributions payable	Employer's contributions
	1a	**1b**	**1c**	**1d**	**1e**	**1f**	
£	£	£	£	£	£ P	£ P	£ P
2083	291	38	36	1718	385.44	175.60	209.84
2087	291	38	36	1722	386.33	176.00	210.33
2091	291	38	36	1726	387.22	176.40	210.82
2095	291	38	36	1730	388.10	176.80	211.30
2099	291	38	36	1734	388.99	177.20	211.79
2103	291	38	36	1738	389.88	177.60	212.28
2107	291	38	36	1742	390.77	178.00	212.77
2111	291	38	36	1746	391.66	178.40	213.26
2115	291	38	36	1750	392.54	178.80	213.74
2119	291	38	36	1754	393.43	179.20	214.23
2123	291	38	36	1758	394.32	179.60	214.72
2127	291	38	36	1762	395.21	180.00	215.21
2131	291	38	36	1766	396.10	180.40	215.70
2135	291	38	36	1770	396.98	180.80	216.18
2139	291	38	36	1774	397.87	181.20	216.67
2143	291	38	36	1778	398.76	181.60	217.16
2147	291	38	36	1782	399.65	182.00	217.65
2151	291	38	36	1786	400.54	182.40	218.14
2155	291	38	36	1790	401.42	182.80	218.62
2159	291	38	36	1794	402.31	183.20	219.11
2163	291	38	36	1798	403.20	183.60	219.60
2167	291	38	36	1802	404.09	184.00	220.09
2171	291	38	36	1806	404.98	184.40	220.58
2175	291	38	36	1810	405.86	184.80	221.06
2179	291	38	36	1814	406.75	185.20	221.55
2183	291	38	36	1818	407.64	185.60	222.04
2187	291	38	36	1822	408.53	186.00	222.53
2191	291	38	36	1826	409.42	186.40	223.02
2195	291	38	36	1830	410.30	186.80	223.50
2199	291	38	36	1834	411.19	187.20	223.99
2203	291	38	36	1838	412.08	187.60	224.48
2207	291	38	36	1842	412.97	188.00	224.97
2211	291	38	36	1846	413.86	188.40	225.46
2215	291	38	36	1850	414.74	188.80	225.94
2219	291	38	36	1854	415.63	189.20	226.43
2223	291	38	36	1858	416.52	189.60	226.92
2227	291	38	36	1862	417.41	190.00	227.41
2231	291	38	36	1866	418.30	190.40	227.90
2235	291	38	36	1870	419.18	190.80	228.38
2239	291	38	36	1874	420.07	191.20	228.87
2243	291	38	36	1878	420.96	191.60	229.36
2247	291	38	36	1882	421.85	192.00	229.85
2251	291	38	36	1886	422.74	192.40	230.34
2255	291	38	36	1890	423.62	192.80	230.82
2259	291	38	36	1894	424.51	193.20	231.31
2263	291	38	36	1898	425.40	193.60	231.80
2267	291	38	36	1902	426.29	194.00	232.29
2271	291	38	36	1906	427.18	194.40	232.78
2275	291	38	36	1910	428.06	194.80	233.26
2279	291	38	36	1914	428.95	195.20	233.75
2283	291	38	36	1918	429.84	195.60	234.24
2287	291	38	36	1922	430.73	196.00	234.73
2291	291	38	36	1926	431.62	196.40	235.22
2295	291	38	36	1930	432.50	196.80	235.70
2299	291	38	36	1934	433.39	197.20	236.19
2303	291	38	36	1938	434.28	197.60	236.68
2307	291	38	36	1942	435.17	198.00	237.17
2311	291	38	36	1946	436.06	198.40	237.66
2315	291	38	36	1950	436.94	198.80	238.14
2319	291	38	36	1954	437.39	199.00	238.39

If the employee's gross pay is over £2319, go to page 61

▼ for information only - do not enter on Deductions Working Sheet, form P11

24

2000-2001

BPP PUBLISHING

Weekly table for not contracted-out reduced rate contributions for use from 6 April 2000 to 5 April 2001

Contribution table letter

B

Use this table for:

- married women or widows who have the right to pay reduced rate employee's contributions for whom you hold a valid certificate CA4139, CF383 or CF380A.

Do not use this table for:

- women aged 60 or over, see Table C
- women for whom you hold form CA2700, see Table C.

Completing Deductions Working Sheet, form P11 or substitute:

- enter 'B' in the space provided in the 'End of Year Summary' box of form P11
- copy the figures in columns 1e and 1f of the table to columns 1e and 1f of form P11. You may copy the figures in columns 1a-1d of the table to columns 1a-1d of form P11 if you wish.

If the exact gross pay is not shown in the table, use the next smaller figure shown.

The figures in the left hand column of each table show steps between the Lower Earnings Limit and the Upper Earnings Limit. The National Insurance contributions liability for each step is calculated at the mid-point of the steps so you and your employee may pay slightly more or less than if you used the exact percentage method.

▼ Employee's Earnings up to and including the UEL	Earnings at the LEL (Where earnings reach or exceed the LEL) 1a	Earnings above the LEL, up to and including the employer's Earnings Threshold 1b	Earnings above the employee's Earnings Threshold, up to and including the employer's Earnings Threshold 1c	Earnings above the employer's Earnings Threshold, up to and including the UEL 1d	Total of employee's and employer's contributions payable 1e	Employee's contributions payable 1f	▼ Employer's contributions
£ Up to and including 66.99	£	£	£	£	£ P	£ P	£ P
			No NIC liability where no entries on form P11 and P14				
67	67	0	0	0	0.00	0.00	0.00
68	67	1	0	0	0.00	0.00	0.00
69	67	2	0	0	0.00	0.00	0.00
70	67	3	0	0	0.00	0.00	0.00
71	67	4	0	0	0.00	0.00	0.00
72	67	5	0	0	0.00	0.00	0.00
73	67	6	0	0	0.00	0.00	0.00
74	67	7	0	0	0.00	0.00	0.00
75	67	8	0	0	0.00	0.00	0.00
76	67	9	0	0	0.00	0.00	0.00
77	67	9	1	0	0.06	0.06	0.00
78	67	9	2	0	0.10	0.10	0.00
79	67	9	3	0	0.13	0.13	0.00
80	67	9	4	0	0.17	0.17	0.00
81	67	9	5	0	0.21	0.21	0.00
82	67	9	6	0	0.25	0.25	0.00
83	67	9	7	0	0.29	0.29	0.00
84	67	9	8	0	0.33	0.33	0.00
85	67	9	8	1	0.54	0.36	0.18
86	67	9	8	2	0.70	0.40	0.30
87	67	9	8	3	0.87	0.44	0.43
88	67	9	8	4	1.03	0.48	0.55
89	67	9	8	5	1.19	0.52	0.67
90	67	9	8	6	1.35	0.56	0.79
91	67	9	8	7	1.51	0.60	0.91
92	67	9	8	8	1.67	0.63	1.04
93	67	9	8	9	1.83	0.67	1.16
94	67	9	8	10	1.99	0.71	1.28
95	67	9	8	11	2.15	0.75	1.40
96	67	9	8	12	2.31	0.79	1.52

▼ for information only - do not enter on Deductions Working Sheet, form P11

25

2000-2001

Weekly table

Employee's Earnings up to and including the UEL	Earnings at the LEL (Where earnings reach or exceed the LEL)	Earnings above the LEL, up to and including the *employee's* Earnings Threshold	Earnings above the *employee's* Earnings Threshold, up to and including the *employer's* Earnings Threshold	Earnings above the *employer's* Earnings Threshold, up to and including the UEL	Total of employer's contributions payable
▼	1a	1b	1c	1d	1e
£	£	£	£	£	£ P
162	67	9	8	78	9.58
163	67	9	8	79	9.70
164	67	9	8	80	9.82
165	67	9	8	81	9.94
166	67	9	8	82	10.06
167	67	9	8	83	10.19
168	67	9	8	84	10.31
169	67	9	8	85	10.43
170	67	9	8	86	10.55
171	67	9	8	87	10.67
172	67	9	8	88	10.80
173	67	9	8	89	10.92
174	67	9	8	90	11.04
175	67	9	8	91	11.16
176	67	9	8	92	11.28
177	67	9	8	93	11.41
178	67	9	8	94	11.53
179	67	9	8	95	11.65
180	67	9	8	96	11.77
181	67	9	8	97	11.89
182	67	9	8	98	12.02
183	67	9	8	99	12.14
184	67	9	8	100	12.26
185	67	9	8	101	12.38
186	67	9	8	102	12.50
187	67	9	8	103	12.63
188	67	9	8	104	12.75
189	67	9	8	105	12.87
190	67	9	8	106	12.99
191	67	9	8	107	13.11
192	67	9	8	108	13.24
193	67	9	8	109	13.36
194	67	9	8	110	13.48
195	67	9	8	111	13.60
196	67	9	8	112	13.72
197	67	9	8	113	13.85
198	67	9	8	114	13.97
199	67	9	8	115	14.09
200	67	9	8	116	14.21
201	67	9	8	117	14.33
202	67	9	8	118	14.46
203	67	9	8	119	14.58
204	67	9	8	120	14.70
205	67	9	8	121	14.82
206	67	9	8	122	14.94
207	67	9	8	123	15.07
208	67	9	8	124	15.19
209	67	9	8	125	15.31
210	67	9	8	126	15.43
211	67	9	8	127	15.55
212	67	9	8	128	15.68
213	67	9	8	129	15.80
214	67	9	8	130	15.92
215	67	9	8	131	16.04
216	67	9	8	132	16.16
217	67	9	8	133	16.29
218	67	9	8	134	16.41
219	67	9	8	135	16.53
220	67	9	8	136	16.65
221	67	9	8	137	16.77

▼ for information only - do not enter on Deductions Working Sheet, form P11

2000-2001

BPP PUBLISHING

Monthly table

▼ Employee's Earnings up to and including the UEL	Earnings at the LEL (Where earnings reach or exceed the LEL) 1a	Earnings above the LEL, up to and including the employee's Earnings Threshold 1b	Earnings above the employee's Earnings Threshold, up to and including the employer's Earnings Threshold 1c	Earnings above the employer's Earnings Threshold, up to and including the UEL 1d	Total of employer's contributions payable 1e
£	£	£	£	£	£ P
1863	291	38	36	1498	183.00
1867	291	38	36	1502	183.49
1871	291	38	36	1506	183.98
1875	291	38	36	1510	184.46
1879	291	38	36	1514	184.95
1883	291	38	36	1518	185.44
1887	291	38	36	1522	185.93
1891	291	38	36	1526	186.42
1895	291	38	36	1530	186.90
1899	291	38	36	1534	187.39
1903	291	38	36	1538	187.88
1907	291	38	36	1542	188.37
1911	291	38	36	1546	188.86
1915	291	38	36	1550	189.34
1919	291	38	36	1554	189.83
1923	291	38	36	1558	190.32
1927	291	38	36	1562	190.81
1931	291	38	36	1566	191.30
1935	291	38	36	1570	191.78
1939	291	38	36	1574	192.27
1943	291	38	36	1578	192.76
1947	291	38	36	1582	193.25
1951	291	38	36	1586	193.74
1955	291	38	36	1590	194.22
1959	291	38	36	1594	194.71
1963	291	38	36	1598	195.20
1967	291	38	36	1602	195.69
1971	291	38	36	1606	196.18
1975	291	38	36	1610	196.66
1979	291	38	36	1614	197.15
1983	291	38	36	1618	197.64
1987	291	38	36	1622	198.13
1991	291	38	36	1626	198.62
1995	291	38	36	1630	199.10
1999	291	38	36	1634	199.59
2003	291	38	36	1638	200.08
2007	291	38	36	1642	200.57
2011	291	38	36	1646	201.06
2015	291	38	36	1650	201.54
2019	291	38	36	1654	202.03
2023	291	38	36	1658	202.52
2027	291	38	36	1662	203.01
2031	291	38	36	1666	203.50
2035	291	38	36	1670	203.98
2039	291	38	36	1674	204.47
2043	291	38	36	1678	204.96
2047	291	38	36	1682	205.45
2051	291	38	36	1686	205.94
2055	291	38	36	1690	206.42
2059	291	38	36	1694	206.91
2063	291	38	36	1698	207.40
2067	291	38	36	1702	207.89
2071	291	38	36	1706	208.38
2075	291	38	36	1710	208.86
2079	291	38	36	1714	209.35
2083	291	38	36	1718	209.84
2087	291	38	36	1722	210.33
2091	291	38	36	1726	210.82
2095	291	38	36	1730	211.30
2099	291	38	36	1734	211.79

▼ for information only - do not enter on Deductions Working Sheet, form P11

2000-2001

Monthly table

C *Contribution table letter*

▼ Employee's Earnings up to and including the UEL	Earnings at the LEL (Where earnings reach or exceed the LEL)	Earnings above the LEL, up to and including the *employee's* Earnings Threshold	Earnings above the *employee's* Earnings Threshold, up to and including the *employer's* Earnings Threshold	Earnings above the *employer's* Earnings Threshold, up to and including the UEL	Total of employer's contributions payable
	1a	1b	1c	1d	1e
£	£	£	£	£	£ P
2103	291	38	36	1738	212.28
2107	291	38	36	1742	212.77
2111	291	38	36	1746	213.26
2115	291	38	36	1750	213.74
2119	291	38	36	1754	214.23
2123	291	38	36	1758	214.72
2127	291	38	36	1762	215.21
2131	291	38	36	1766	215.70
2135	291	38	36	1770	216.18
2139	291	38	36	1774	216.67
2143	291	38	36	1778	217.16
2147	291	38	36	1782	217.65
2151	291	38	36	1786	218.14
2155	291	38	36	1790	218.62
2159	291	38	36	1794	219.11
2163	291	38	36	1798	219.60
2167	291	38	36	1802	220.09
2171	291	38	36	1806	220.58
2175	291	38	36	1810	221.06
2179	291	38	36	1814	221.55
2183	291	38	36	1818	222.04
2187	291	38	36	1822	222.53
2191	291	38	36	1826	223.02
2195	291	38	36	1830	223.50
2199	291	38	36	1834	223.99
2203	291	38	36	1838	224.48
2207	291	38	36	1842	224.97
2211	291	38	36	1846	225.46
2215	291	38	36	1850	225.94
2219	291	38	36	1854	226.43
2223	291	38	36	1858	226.92
2227	291	38	36	1862	227.41
2231	291	38	36	1866	227.90
2235	291	38	36	1870	228.38
2239	291	38	36	1874	228.87
2243	291	38	36	1878	229.36
2247	291	38	36	1882	229.85
2251	291	38	36	1886	230.34
2255	291	38	36	1890	230.82
2259	291	38	36	1894	231.31
2263	291	38	36	1898	231.80
2267	291	38	36	1902	232.29
2271	291	38	36	1906	232.78
2275	291	38	36	1910	233.26
2279	291	38	36	1914	233.75
2283	291	38	36	1918	234.24
2287	291	38	36	1922	234.73
2291	291	38	36	1926	235.22
2295	291	38	36	1930	235.70
2299	291	38	36	1934	236.19
2303	291	38	36	1938	236.68
2307	291	38	36	1942	237.17
2311	291	38	36	1946	237.66
2315	291	38	36	1950	238.14
2319	291	38	36	1954	238.39

If the employee's gross pay is over £2319, go to page 61

▼ for information only - do not enter on Deductions Working Sheet, form P11

Working out employer's contributions due on earnings above the Upper Earnings Limit

The last figure in the left hand column in each table is the Upper Earnings Limit (£535 in the weekly tables or £2319 in the monthly tables). This is because employee's contributions are not payable on earnings above the Upper Earnings Limit. However, employer's contributions are still payable.

To work out employer's contributions due on earnings above the Upper Earnings Limit:

Step	Action	Example (based on Table A with total monthly earnings of £4479.29
1	subtract the upper earnings limit figure from the total gross pay	£4479.29 - £2319 = £2160.29
2	round the answer down to the nearest whole £	Rounded down to £2160
3	look this figure up in the 'additional gross pay table' on page 62	Look up £2160
4	if the figure is not shown in the table, build up to it by adding together as few entries as possible	Amount Employer's contributions £2000 £244.00 £100 £12.20 £60 £7.32 **Total** **£263.52**
5	add the employer's contributions worked out to the total contributions due for earnings at the upper Earnings Limit - column 1e of the main table	**Total** payable by employee **and** employer is: £263.52 (further employer NICs) + £437.39 (due for employer and employee on earnings at UEL) = **£700.91**
6	record the figure resulting from Step 5 in column 1e of form P11	**On form P11 record:**

Col 1a	Col 1b	Col 1c	Col 1d	Col 1e	Col 1f
291	38	36	1954	700.91	199.00

2000-2001

206

Additional gross pay table

Earnings on which contributions payable 1a £	Total employer's contributions payable 1b £		Earnings on which contributions payable 1a £	Total employer's contributions payable 1b £		Earnings on which contributions payable 1a £	Total employer's contributions payable 1b £
1	0.12		56	6.83		3000	366.00
2	0.24		57	6.95		4000	488.00
3	0.37		58	7.08		5000	610.00
4	0.49		59	7.20		6000	732.00
5	0.61		60	7.32		7000	854.00
6	0.73		61	7.44		8000	976.00
7	0.85		62	7.56		9000	1098.00
8	0.98		63	7.69		10000	1220.00
9	1.10		64	7.81		20000	2440.00
10	1.22		65	7.93		30000	3660.00
11	1.34		66	8.05		40000	4880.00
12	1.46		67	8.17		50000	6100.00
13	1.59		68	8.30		60000	7320.00
14	1.71		69	8.42		70000	8540.00
15	1.83		70	8.54		80000	9760.00
16	1.95		71	8.66		90000	10980.00
17	2.07		72	8.78		100000	12200.00
18	2.20		73	8.91			
19	2.32		74	9.03			
20	2.44		75	9.15			
21	2.56		76	9.27			
22	2.68		77	9.39			
23	2.81		78	9.52			
24	2.93		79	9.64			
25	3.05		80	9.76			
26	3.17		81	9.88			
27	3.29		82	10.00			
28	3.42		83	10.13			
29	3.54		84	10.25			
30	3.66		85	10.37			
31	3.78		86	10.49			
32	3.90		87	10.61			
33	4.03		88	10.74			
34	4.15		89	10.86			
35	4.27		90	10.98			
36	4.39		91	11.10			
37	4.51		92	11.22			
38	4.64		93	11.35			
39	4.76		94	11.47			
40	4.88		95	11.59			
41	5.00		96	11.71			
42	5.12		97	11.83			
43	5.25		98	11.96			
44	5.37		99	12.08			
45	5.49		100	12.20			
46	5.61		200	24.40			
47	5.73		300	36.60			
48	5.86		400	48.80			
49	5.98		500	61.00			
50	6.10		600	73.20			
51	6.22		700	85.40			
52	6.34		800	97.60			
53	6.47		900	109.80			
54	6.59		1000	122.00			
55	6.71		2000	244.00			

2000-2001

62

Earnings limits and National Insurance contribution rates

	Employee's contribution			Employer's contribution	NIC rebate on earnings above the LEL, up to and including the Employee's Earnings Threshold	NIC rebate on earnings above the LEL, up to and including the Employer's Earnings Threshold
Earnings limits	Contribution Table letter D	Contribution Table letter E	Contribution Table letter C	Table letters D, E and C		
Below £67.00 weekly **or** Below £291.00 monthly **or** Below £3484.00 yearly	Nil	Nil	Nil	Nil	Nil	Nil
£67.00 to £76.00 weekly **or** £291.00 to £329.00 monthly **or** £3484.00 to £3952.00 yearly	0%	0%	Nil	0%	1.6% on earnings from £67.01, up to and including £76.00 (or monthly or annual equivalents)	3% on earnings from £67.01, up to and including £84.00 (or monthly or annual equivalents)
£76.01 to £84.00 weekly **or** £329.01 to £365.00 monthly **or** £3952.01 to £4385.00 yearly	8.4% on earnings above the Employee's Earnings Threshold	3.85% on earnings above the Employee's Earnings Threshold	Nil	0%		
£84.01 to £535.00 weekly **or** £365.01 to £2319.00 monthly **or** £4385.01 to £27820.00 yearly			Nil	9.2% on earnings above the Employer's Earnings Threshold		
Over £535.00 weekly **or** over £2319.00 monthly **or** over £27820.00 yearly	8.4% on earnings above the Employee's Earnings Threshold, up to and including the UEL then **NIL** on earnings above the UEL	3.85% on earnings above the Employee's Earnings Threshold, up to and including the UEL then **NIL** on earnings above the UEL	Nil	9.2% on all earnings above the Employer's Earnings Threshold, up to and including the UEL, then 12.2% on all earnings above the UEL		

2000-2001

5

Monthly table for Contracted-out Salary Related standard rate contributions for use from 6 April 2000 to 5 April 2001

D *Contribution table letter*

Use this table for:

- employees in your Contracted-out Salary Related Scheme or the salary related part of your Contracted-out Mixed Benefit Scheme, who are age 16 or over and under State pension age (65 for men, 60 for women).

Do not use this table for:

- married women or widows who have the right to pay reduced rate employee's contributions, see table E
- employees who are State pension age or over, see leaflet CA38
- employees for whom you hold form CA2700, see table C
- employees who have an Appropriate Personal Pension, see leaflet CA38
- employees contracted-out in a Contracted-out Money Purchase Scheme, see leaflet CA43.

Completing Deductions Working Sheet, form P11 or substitute:

- enter 'D' in the space provided in the 'End of Year Summary' box of form P11
- copy the figures in columns 1a-1h of the table to columns 1a-1h of form P11 on a line appropriate to the tax month in which the employee is paid.

If the exact gross pay is not shown in the table, use the next smaller figure shown.

The figures in the left hand column of each table show steps between the Lower Earnings Limit and the Upper Earnings Limit. The National Insurance contributions liability for each step is calculated at the mid-point of the steps so you and your employee may pay slightly more or less than if you used the exact percentage method.

▼ Employee's Earnings up to and including the UEL	Earnings at the LEL (Where earnings reach or exceed the LEL)	Earnings above the LEL, up to and including the employee's Earnings Threshold	Earnings above the employee's Earnings Threshold, up to and including the employer's Earnings Threshold	Earnings above the employer's Earnings Threshold, up to and including the UEL	Total of employee's and employer's contributions payable	Employee's contributions payable	NIC rebate due on amount in column 1b	NIC rebate due on the sum of the amounts in columns 1b and 1c	▼ Employer's contributions
1a	1b	1c	1d	1e	1f	1g	1h	
£	£	£	£	£	£ P	£ P	£ P	£ P	£ P
Up to and including 290.99			No NIC Liability, make no entries on forms P11 and P11						
291	291	0	0	0	0.00	0.00	0.00	0.00	0.00
295	291	4	0	0	0.00	0.00	0.06	0.12	0.00
299	291	8	0	0	0.00	0.00	0.13	0.24	0.00
303	291	12	0	0	0.00	0.00	0.19	0.36	0.00
307	291	16	0	0	0.00	0.00	0.26	0.48	0.00
311	291	20	0	0	0.00	0.00	0.32	0.60	0.00
315	291	24	0	0	0.00	0.00	0.38	0.72	0.00
319	291	28	0	0	0.00	0.00	0.45	0.84	0.00
323	291	32	0	0	0.00	0.00	0.51	0.96	0.00
327	291	36	0	0	0.00	0.00	0.58	1.08	0.00
329	291	38	0	0	0.00	0.00	0.61	1.14	0.00
331	291	38	2	0	0.34	0.34	0.61	1.20	0.00
335	291	38	6	0	0.67	0.67	0.61	1.32	0.00
339	291	38	10	0	1.01	1.01	0.61	1.44	0.00
343	291	38	14	0	1.34	1.34	0.61	1.56	0.00
347	291	38	18	0	1.68	1.68	0.61	1.68	0.00
351	291	38	22	0	2.02	2.02	0.61	1.80	0.00
355	291	38	26	0	2.35	2.35	0.61	1.92	0.00
359	291	38	30	0	2.69	2.69	0.61	2.04	0.00
363	291	38	34	0	2.94	2.94	0.61	2.16	0.00
365	291	38	36	0	3.11	3.11	0.61	2.22	0.00
367	291	38	36	2	3.73	3.36	0.61	2.22	0.37
371	291	38	36	6	4.43	3.70	0.61	2.22	0.74
375	291	38	36	10	5.14	4.03	0.61	2.22	1.10
379	291	38	36	14	5.84	4.37	0.61	2.22	1.47
383	291	38	36	18	6.54	4.70	0.61	2.22	1.84
387	291	38	36	22	7.25	5.04	0.61	2.22	2.21
391	291	38	36	26	7.95	5.38	0.61	2.22	2.58
395	291	38	36	30	8.66	5.71	0.61	2.22	2.94
399	291	38	36	34	9.36	6.05	0.61	2.22	3.31

▼ for information only - do not enter on Deductions Working Sheet, form P11

ORDER FORM: AAT DIPLOMA IN PAYROLL ADMINISTRATION

Any books from our AAT range can be ordered by telephoning 020-8740-2211. Alternatively, send this page to our address below, fax it to us on 020-8740-1184, or email us at **publishing@bpp.com.** Or look us up on our website: www.bpp.com

We aim to deliver to all UK addresses inside 5 working days; a signature will be required. Order to all EU addresses should be delivered within 6 working days. All other orders to overseas addresses should be delivered within 8 working days.

To: BPP Publishing Ltd, Aldine House, Aldine Place, London W12 8AW

Tel: 020-8740 2211   Fax: 020-8740 1184   Email: publishing@bpp.com

Mr / Ms (full name): _____

Daytime delivery address: _____

_____

Postcode: _____   Daytime Tel: _____

Please send me the following quantities of books.

		10/00 Text		10/00 Kit		10/00 Both	£
Payroll administration NVQ Level 2	£29.95	☐	£15.95	☐	£44.95	☐	☐
Payroll administration NVQ Level 3	£29.95	☐	£15.95	☐	£44.95	☐	☐

Relevant titles from the AAT's Education and Training scheme

NVQ2 Unit 20: Working with Information Technology (8/00)	£9.95	☐			£ ☐
NVQ3 Unit 21: Using Information Technology (5/00)	£9.95	☐	£9.95	☐	£ ☐
Unit 22/23 Achieving Personal Effectiveness (incorporating Health and Safety)	£9.95	☐			£ ☐

Postage and packaging:
UK: £2.00 for each book to maximum of £10
Europe (inc ROI and Channel Islands): £4.00 for first book, £2.00 for each extra
Rest of the World: £20.00 for first book, £10 for each extra

Total books = £ ☐

P & P £ ☐

GRAND TOTAL £ ☐

I enclose a cheque for £ _____ (cheques to BPP Publishing Ltd) or charge to Mastercard/Visa/Switch

Card number ☐☐☐☐☐☐☐☐☐☐☐☐☐☐☐☐☐☐

Start date _____   Expiry date _____   Issue no. (Switch only)____

Signature _____

REVIEW FORM & FREE PRIZE DRAW

All original review forms from the entire BPP range, completed with genuine comments, will be entered into one of two draws on 31 January 2001 and 31 July 2001. The names on the first four forms picked out on each occasion will be sent a cheque for £50.

Name: _____   Address: _____

_____

_____

How have you used this Assessment Kit?
(Tick one box only)

☐ Home study (book only)

☐ On a course: college _____

☐ With 'correspondence' package

☐ Other _____

Why did you decide to purchase this Assessment Kit? *(Tick one box only)*

☐ Have used BPP Texts in the past

☐ Recommendation by friend/colleague

☐ Recommendation by a lecturer at college

☐ Saw advertising

☐ Other _____

During the past six months do you recall seeing/receiving any of the following?
(Tick as many boxes as are relevant)

☐ Our advertisement in *Accounting Technician* magazine

☐ Our advertisement in *Pass*

☐ Our brochure with a letter through the post

Which (if any) aspects of our advertising do you find useful?
(Tick as many boxes as are relevant)

☐ Prices and publication dates of new editions

☐ Information on Tutorial Text content

☐ Facility to order books off-the-page

☐ None of the above

Have you used the companion Tutorial Text for this subject?   ☐ Yes   ☐ No

Your ratings, comments and suggestions would be appreciated on the following areas

	Very useful	Useful	Not useful
Introductory section (How to use this Assessment Kit etc)	☐	☐	☐
Practice Questions	☐	☐	☐
Deveolved Assessment Style Questions	☐	☐	☐
Specimen Central Assessment	☐	☐	☐
Content of Answers	☐	☐	☐
Layout of pages	☐	☐	☐
Structure of book and ease of use	☐	☐	☐

	Excellent	Good	Adequate	Poor
Overall opinion of this Kit	☐	☐	☐	☐

Do you intend to continue using BPP Assessment Kits/Tutorial Texts/?   ☐ Yes   ☐ No

Please note any further comments and suggestions/errors on the reverse of this page.

Please return to: Nick Weller, BPP Publishing Ltd, FREEPOST, London, W12 8BR

REVIEW FORM & FREE PRIZE DRAW (continued)

Please note any further comments and suggestions/errors below

FREE PRIZE DRAW RULES

1   Closing date for 31 January 2001 draw is 31 December 2000. Closing date for 31 July 2001 draw is 30 June 2001.

2   Restricted to entries with UK and Eire addresses only. BPP employees, their families and business associates are excluded.

3   No purchase necessary. Entry forms are available upon request from BPP Publishing. No more than one entry per title, per person. Draw restricted to persons aged 16 and over.

4   Winners will be notified by post and receive their cheques not later than 6 weeks after the relevant draw date.

5   The decision of the promoter in all matters is final and binding. No correspondence will be entered into.